A Species of Insanity

A Species of Insanity

The Story of Drug Kingpin Jerry Allen LeQuire

Richard Biggs

CreateSpace

Copyright © 2015 RICHARD BIGGS

The moral right of the author has been asserted.

All rights reserved.

No part of this publication may be reproduced, stored in a retrieval system, or transmitted, in any form or by any means, without the prior permission in writing of the publisher, nor be otherwise circulated in any form of binding or cover other than that in which it is published and without a similar condition including this condition being imposed on the subsequent purchaser.

Published by createspace

ISBN: 1519176783

Typesetting services by BOOKOW.COM

Preface

This is a true story based on recollected events from four years of interviews with Jerry LeQuire at four different federal prisons. I also drew on the evidence of volumes of trial transcripts and other documents. Some of the information was kindly presented by a few of those who had first hand knowledge of events and conversations. Since most of the story occurred over thirty years ago, it was impossible to verify every statement but an honest effort was given. In that regard, Jerry's memory seemed intact and his statements meshed with other accounts.

In some cases, I didn't use the real names of incidental characters because of my concern for their privacy. These characters are referenced by only a first name. The book is narrative non-fiction and some of the scenes have been enhanced, based on real events and facts. Also, some of the language is graphic because of an attempt to be true to the characters.

Chapter 1

Maryville, Tennessee is located at the foot of the Smoky Mountains, bounded by the Tennessee River and Knoxville, a beautiful place that has been selected as one of the 10 best small towns in America in which to live. The local accent is mixed with accents from all over the nation because of its easy access to high-tech companies such as the Oak Ridge National Lab. The land is fertile, with magnificent views of the mountains; the home of Maryville College, a prestigious liberal arts school, and Maryville High where football championships are as expected as frost in the winter.

Maryville is a town in transition; impacted by the move to large malls, its downtown was once deserted but recent years have seen a change as streets have been remodeled, new businesses arrived, along with parking to accommodate visitors. It has changed from an old south kind of place to a modern town with progressive leaders. Pool rooms have been replaced, theaters turned into restaurants, coffee shops dot the landscape. On the outskirts are two Walmart's, Dicks Sporting Goods, Home Depot and Lowes, and enough grocery stores to feed a small army.

The town has one newspaper, the Daily Times, and is staffed by people like Melanie Tucker, an attractive woman who reports on everything from crime to food trends. The newspaper, itself, is a family owned business that has been serving Maryville and surrounding communities for decades.

The school system of Maryville is especially excellent. The school puts out more than its share of Merit Scholars and its orchestra is annually one of the best in the state. It is a well-rounded school that demands the best from its students. Maryville is a great place to live.

But in the early 1980s, few in the nation had ever heard of Maryville, except as a passageway to the Great Smoky Mountains National Park and as the sister city to Knoxville and the University of Tennessee. And the inhabitants were seemingly content to leave it that way. About the only drama that had passed through the town had been the emergence of Lamar Alexander as a serious player in the national political arena. But then, in the fall of 1983, the people of east Tennessee, and Maryville in particular, awoke to the startling news that one of their own, Jerry Allen LeQuire, had been arrested for operating a drug ring that smuggled cocaine from Medellin, Colombia to south Florida. One of his several planes had been intercepted in Alabama carrying cocaine with a street value of $20,000,000. Subsequent stories painted him as the head of an extensive operation that brought him nearly $400,000,000 in revenue, making him one of the largest drug smugglers in America. Afterward, when the realization had finally set in, the townspeople wondered how the man they had known could have become entangled with a drug cartel. Bobby Brown, a childhood friend, tried to see if there was anything that would point to this end. Others went through the same exercise. And they, along with Bobby, also wondered where he had hidden the $280,000,000 the feds claimed he had stashed. As it turned out, no matter the speculation, both public and private, the answers were not simple.

CHAPTER 2

Jerry said he needed to talk to her about something but she had to promise not to go ballistic. She said, I know, you want to break up. Well, that's okay because I want to break up with you, too.

"Then, it's settled," he said.

She shot him the finger and walked away from the bar, her butt twitching under the short skirt. Fortunately for her, she didn't look like any of the Finleys.

"You got a nice thing going with her," Larry Jones said. "And those are nice cowboy boots you're wearing, too. New?"

Jerry nodded and told him he was breaking up with her, and don't say anything about passing up a nice piece of ass like that because he wasn't in the mood. But he knew that Jones liked to talk, especially about women.

"Is it alright if I tell Jimmy he can go after her now? He's interested."

Jerry said he didn't care what he told Jimmy because Jimmy was a piece of shit that he didn't give a damn about. Jones said he better keep that opinion to himself because Jimmy had a mean disposition. And what am I, Jerry said, Mr. sunshine? Then he walked to the table where Babe Finley was sitting.

Finley was the owner of the Wagon Wheel Tavern, a Maryville honky-tonk where weekends were like the wild-west. He and Jerry were friends because they both liked to hustle suckers, either in cards or shooting pool.

"You get my daughter pregnant and you're my son-in-law," he said.

"That's warning enough," Jerry said. "I want be living there anymore."

Well, she'll just find someone else, Finley said. He pointed toward a young man leaning against the bar and said Jerry should tell him that if he causes anymore trouble, he'll not be allowed back again. Jerry looked at the man, whose name was Chili, and said he'd be glad to tell him because he had been looking for an excuse to bust him in the mouth. What'd he do to you? Finley said. I never liked the way he looks, Jerry replied. Jerry was tall, over six feet, slender, with arms rippling with muscles, and blessed with a bad disposition. He managed the Wagon Wheel, which meant he had to take care of a lot of trouble.

"Just don't shoot him," Finley said. "I'm tired of shootings; they're giving the place a bad reputation. Now, take care of Chili."

That night Chili didn't want any trouble so he kept his mouth shut when Jerry talked. And then when Larry Jones came over, he turned and left. "Something I said?" Jones said.

Jerry told him not to worry about it. I can't go with you to Kentucky this weekend, he added. Jones, who took stolen cars and fixed them up for resale, had asked him to accompany him to Corbin where he was getting rid of a two-year old Ford that had been stolen in Chattanooga. Jones said he thought they had already agreed Jerry would help.

"I don't want any part of the chop shop business," Jerry said. "It's just a disaster waiting to happen."

Jones slugged down a beer. "Think so? I ain't been caught yet."

Jerry grinned at him. He had been friends with the big redhead for years but admitted he might be a bit short with his thinking. He heard a noise from the back and said, "Oh, hell." Two men had squared off and the skinny one had pulled a knife. He walked over and said, "Why don't you put that away? Otherwise, something's going to happen we all might regret." The man looked at him, his expression saying who the hell you think you're talking to, trying to look tough. But Jerry had seen tough before and this wasn't it. He was tired of hearing guys try to be something they weren't. And what was with a knife? If you wanted to kill someone, shoot the son of a bitch. Now take it outside, he told them, putting the knife in his pocket when the man handed it to him. Jerry walked over to the bar and stashed it with all the other weapons, then told the bartender to make sure they didn't kill each other.

Chapter 2

Finding an end seat, she sidled up to him a few minutes later. You really breaking up with me, Jerry? He said it could be a mutual thing.

"It don't seem mutual," she said.

"Your daddy thinks it's a good idea."

"Well, damn," she said, "this caps off a perfect day."

"Jimmy's interested in you, if that's any consolation."

She said, "Are you serious? Why would I go with Jimmy?"

He shrugged. "Just what I hear."

She shot him the finger again. "Well maybe he's better in bed than you," she said.

Jerry looked around, checking the action. For a Friday night, it was calm. Two men walked through the door, one he didn't recognize, odd because almost all of the customers were regulars. The man, wearing a leather jacket and blue jeans, sat down at the bar and ordered a beer. He had a northern accent. He turned to glance at a pretty young woman carrying beer to one of the tables. "How about a y'all, honey," he said. The girl, Nancy, ignored him but gave Jerry a who is this jerk look. When she returned to pick up more beers, the man said, "I'm still waiting for that y'all."

Jerry just watched. Barmaids were used to jerks but this one was starting to get under his skin. The man reached over and touched her arm and she told him not to touch what he couldn't afford. The man said, "Come here honey, I've got something I'd like you to meet."

Jerry said, "She told you not to touch."

"What?"

Nancy told the man that if he touched her again she would kick him in the nuts. The man grabbed his crotch and said first she had to feel them. Jerry walked over to him. "Time for you to shut up partner," he said.

"Are you going to make me? I don't think so."

The man's friend put his hand on his shoulder and said it was time for them to be somewhere else, looking at Jerry with caution. Jerry said that would be a smart choice. Jerry heard the man say when they left, "I would've kicked that hayseed's ass." And his friend said he didn't think so.

Two weeks later, Jerry heard that she was sleeping with Jimmy and had told him some shit that made Jimmy want to kill him. He talked to her about it and she said, I just told him that you told people I like kinky sex, that's all. Now why would I tell anyone that? he said, though she did. Your daddy would shoot me. I just repeated what I heard, she said. He talked with Babe about it but got no relief other than Jimmy was bad so he should carry a gun with him.

"If he comes in here I'll probably have to kill him," Jerry said.

"Just don't shoot my daughter."

Jerry went home and grabbed the bourbon bottle and poured a drink. Then he fell onto the couch, kicked off his shoes and took a long drink. If he had to kill Jimmy that's what would happen, he didn't much care. Now, in his late twenties, he'd come to peace with himself. You just did what you had to do and to hell with the consequences. In high school, he didn't think twice about dropping out of school to marry. It was the same when he decided to divorce. You couldn't look back. Jail, prison— none of it made any difference as long as you remained true to yourself. So dead or not, that was Jimmy's choice, not his.

He'd seen big men, small men, in-between men, cry when someone pointed a gun at them. You never knew how you would react until it happened. The first time someone had pointed a gun at him with malice, he had nearly pissed in his pants until anger took over and all he could think of was a way to take the gun and ram it down his throat. Once, he had fired five times into the back of a car just because they passed him up and shot the finger. Something inside had just snapped. But in all honesty, it felt good.

It sometimes occurred to him he might try to control his emotions a bit more now that he was getting older, be more diplomatic, but that was going to have to wait until he got into a more civilized business.—he had no idea what that would be but he was always thinking. He took another drink and decided to call it a night.

Chapter 2

He imagined different ways Jimmy might try to find him. It was doubtful he would show up at the Wagon Wheel, walk in with his gun and start firing. Much too dangerous and while Jimmy didn't forego danger, he wasn't that stupid. It would probably be when he least expected it, like when he was leaving his mother's house in Maryville, or maybe leaving a restaurant, someplace when his guard was down. That was more his style, grinning at him as though to say, gotcha.

It happened two days later. He pulled into his usual mom-and-pop grocery store and scribbled down a reminder on a notepad to buy something for his daughter for her birthday, then walked toward the store. It was one of those places with sawdust sprinkled on the floor where you had to be careful not to slip. When he opened the door, he saw two men looking at him and one of them was Jimmy. Instinctively, he reached for his gun.

"No need for that," Jimmy said, moving to his left. "I hear you're looking for me." He was well-built, with brown hair cut short.

"Not me. I don't ever look for trouble. How about you? She's sleeping with you so what do you need from me? And tell your buddy to keep his hands where I can see them."

"He's got nothing to do with this."

"Then tell him to stay where he is," Jerry said. "How about if I just back out of here and you wait five minutes. That sound all right?"

"If that's what you want."

Jerry eased toward the door, then saw a hand move, coming up with a gun. Jerry dropped to the floor and fired two shots from his .38. The first one missed, but the second brought a scream. Two shots fired in Jerry's direction shattered a wood cabinet behind him. Then another shot, and he felt the intense pain in his leg, like a hot iron had hit him. He saw Jimmy moving forward and fired three more shots. Jimmy fell to the floor, yelling in pain. Jerry heard another noise and saw the other man crawling behind a counter, his body leaking fluid. Jerry stumbled out of the store and to the car. He needed to get to the hospital before the cops showed up. What a fucking mess.

Fifteen minutes later, he dragged his leg into the emergency room. The attendants rushed him past the waiting room to tackle his wound. Though the bullet had missed the bone, the doctor said he might walk with a limp for a while. He also mentioned that a detective was outside.

"You can't talk with me," Jerry said, a few minutes later. "I've been drugged."

The Maryville detective said, "Tell that to someone who cares. You're in deep shit, LeQuire."

"Yeah? Besides being shot and having to listen to you, I don't know what you're talking about."

"Ever hear of assault with a deadly weapon?"

"What assault?" Jerry had heard that the other two were in the hospital getting patched up. "Did anyone say it was assault?"

"I know being stupid can be a drag, but think about the upside." The detective looked past him toward the door. "Every day in prison will be a new experience. But if you cooperate, maybe I can get you a break."

Jerry smiled. "That'd be the first time. Anyway, there's not much I can say because I have no idea how I got shot. Did you find a gun?"

"Did I find a…" The detective laughed. "Oh yeah, it was on the floor with a bow around it. What I did find, though, was a store shot to pieces. And two punks leaking oil."

"Maybe they know what happened, maybe the same person who shot me, shot them. Fuck, there might be a serial shooter loose in Blount County."

"Why'd you shoot them, LeQuire? I hear it's over a woman. Is that it?"

"You know me, would I get mad over a piece of ass? I'm telling you, you need to find this guy before he shoots someone else."

"So, let me get this straight. Someone walks into the store and starts shooting with two different guns. Shoots you with one and the other two with another. Then, just walks out like it's nothing."

"Ask the store owner."

"He didn't see a thing."

Chapter 2

Jerry's smile broadened. "Man, you're having a bad day aren't you? Now, you going to charge me with something or not? My leg hurts, and I need some rest."

"You know you're a real son of a bitch, LeQuire, and it's just a matter of time."

"But not today, huh?"

"I'm just going to let you sons of a bitches kill each other," the detective said. He turned to the cop by the door. "Let's get the hell out of here."

Jerry had the store fixed up and paid the owner for keeping his mouth shut. He spent some time looking for the two men until hearing they wanted no more trouble. Still, he never went anywhere without carrying a piece.

Chapter 3

They sat at one of the chairs inside the dimly lit bar, across from the restaurant, down from the Jefferson City courthouse, Franklin Park with the glass of beer and pretzels and Jerry with a soft drink and hamburger.

From time to time people would nod in their direction, say something to Park or just stare, a reminder of Park's power in the small, east Tennessee town where usually the most exciting event was a Saturday afternoon football game featuring the small Baptist school, Carson Newman College.

"How long you been a lawyer?" Jerry said.

The 68 year old laughed. "How long? About all my life. You should've known me sooner. Just yesterday I was thinking about your bonehead acts. Cattle rustlng, really? Did that bullet in your leg affect your brain?" Jerry said it was done and no need to bring it up again. And how about that time you shot into the back of the car? Park said. Way I heard it you told the Judge the gun went off accidently and he laughed and said, five times Mr. LeQuire? By god, I wish I'd been there, I surely do.

"Is that why you wanted to talk, to make me feel good?"

"Just having a little fun, son." He waved for another beer. "So, how you doing? Haven't seen you in awhile. Everything good? You know you can't go through life shooting pool and playing cards with suckers. You need a plan." He waved at a tall man walking toward the door.

"I was thinking about going in the smuggling business," Jerry said, "marijuana."

Park leaned forward. "Now that's more like it. How you going to do it?"

Chapter 3

"With a boat, but don't ask me a ton of questions because I'm still working it out."

"This a big boat you're talking about?"

"Whatever I can afford. I figure I can take a couple of men and go to Jamaica."

"Uh huh. What's the profit?"

"In the neighborhood of $250 grand."

Park rubbed his chin. "I might be able to help you out for a percentage," he said. "I could call in some favors so the authorities would look the other way. Maybe some other things. So, tell me more."

"Like I said, I'm still working on it." The man could get on your nerves with his questions. They had met through a mutual friend who had been defended by Park in a murder trial. The prosecution had an eyewitness, but at the trial she changed her testimony and said it was self-defense.

"Also," Park said, "I'd have to be a silent partner. I wouldn't want my reputation to be tarnished, especially after that son of a bitch Waymon Poole's been going out of his way to paint me a mobster. By the way, I dream about someone putting a bullet in his fucking head."

Poole was the recently appointed Sheriff, with a charter to clean up the county. Park had tried to talk City Council out of the appointment. Angered, he had publicly stated they would live to regret the decision.

"He has no idea of what I'm capable of," Park said. "If he thinks he can bully me, he's got a hard lesson to learn. You know the son of a bitch ran me out of the courthouse because I was carrying a gun, don't you? I said, 'How can I kill your sorry ass if I'm not carrying?' His face turned beet red, and he told the cop to arrest me if I didn't leave."

"So, he's a prick. Pricks come and go; forget him."

"Almost sounds like you're giving me a lecture."

"I'm just saying it's bad to threaten a sheriff," Jerry said.

"I had to let him know it's not over till it's over. They're looking into his past so I think it's just a matter of time. The son of a bitch had to know he couldn't get away with saying I'm a crook."

"What's really bothering you isn't words," Jerry said. "It's thinking you're losing control."

"What the fuck you know about it?"

"Oh yeah, that's right. I just got off the watermelon truck and don't know anything about you. I've never seen you get mad before either."

They exchanged stares before Park said, "Hell, this is depressing. Let's get back to smuggling. I'm telling you straight up if you're gonna run a business you need to limit your relationships with men like Red Shoes and Jacky Laymon. While my business makes me a part of thugs, you got no excuse. You want to smuggle, act like a fucking businessman. You see what I'm saying?" He didn't wait for a response. "Now, tell me about this guy who wears red shoes. Is he really connected to the mob?"

Jerry nodded, anything to avoid a lecture. Park liked handing out advice and it got old. "In Detroit," he said. "He's a bookie with his hands in a lot of stuff, a little like you. One day he has a plan to rob this guy who supposedly has a lot of money. He brings in these guys from Detroit and tells them what to do. I'm supposed to be the driver for which I'll get ten grand. I'm supposed to take them to an airport in Lexington, Kentucky, after it's over.

"So, they go into this place and a few minutes later they run out, yelling for me to drive. One of them sticks a .45 against my head and says there was no money but there sure the hell were a lot of men with guns. I'm thinking that I'm dead, so I start talking. Finally, they're convinced I had nothing to do with it, so they let me live. When I tell Red Shoes about it, he gets angry and says they're dead. A week later, they were."

"And Laymon, what about him?"

"We went back a little," Jerry said, wiping mustard from his mouth. "But when they sent him to prison for murder I lost touch, so you can imagine my surprise when he shows up one day at my house and asks if I'll hide him."

"How'd he escape?"

"I really never got a clear answer on that," Jerry said. "Anyway, in 1975 he and two other men attempted a robbery, and when it went sideways,

Chapter 3

they got pissed and tried to kill him. On Christmas Eve he heard they were going to be at the Red Lantern Tavern in Newport. He went there with a carbine and began shooting until his rifle jammed. When it was over, three were dead and Jacky was shot. A man dragged him outside and ran over him several times until he was dead."

"That's pretty much what I heard," Park said. He patted the waitress on her butt when she brought the beer. "I think I might get some of that, later."

"She's a little young. You need to be careful, Franklin." He'd fixed Park up with several women, a few times with bad results, and knew his sexual appetite.

"The hell with you, son. Don't pull that righteous shit on me." He paused a moment and looked around. "Now, what I wanted to talk about—What do you know about making bombs?"

"What?"

"You're street smart, so I figure you know how to make one."

"What do you need a bomb for?" Jerry said.

Park grinned. "Why you think? I want to scare the shit out of some people."

"You want to scare, shoot a .45 next to their ear. Bombs aren't the way to do it. What do you know about bombs, anyway?"

"Why the hell you think I'm asking you?" Park snipped off the end of a cigar and lit it with a gold plated lighter.

Jerry's bladder was about to explode so he said he had to go to the john. "If you're talking about scaring who I think you are, you'll be the first person the police look at."

"So what? They don't have the balls to do anything about it. This is my goddamn town."

"You don't own the FBI and ATF," Jerry said. "They'll make Waymon Poole look like amateur night."

"You let me worry about that."

Jerry walked away from the table, hearing Park say, "As long as I'm here, not even the FBI can touch me."

Coming back from the bathroom thinking of Park's plan, he knew that no matter what he said wouldn't change his mind. It was an insane idea.

Park was still talking. "Just between you and me, Poole is a dead man. I've already made arrangements."

Jerry looked at him a moment. "Okay, so that ends it. You don't need the bombs."

"To the contrary, I need them more than ever."

Here was a man who had everything and he was risking it on grade school revenge. "Tell me why, Franklin."

"Why? Because they have to know that I'm the goddamn boss of this town," Park said. "Now, I've done a lot of things for you so I want you to come over to my house and show me how to make a goddamn bomb. I'll build the fucking thing myself."

At home, Jerry sat in the dark of his truck, thinking about his life. He had to get away from all this crap, Park with his bombs, Jones with his stolen cars, the Wagon Wheel buddies. In his idiotic ramblings, Park said one thing that was true: he needed to move forward with his life. He picked up the phone and made the call. "John, if you're still interested in what we discussed earlier," he said, "I've decided to go ahead."

Jerry finished the conversation, scribbled down the place they had agreed to meet, then grabbed the worn map and spread it across the Formica table in his kitchen. He looked at the red-circled islands and ran his finger along the route from Florida to Jamaica. Ever since he had helped unload marijuana from a plane, and ran his fingers through the wad of hundred dollar bills he'd been paid for his help, he'd wondered why he wasn't in the marijuana business himself. He figured he could buy a boat and travel from south Florida to the Bahamas, then to Haiti, and finally to Jamaica to buy the weed. He had gone over the route so many times he knew the coordinates by heart.

It would be dangerous with a lot of problems. First he knew nothing about the ocean except what he had read; secondly, he would need a crew and right now the only one he was sure was dumb enough to go along

Chapter 3

was Larry Jones; and third, he didn't have a boat, though he hoped that problem would soon be solved.

He stood up and walked to the window, watching the shadows dance across the small lawn. A wave of fear washed over him. He liked Park, considered him one of his best friends, and it was tough seeing him like this. His bombing plan would be an avalanche taking down everything in its path. How are you supposed to handle such uncertainty?

Jerry moved away from the window and walked to the bedroom where Bonnie was sleeping. He tucked the covers about her carefully and then kissed her gently on the forehead. The moonlight filtering through the blinds created a sliver of gold on her face, such a gentle person, never questioning, always faithful.

Then he moved back to the maps and went over them once again.

The next day, Jerry parked his truck in the driveway of a brick house surrounded by manicured grass. The front door opened and a woman in her early-thirties stepped out and introduced herself. "John's waiting inside," she said.

He followed her into the foyer, across hardwood floors, and finally to a paneled room. He thought she probably came from rich parents, with everything she wanted growing up. She had that look.

"Beer okay?" John asked as she left the room. He was about Jerry's age, shorter, with a similar look as his wife – privileged.

"Fine," Jerry said, making himself comfortable in the leather chair. "Your wife's attractive."

John nodded. "Let's leave her out of this. Now, tell me more about your plan."

"Pretty much like I said before. Except now I've decided on the boat. How's a 26 foot Sea Ray sound to you?"

"Sounds small."

"Yeah, but with no experience, it's about all I'm willing to bite off. But if you're willing to get me a bigger one, I'll sure listen."

John thought about it. "Didn't Jones say something about a custom-made boat?"

"I don't know what he said. He's confusing me lately."

"Then why is he coming with us?"

"Us?"

"Yeah, I'll spring for the boat," John said. "I'll even go with you."

Jerry smiled. "When?"

"I can get the boat Friday? That soon enough? Now, let's talk about Jones. You think he's dependable?"

"What he is is my friend." He hoped the man understood the value of loyalty, but he thought about what Park said about associations, and he wasn't sure if he could afford having Larry Jones working for him. Some of Jerry's buddies were content hanging out in poolrooms, playing for free beer, and he was starting to put Jones in that camp. "I'll care of Jones."

John wasn't pleased. "You can't have problems in the middle of the ocean."

"I said I'll take care of it. You ever been to sea?"

"I cruised the Bahamas once," John said.

"You ever been at sea on a 26-foot boat?"

"Yeah, on a fishing trip from Miami," John said.

Jerry grinned at him, thinking he'd probably be the first one to bail out.

"I'm not the one you should worry about, Jerry."

The man knew nothing about anything, living in his fine house with his pretty wife and new car. Worry? What did he know about worry? If Jerry had learned anything in his life it was not to depend on anyone for success. If necessary, he'd make the damn trip alone, that's the way he felt. He just needed to get away before Franklin Park did something stupid.

"It's a high risk job," Jerry said. "I worry about everything. So, right now I'm wondering if you can be ready to go to Florida in three weeks. That's what I'm worrying about today."

Chapter 3

The man stared at Jerry a moment as though trying to decide something. "I'll be ready," he said. "Now, tell me something. Is the story about you in that bar on Clinton Highway true?"

"Which story?"

"The one about you walking up to the man with a gun pointing at you, then hitting him in the side of the head with a beer bottle, and taking the gun and pistol whipping him," John said.

"No, the gun was pointed at someone else."

Jerry signed up for a Coast Guard course in boating, but before the first class he heard that two bombs had been discovered outside the houses of two Jefferson City council members. They were attached to clocks but for some reason neither had exploded. Jerry was furious but Park assured him there was nothing to worry about because as long as he was alive no police would bother him or his friends.

But on August 31, 1978, Park was murdered in his home. And Jerry knew he was in trouble.

The funeral was a scene from *The Godfather*, with Waymon Poole in the role of the lead FBI agent. His men took pictures of everyone, along with the license number of their cars. A day later, he announced that they were making progress in both the murder and bombing investigation.

CHAPTER 4

By mid-afternoon, they had reached south Florida. Jerry had pulled the boat trailer into a motel where they would stay until leaving for the Bahamas, then walked outside and stared at the *Sea Ray*. It was going to be his home for at least a week. Now he wondered if he'd be making the trip alone because as soon as they had seen the ocean, the complaining had started. It's too small for big water, what if a storm comes, and on and on. It was nauseating. He had tartly reminded them that the water wasn't any bigger than it was when they left Tennessee, when they had been excited. He looked back where they were huddled together and cursed. Well, if they wanted to drop out, to hell with them. He was still going.

The next morning the first bad news came when John said his wife had been a car wreck and he needed to return home. Jerry didn't believe him but saw the man was determined. So now there were three.

"It's a lot of water, Jerry," Larry Jones said. Jones was the only one he believed he had any chance of keeping. Jones knew how much he was needed and they had been friends forever. But over the past couple of years, he'd seen a change in him, walking around with a chip on his shoulder, like he was beginning to realize that life was catching up with him. Jerry and Jones were old buddies in business together, except Jerry was the boss, and he thought this bothered Jones. But Jones could never be the boss because he became too caught up in emotion. He would rather do something and ask questions later, than plan. A few weeks ago Jerry had said, "You see a chance to make a thousand dollars if you steal a fur coat from a checkroom, but it belongs to a crime boss, would you

Chapter 4

do it?" Jones told him he wasn't that dumb. Jerry said, "But what if the smartest man in the world assured you the boss didn't give a damn about the coat?" Jones laughed and said he didn't give a shit, he still wouldn't do it. Then Jerry said, "And if I told you to do it?"

Jones shrugged.

In Jones, he had someone who was just a good old boy and what he needed was someone with a stake in the venture. Wasn't that what Franklin Park had tried to tell him? He filled his glass with whiskey and began looking at his map.

As they walked to the boat the next morning, they passed a large shirtless man mopping down the deck of a sailboat. Jones said, "You ever wonder what somebody eats to get that big? Christ, how'd you like to feed that guy?"

"What I'd do if I was you," Jerry said, "is keep that to myself, unless you want to end up in a hospital."

"Shit, I'm shaking," Jones said.

"Get in the damn boat."

The trip began calmly, with a slight breeze and gentle swells. Jerry was enjoying the ride, but he could tell that the others were not. He admitted that being in the middle of water with nothing in sight except for an occasional ship or an overhead bird was unsettling. And he could see that the bobbing of the boat was making them sick.

Then the sea became rougher from an approaching storm, throwing the small boat around. "I'm not fucking doing this anymore," one of the men said as they approached the first island. "Think anything you want, but I'd rather spend the rest of my life sleeping in a box than riding another mile in this boat."

The way he said it made Jerry laugh. "Tell you what, sleep on it and let me know in the morning."

"The moment we get close to land, I'm going ashore, even if I have to swim, and I could sleep a week and wouldn't change my mind."

They anchored in the shelter of an island and spent the night. Jerry hoped the man would change his mind in the morning but he didn't, so

Jerry took him to shore and wished him luck. Now, there was just he and Jones.

"You know what I like?" Jones said, "crossing the ocean with someone who knows about as much about boating as me, which is zilch. Oh, I forgot, you took a Coast Guard class. That makes it better."

It was too hard to read his face. Jerry said, "You want to go somewhere for a steak. It might be the last good meal we'll get in a while."

"Or we could postpone this until we get more help."

The waitress put the coffee on the table. Jerry waited until she was gone before saying, "Look, we're talking about $250,000, and if you'll help I'll up your percentage."

"What good does it do if we're dead," Jones said.

Jerry flipped out a sheet of paper. "Here's my plan. Read it and then decide if I know what I'm doing."

Jones scanned it twice, then looked away for a moment.

Jerry said, "It's foolproof. All we have to do is make it to Jamaica and back. We have all the necessary documents. After that the pipeline is set up forever. We can buy a bigger boat, experienced men, everything we need to become a first class organization."

Jones smiled. "Fifty-fifty?"

"You think so?"

"Why not? You can be the brains and I'll be the brawn," Jones said.

"I didn't know you were that ambitious."

"I've got a few connections that might make it easier."

Jerry finished the coffee. "Is that right? Tell me about it."

"I have contacts with the FBI."

Jerry grinned "Then you'll go with me to Jamaica?"

"It's crazy to do that. I can see it now. Look, we should go back to Tennessee and get a bigger boat," Jones said. "Then we'll get a captain who understands the water."

"And why are you waiting until now to say this?"

"What difference does it make?"

Chapter 4

"What I'm thinking is that you hoped to catch me in a vulnerable moment, like not having any helpers, and try to fucking blackmail me. You're smarter than I thought, Larry. How did you know the others would bail?"

"I—I don't know what you're talking about."

"We've been friends for a long time, so I'm willing to cut you some slack, but don't ever try that shit on me again. I might consider letting you go in with me, but there's no way in hell it'd be fifty-fifty, not with me taking all the risks."

"I could spring for some money," Jones said.

Jerry's expression remained patient, solemn. "Come up with two hundred grand, and we'll talk about it. Otherwise, I'm not interested."

"I could do ten."

"Okay, for ten, I'll give you five percent and you handle the ground crew—help with distribution, that sort of thing."

"Fuck five percent, Jerry. Five percent of $250,000 is—well, it's not enough."

"You'd get your money back in one trip."

"Thirty percent, and I'll go with you to Jamaica," Jones said, shaking his head.

"Almost three months we've talked about this and now you're trying to leverage me. Look at me, Larry. Do you think this is going to work with me? How long have we known each other? I'd sooner drown in this boat than give a damn inch to your blackmail."

"You keep saying that, but it's not blackmail. We're talking business."

"Business we could've discussed in Tennessee," Jerry said.

"It's still business. Besides, you're the person who wants something. I'm willing to admit that I'm too scared to keep going because I can see the problems ahead. But under the right circumstance I'd be willing to take the risk."

"And you don't think this is blackmail?"

Jones grinned. "We could be a good team," he said, "just like in the past."

The dipshit was serious, sitting there like he had all the cards, running his fingers through his hair. How long had he been thinking about this? Had he talked with the others and worked something out, maybe expand the operation so they could get a bigger cut? He doubted that one of them would go along with the idea but wasn't sure about the other. He looked hard at Jones and saw the smirk he wanted to slap away.

"Tell you what. I'll stay behind and you go to Jamaica to get the marijuana, and when we sell it I'll make you my partner."

Jones looked surprised. "Shit, I don't know anything about boats or maps."

"Then what good are you? Matter of fact, I don't know why I'm talking to you." Jerry pushed away from the table. "Here's my offer. You wait for me on Great Inagua and help with the refueling and I'll pay you half of what you expected to get. Then when we get back to Tennessee we'll talk about this other shit."

"There's not much there except niggers," Jones said.

The island was the southernmost island in the Bahamas and was where Jerry wanted to take the boat, which would be filled with bales of marijuana, for the final refueling before reaching Florida.

"Take a book."

After some haggling, Jones agreed. That night, Jerry kept seeing the smirk on his face, like he thought he'd done something. And he went to sleep thinking he should never again have anything to do with him.

The next morning, Jerry dropped him off at Great Inagua. There wasn't much on the island except a salt factory so maybe Jones would stay out of trouble. The sky was darkening again, so he waited a couple of hours to see if the weather would break. When the skies cleared enough to give him hope, he set off alone on his long journey.

His uncertainty was dampened by his anger at being left alone. He was a devotee of loyalty and believed strongly in your word, but staying mad would solve nothing, and he needed all his wits for the journey ahead. So he dismissed the bad thoughts and concentrated on guiding

Chapter 4

the small craft toward Haiti. He was good at reading maps and direction, and knew he would need all that skill.

The trip was uneventful, and in the early evening the coast of Haiti appeared off to his right, a hazy figure in a deepening fog. He stood up in the boat and surveyed the scene, but his wobbly legs gave way and he stumbled against the side of the boat. He was weary to the bone and needed a good night's sleep. The sea was beginning to churn and the *Sea Ray* was struggling against the waves.

Eventually, he found a place to dock and climbed out of the boat. His legs were weak, and he stumbled like a drunk. After refueling, he got something to eat and immediately felt better. Then his conversation with Jones re-entered his thoughts. What the hell was that part about having FBI contacts? He might be an idiot but to say he was pals with the law was out of character. It didn't make sense. The thought was chilling. Jones tied to the FBI – my god, what would be next? He took another drink. It was crazy thinking Jones would spy for the feds. He hated the law, always had. He finished his drink and walked outside.

In a few minutes, he found an elderly black man who was curious why a white man had come to Haiti in a small boat. Jerry explained that he was going fishing, and the man laughed. "Not fish here, I bet." He pulled out a bottle and offered a drink. Thirty minutes later, they were good friends.

"Is the storm going to miss us?" Jerry asked.

The black man grinned. "Maybe so, maybe not. Weather come and go, as God wills."

They were walking toward the boat when an old man, holding a young girl by the hand, approached. She was maybe eleven or twelve. He smiled through broken teeth and said, "You want to take girl to America. She be good for man. She good girl."

It took Jerry a moment to understand that he was offering her services. "Get the hell out of here," he said.

The man shrugged and walked away. The elderly black man, who had been observing this, smiled but said nothing.

"Was that what I think?"

The man nodded. "Life comes hard. Decisions come harder."

Jerry went to sleep thinking of this. In the morning, he awoke to a black, threatening sky. The bad news was waiting. From the Bahamas he had known little except worry. It wasn't the lurching motion of the small craft, but the concern of what was ahead. Being alone on the open sea was not something he had planned for and he worried that it might be more than he could handle. A small measure of reassurance was that he would have no one to worry about except himself – but it was certainly a small measure.

He had hoped for sunshine today, as the storm whipped through the night, but it seemed to stall overhead. And as he cleared the harbor, as though waiting for his arrival, the winds began to increase. He gripped the wheel tightly and checked his bearings again. The water was grey green, shrouded in a light fog, and almost before the land disappeared, the ocean rose against the boat, causing it to heave, letting him know it was in control now. And his fear was filled with rage, not at the storm but at those who had deserted him. It came over him like a coat and he released his anger through a piercing scream, dampened by the wind and pelting rain.

The rain was like tiny needles on his face, stinging, blinding him from the water that rushed toward the boat. He was shocked because it all happened so fast. The incessant pounding of the waves, one after another, pummeled the *Sea Ray*, tossing it from side to side, playing with a toy until weary and discarding it. The engine hesitated several times before catching its breath against the onslaught of the waves. The fog was now so thick that all he could see was the tiny beam of light coming from the lighthouse on Navassa Island. He held on to it like a beacon of hope. As the storm increased it became the only hope he had. Navassa was a small, uninhabited island about fifty miles from Haiti, and if he could make it there, he could find shelter.

There were times when he was sure the *Sea Ray* would break in two, and by then he knew it wasn't meant for weather like this, but he fought

Chapter 4

to keep the boat headed into the waves because the first time one hit him sideways, it was over. Still, the boat was being slammed so hard he wondered how much more punishment it could take, creaking under the strain, groaning as each wave passed over.

Time and distance seemed to hold back, but as the storm raged the light on Navassa was getting a little closer, a sliver of life to embrace, so while the howling of the wind made it nearly impossible to hear his voice, the outline of the island crept ever larger in view and kept his spirits from drowning in the darkness of despair. I might make it, he thought.

It was long odds that he would return alive, for even if he reached the island he still had a long way to go, and then there was the return trip. But he had fought against odds all his life. *I can do this*, he thought. *I am going to do it. And the others can go to hell.*

The wind was screaming in an unknown tongue as land grew nearer, a small island, about 2 square miles and uninhabited, but big enough to provide shelter from the storm as he took the boat around the tip, the wind calming and the waves receding. A sense of relief swept over him as he dropped the anchor and leaned back in the seat, praying he would never have to go through something like that again.

He checked the boat to see if everything was intact, pleased that it had held up so well under the stress. There was a little water in the cabin, but the bilge pump took care of it. He spent the night getting small pieces of rest.

By the next morning, the seas were calmer as he headed toward Morant Point. The skies were still dark but held off, so he made good time. It was twice the length of the trip he had made the previous day but was traveled in about the same time, and he soon saw the famous lighthouse in the distance.

He was concerned that after his delays, the Jamaicans would not be there, and as he cruised through the harbor, his fears seemed justified because they were nowhere in sight, nor should they be because punctuality was important, as they had told him before. With low fuel and forced to go ashore, he found a place to dock and began walking.

The skies had cleared, and being able to walk in sunshine was nice, though his legs were unsteady, causing him to weave and bringing amused looks for others. He knew that he looked strange, a white man carrying a fuel can, wobbling like a drunk, so he tried to act friendly by waving at those he saw. Still, it wasn't long before the police became curious.

"Do you have papers?" they said, politely.

He showed them. After some examination, they wondered where the other men were.

"They backed out at the last minute," he said. He said he had come to scuba dive and offered to show them the gear on the boat. He was actually a good scuba diver.

"Why don't you come with us while we check your credentials, Mr. Martin?" they said.

"Am I under arrest?"

"No, no, we just need to detain you until verification."

The detainment lasted a few days, but that was fine with Jerry because he needed the time to recover. They took him to Kingston, along with the boat, and finally let him go free. He had some minor repairs done to the boat before deciding it was time to return home. As he walked down the dock, a man came alongside and said, "Mister Martin, we are waiting in the harbor."

He couldn't believe it. "What?"

The Jamaican smiled. "We thought you had drowned," he said.

When Jerry reached them in the harbor, they looked at the boat and smiled. "Small boat for ocean, mon," one of them said.

"Yeah, tell me about it," Jerry said.

They loaded the boat with marijuana bales and told him he should hurry because another storm was on the way.

"How big?" Jerry said.

"Pretty big." He glanced at the boat again. "Small boat."

Jerry cursed his luck and set his bearings for the trip. He glanced anxiously at the sky, pewter, not threatening, futilely trying to convince

Chapter 4

himself that the Jamaican was wrong. He had 600 pounds of marijuana stashed in the cabin and didn't know what the added weight would do to the boat, perhaps make it even more unsafe. Strained as it was to handle heavy seas, he could only imagine what more weight would do.

But the weather held off for most of the morning, and his optimism increased. Maybe the worst had passed him by. But then the sky began to darken. In the distance, he saw lightning, and soon the rain came, dark clouds rolling in like waves of doom. He made sure the door to the cabin was tightly fastened, took a look at the marijuana bales, seeing they were packed in tight, and prepared for the worst. It wasn't long coming. The lighting was the first indication, a waterfall of distant light illuminated the horizon, tiny fingers of death reaching down, pulsing the water and casting fingers of shadows across the surface. Then, the mountain of water came toward him.

He was certain he was going to die.

Chapter 5

For several hours, the storm raged, an endless nightmare, washing the cabin door open, bales of marijuana floating at his feet, the wheel lurching in his hands, tossing the boat around like a kite in a whirlwind. A deflated life raft brushed against his leg and mindlessly he began trying to inflate it, a useless act because nothing would save him, not even a God he doubted existed or cared. He saw a mountain of water rise up and slam over the boat, nearly washing him overboard, and he wondered why he had held on. Just let go and end the misery.

By now, he had no idea of what direction he was going and didn't care. His thirst for survival was waning. Then finally, relief came in the manner of unconsciousness. He felt the energy leaving and wrapped his arms around the wheel, holding tight the best he could, not caring or knowing, just instinct.

Ten hours of fight had taken its toll, and he woke up when a wave splashed against his face, slumped in the floor of the boat, drenched in water, and something that smelled of seaweed. He pulled himself upward and checked his bearings. Where the hell was he? The sky was clearing and he grabbed his binoculars and scanned the horizon. Finally, he saw the faint outline of Haiti. He checked the compass. My god, he thought, I'm somewhere between Haiti and Cuba. Could I be this lucky? He checked again, certain he was right, then set a course toward Great Inagua.

How odd it was, he thought, waking up in the middle of an ocean, almost as if nothing had happened. Was it fate? But he didn't believe in

Chapter 5

fate or much of anything for that matter. Life was up to him. Still, as he thought of the past day, it made him wonder.

He felt like hell, sea salt caked his face, sick to his stomach, and dehydrated. He thought he had lost some marijuana bales and wasn't sure what the salt water had done to those remaining. But he was alive – and a helluva lot smarter.

When the small island came into view, he eased the boat toward shore and waited for Larry Jones to appear. He didn't expect him to be there but after this trip, still being alive, miracles could happen. But not with Jones. After a couple of hours, he accepted that he had skipped out on him, so he anchored the boat and waded ashore to get fuel.

When he reached land, weariness forced him to sit down. He had looked forward to Jones waiting with drink and food. He looked up at seagulls overhead and wondered how it felt to fly. A few curious onlookers offered him water, and with his salt-caked face, he must have looked like a snowflake in a sea of color. Gathering his strength, he pushed to his feet and began walking with the empty fuel cans. A few minutes later his fear was realized when the police arrived.

"What are you doing here?" they asked.

He had to lie. "I don't remember."

"Where's your boat?" Their tone was belligerent and angry.

"What boat? I just said I didn't remember."

One of them hit him with a baton. "I'll ask again: what are you doing here?"

"I've been to Haiti and got caught in the storm," he said. "I hit my head on the boat." He showed a cut place on his temple.

This went on for several minutes before someone ran up saying they knew where his boat was. And then they found the marijuana.

"It's not my boat," Jerry said.

Then the man hit him again. "Your boat, your marijuana. Now, you come with us and see how we treat marijuana man."

The next blow was to the stomach, sending him to his knees. Then another blow struck the side of his head. "Who is with you?" they demanded. "Where are they hiding?" When he said he was alone, they hit him again.

"We take you somewhere to talk," the policeman said.

Somewhere was a small, primitive cell, with a hole in the floor for the bathroom. They began beating him on arms and shoulders, carefully avoiding his face. Once, he was certain they had broken a rib; the pain was horrible. "Confess and tell us about the others," they demanded. Finally, he passed out.

A few hours later they returned, two men, one slightly built and the other fat. He assessed them carefully, measuring the distance between them, calculating how quickly he could hit them both and escape. He had to do it while he still had the strength. He was prepared to make his move when a third man arrived and whispered something to them. The news seemed to disappoint them. One of them kicked him in the side and said, "We move you tomorrow."

He wondered what was going to happen next. Were they taking him somewhere for more advanced interrogation? Maybe to be executed? His mind raced with possibilities. Someone brought food and water and he devoured it like an animal. Perhaps, he thought, someone important was going to see him. It was hope.

The next day, they cleaned him up before taking him to Nassau to appear before a magistrate. "We can either put you in jail for a long time, or you can pay a fine of twenty-five hundred American dollars."

"What about the boat?" Jerry asked.

"What boat?"

"Honest to God, Jerry," Jones said, "I thought you'd drowned in the storm. I mean, who could survive something like that? For Christ's sake, you don't think I'd run out on you if I thought you were alive, do you?" He slapped him on the back. "God damn, I can't believe you made it."

Jerry heard the words but they meant nothing to him. His ribs were sore from the beatings and his knees hurt from being hit by the batons, so

Chapter 5

Jones' actions would have to be sorted out later. He mumbled something and walked away.

"Wait a minute. Didn't I save your life once? You just going to throw all that away?"

"You're saying that makes up for hanging me out to dry?"

"What'd you expect, Jerry? You leave me on an island with nothing but niggers who look at me like I'm a piece of white meat. Tell me you wouldn't done the same. You think I betrayed you but no man in his right mind would've thought you weren't dead."

"You got a yellow streak the size of Louisville Road. What's got into you, man?" He saw Jones straighten up, raise his hand in anger. "What? You going to hit me now?"

Jones turned away, the old Jones not wanting confrontation. "What do you want from me, Jerry?"

"What you owe me is an apology. I decided in jail that I was going to give you some benefit of the doubt, but you need to know that I'm not going to trust you with anything important until you prove you've earned it. So here's a piece of advice. Never try to excuse what you did because there isn't any. Now let's leave it on that. Okay?"

Driving home in the truck, he tried to sort out things. When he was being held captive he relived his experience with the boat, deciding he never wanted to go through that again. So if he wanted to continue smuggling, he was going to have to find another way. And he needed to act soon because he'd heard that a suspect for Park's murder had been taken into custody and supposedly confessed, after first saying someone had hired him to kill the lawyer. There was also a rumor than the authorities were nearing an arrest for the bombings. He could feel it was only a matter of time before the knock came on his door.

"Thirty hours at the most," the flight instructor said to him. "If you don't have your license by then, I'll refund your money."

Jerry smiled. He had no intention of getting a license.

Flying came easy to him. His excellent hand-eye coordination was a benefit, but the greatest help was his determination to listen closely to his instructor, and not being hesitant to ask questions. After 11 hours of instruction he felt confident enough to fly by himself.

The only remaining item was the ground crew and getting a plane. "You're trusting Larry Jones again?" Bonnie said. "I can't believe this. How many times does he have to betray you before you see what he is?"

She had a point but Jones was good at some things, and working on the ground crew should be right up his alley. It didn't require bravery or intelligence. All that had to be done was to unload the marijuana and put it into a vehicle. Anyway, unless Jerry decided not to land at the Maryville airport, where he could take the plane into an enclosed hangar, the ground crew wouldn't be required.

Through a friend, Jerry obtained the proper identification of a man living in a nearby county. From this point on, he was to be known as Richard Martin.

Chapter 6

The first thing he noticed about the banker was his hair seemed wet, slicked down with a cream but trimmed short with no sideburns. His name was Ralph, early thirties, wearing a dark blue suit and patent leather shoes. He'd arrived in a year-old Mercedes, black, and parked in front of the restaurant. He stopped and shook hands with a man, made small talk for a few minutes, then spotted a brown skinned girl wearing a short skirt and halter-top. He kissed her lightly on the cheek and let his hand find her nicely formed butt. She smiled at him and said something Jerry couldn't quite pick up by reading her lips, but didn't move away from his hand. Then he turned toward where Jerry was seated and nodded recognition.

Ralph was a successful banker at one of the largest banks in east Tennessee. Jerry met him through someone who had done business with him for a few years. He was a little less than six feet, brown hair, maybe 175, and a boyish face. As he talked, he continued to look at Jerry, giving him his full attention. He checked his Rolex and pulled away from the girl. She said something which looked like "Call me," and walked away.

"Nice," Jerry said, when Ralph sat down in the expensive chair.

"A great fuck, among other talents. "Good to see you." He ran his fingers along the sleeve of Jerry's coat. "Silk?"

Jerry shook his head. "Linen. When I get your kind of money, I'll buy silk."

Ralph laughed, then waved at a fat man who had just entered the private club. "Christ, that suit looks like he's attending a convention," he said.

"Or a limo driver," Jerry added, smiling.

"That's good." He finally pulled off his sunglasses and carefully placed them on the table, looking up as a tray of coffee arrived, along with cream and sugar. "I got these from Italy, special order. You want me to order you a pair next time?"

"Got more than I can keep up with now," Jerry said. He put one sugar into the coffee and stirred it with the tiny spoon. Looking around, he knew several people in the room, though they wouldn't look at him.

Ralph signaled the waiter. "Two porterhouses..." He looked at Jerry. "Medium rare okay?"

"Yeah."

"And two Jack's on the rocks. I got that right, didn't I?"

"Jack is fine," Jerry said, watching him take charge like he ran the world. Well, maybe he did in Knoxville. "And a couple of olives, too."

"I heard about what happened in Jamaica. Sounds to me like you're lucky to be alive." He sipped the coffee. "Otherwise, how's it going?"

"Couldn't be better," Jerry said. "Who told you about Jamaica, if you don't mind my asking?"

Ralph shrugged. "I've got a lot of ears around here, you know that. I know you lost your boat and started taking flying lessons, for instance. How's that coming along?"

"See, you say things like that and I wonder who the hell you're talking to," Jerry said.

"Hell, Jerry, there's not a whole lot in this town I don't know." He paused as someone passed and spoke to him. "I assume you're planning on expanding your business model and I would be interested in helping."

"You're interested, give me the keys to the bank, then."

"You should've come to me before buying that ski boat. Maybe we could have worked out something bigger." Ralph smiled. "But hindsight's always twenty-twenty, right? So, how big an operation are you thinking about?"

Chapter 6

"One plane and a crew," Jerry said, "and don't ask who they are. All you need to know is that they're reliable." Which was true except for the question mark surrounding Jones.

"How many flights a week?"

"One."

And the plane you're considering?"

"A Beech Baron."

Ralph nodded. "I'm familiar with it."

Jerry could see his mind figuring how much it could hold and what the profit would be. "What are you offering?"

"How about a line of credit at zero interest and my willingness to take care of washing your money."

"For how much?"

"Say ten percent after you get going good—nothing to begin with." Ralph looked at him and when Jerry didn't comment, said, "When the money comes to you it will look so clean they'll think you got it preaching."

"You know what could happen if I learn you're fucking with me, I assume."

"Your reputation is such," Ralph said, nodding. "Consider this a legitimate business offer."

"I'm not saying I will or I won't accept the offer, but I'll definitely think about it," Jerry said. He accepted the drink when it arrived and slugged it down. It would be good when he expanded his business to have a banker in his pocket.

"Good, now how's the flying coming along?"

"Not bad."

"Not bad might not be good enough when you fly into the rugged mountain terrain of Jamaica," Ralph said. "I've been there and can tell you that it's nothing like east Tennessee." He let his gaze move toward the door where a beautiful woman, held closely by an elderly man, entered.

"Christ, is there anybody you're not screwing?" Jerry said.

35

"She's a lawyer," Ralph said. "She's screws; she doesn't get screwed. And speaking of getting screwed, what's going on with the Jefferson City thing. Did Franklin plant those bombs?"

"You need to ask him that."

"I guess I could have a séance," Ralph said. He smiled at Jerry over the glass. "They'll come after you. It's the way they do things."

"I figure as much but not much I can do about it."

"Any evidence to implicate you?"

Jerry frowned. "When did that become a requirement?" He thought about it a moment, trying to make the worry disappear. "I think I'll be ready to start business in a few weeks."

The steaks arrived and Ralph sliced it tentatively with the knife. "I'm glad to see you dressed up today," he said. "I admire a professional look. This has to be run like a business if you want to make any money. You can't be just another outlaw trying to make an easy score."

Jerry looked at him and grinned. "They teach you that in business school or did you come up with by yourself?"

"Come on, damn it, you know what I mean," Ralph said. "I'm saying you can't go off and do some half ass thing like try to take a boat to Jamaica if you want to make money. You've got to think things through, talk with people. You need to set up an organization so you'll have resources. For instance, if it involves money, then come to me. If it involves something else, have someone available who knows about such matters. This isn't a small time pool hustling, card cheating operation. You'll have plenty of big boys looking to catch you, so you can't afford to make even one mistake." He took another drink. "That's my lesson for today, take it or leave it."

Jerry lifted his glass and said, "Let's drink to it."

The next day, Jerry flew into Miami and rented a car, making the drive to Marathon, Florida without any difficulty. The town was in the middle of the Florida Keys and about as remote as he could desire for a place to refuel his plane on the trip from Jamaica. He talked with a man at

Chapter 6

the airport and learned the hours that someone was there to refuel. He could fly in at night and refuel in the morning.

He had thought about trying to purchase a plane with enough fuel capacity to fly nonstop, but that size plane would stretch his limited flying ability. Someone had told him about the Marathon Airport as a midway point, so he decided to check it out. It seemed to have everything he needed.

With that done, he flew into Jamaica to establish contacts for the marijuana.

"What can I expect to find for a landing strip?" he asked the Jamaican who met him at the airport. "How primitive is it going to be?"

"Depends on which site." He talked more like a south Floridian than a Jamaican. "The marijuana is collected at different sites, from different growers, so you'll fly into possibly four different places. Some sites are better than others." He glanced at Jerry. "I assume you're an experienced pilot."

Jerry could do little more than smile. What had been nothing more than a mere idea a month ago was getting ready to happen. And he had no experience, but he had an abundance of optimism.

"Well," the man continued, "you should expect the fields to be uneven, perhaps even rocky, and goats will be running across some of the sites, though the men will do their best to keep them away."

"What about police?"

The man shrugged. "For the most part, that should be no problem," he said. "They are paid well, but from time to time the state police enjoy making a show."

"And how is the money handled?"

"You'll give me half when you place the order, at which time I'll take you to the site. It will give you the chance to look it over and make your plans. Then, when the plane is loaded, the rest of the money is due."

"What if I don't like the landing site? Do I get my money back?"

"No, it's the risk you take."

Jerry nodded, staring at his reflection in restaurant window. The suit was hot but he needed to look good. "We have a deal," he said.

The man handed him a business card. "Call this number when you're ready."

Over the course of the next few weeks, as Jerry continued with his flying lessons, his stomach churned with excitement. Yes, he could fly the plane into Jamaica and soon become a wealthy man – or a dead one.

The Baron was an easy plane to fly, much better than what he flew while taking lessons, and it wasn't long before he felt confident enough to start the new business. So, he traveled to Jamaica to view the landing site.

It was about as he expected, little more than a field, uneven, with rocks outlining the runway. If he hadn't been warned he would have seen desolation, but having had time to think about it, it looked like something he could handle. Not even the falling rain could deter his spirits. He pointed to the goats.

"We keep off runway, mon," the tall Jamaican said, grinning. "You see."

Jerry had come to like the Jamaican enthusiasm, even if it might be misplaced. "What if I just shoot them?" He showed his 9mm in his waistband. He'd been warned about gangs hijacking the marijuana as it was loaded.

"Need bigger gun," the Jamaican said.

"It's big enough."

"That's because you don't understand the problem," the Jamaican said.

"And what did you say then?" Bonnie asked the next day. They were in the living room, drinking iced tea from paper cups she had purchased at the grocery store so she wouldn't have to wash dishes.

"I told him I could buy one. He thought it was funny and the next thing I know he pulled this rifle – I think it was an old. .22 – and shot at one of the goats. The goat never moved."

"He probably missed it deliberately," she said.

Chapter 6

"Maybe, but the gun was real old. I have a hunch it hadn't been fired in a long time. He seemed surprised by the sound."

"You seem happy," she said. "I think you must like these people."

"They're friendly. One of them looks like Tony Curtis." He thought about it a minute. "You want to go out for dinner?"

"I don't want to get dressed, if it's okay. We could order pizza."

He shrugged. "Okay. You want to go flying tomorrow? We could fly over the mountains."

She said, "I'd like that. I could pack a picnic and we could have lunch in the sky."

"Or I could put it on autopilot and we could screw."

She shook her head. "That would scare me to death."

"Me too," he said. "Did Gerald call?"

Gerald was his lawyer, also his friend. "Yes, I almost forgot. He said you need to come by to see him when you have time."

"That's what he said, I should come over? Nothing else?"

"Yeah."

"Did he sound worried?"

"He always sounds worried," she said.

Jerry decided to forego the pizza for a drive to his lawyer's house. They had been friends since childhood, played ball together, but Gerald went one way with his life and he went another. Jerry said, "What was so important you couldn't tell me over the phone?"

"Big brother might be listening."

"What makes you think so?"

"Intuition," Gerald said. "The police have been nosing around in Jefferson City, asking a lot of questions with people you know. And I thought someone might've been following me the other day."

"Well, it's something to think about. I'll make it a point not to talk about anything important on the phone. What else you hearing about Jefferson City?'

Gerald stretched out his lanky frame and said, "They're trying to find enough to bring you to trial. But I hear they're struggling."

"Because I didn't to it," Jerry said. "Fuck."

"Maybe one of your fingerprints on one of the clocks?"

"They look around," Jerry said, "they'll find my fingerprints all over the place. How many times was I there, twenty or so?"

"But the clock was part of the detonator."

"Yeah? So what. I'll find five people who'll swear they saw me fool with those clocks over a year ago."

"You might need them," Gerald said.

"If I was going to hurt those people, you think I don't know better ways to do it? It's stupid to even think of me. Damn insult is what it is."

Gerald shrugged. "You find that place in Florida to refuel."

"On Marathon, in the middle of the Key's," Jerry said. "It pisses me off to think they believe I'm that stupid." He exhaled. "I tried to talk Franklin out of it. Shit!"

"You can't let anyone hear you say that. In fact, from here on, don't comment on it at all, even to Bonnie. The less she knows, the better."

"We don't talk about it. You're sure they found my prints on the clock."

"That's what I heard," Gerald said.

"Son of a bitch! I remember playing with it on a couple of occasions, trying to get it to work right. But there's probably other prints on it, too."

"Doesn't matter if they're trying to get you. Yours are the only ones they're interested in." Gerald took a deep breath. "It's a small town and they want revenge for all the things Park did when he was alive. If you go to trial, we'll have our work cut out for us. But on the other hand, so will the prosecution. Beyond reasonable doubt is a heavy burden to prove."

"That damn clock!" Jerry said.

"Maybe it's nothing. You okay with flying with so little experience?"

"I got more than I had with the *Sea Ray*," Jerry said.

Gerald laughed. "You're something else, Jerry. Sometimes I think you'd do anything for a dollar." He paused for a moment. "You trust this banker?"

Chapter 6

"I think he knows what'll happen if he gets cute," Jerry said. "He's looked at my record."

"Well, speaking of which, don't tell what you're doing. I'm better off not knowing. I'll just handle the legal stuff."

"You make this shit in Jefferson City go away and you'll be my hero, then you won't have to worry."

"What does that mean?"

"It means," Jerry said, "I'll give you enough money to not worry about what anybody thinks."

Chapter 7

A thin mist covered the Blue Mountain range of Jamaica as Jerry approached in the plane. The mountain rose quickly as he approached from the ocean and now was at 3000 feet elevation. The mountain was beautiful from the sky, much like the Smokies, with its blue haze. The region received over 300 inches of rainfall a year and provided Jamaica with most of its water. The region produces some of the best coffee beans in the world, also some of the best marijuana. And marijuana was what interested Jerry today.

He rechecked the coordinates to make certain he was headed the right direction, knowing that with his inexperience he could easily make a mistake. The land was a labyrinth of streams and lakes, dense trees everywhere he looked, and without the proper map coordinates nothing made sense to him. He swooped down through a valley and saw the abandoned school house, one of the landmarks. Soon, the landing area came into sight and he circled the field to let them know to open the gate. The field was L-shaped and narrow. Two wrecked planes were on either side as a needless reminder that he needed to be careful. The runway was short so he had to get down in a hurry. When he dropped too fast, the plane bounced three times before finally rolling to a stop. Only then did he breathe.

"Good landing, mon," one of the workers said, grinning.

Jerry got out of the plane and watched as they packed the 1200 pounds of marijuana inside. He walked over to where a man who owned most of the load was watching quietly from a folding chair. He had thick, graying hair and a leathery face. He was in his late fifties and had the

Chapter 7

tough look of a man who had worked hard all his life. He was worrying about a storm. "I can smell it in the air," he said. "This time of year it smells like the devil's coffee. In one place it might be sunny and across the valley lightning fills the sky." He held up a finger. "No one around here knows the weather like me."

Jerry couldn't see any sign of a storm but sat down beside him to talk.

"Did you know," the man said, "that there is nothing wrong with using marijuana? It causes less harm than drink and makes you feel much better. What is wrong with feeling better?" He pointed to the plane. "You make many trips. Good plane." He looked at the sky for a second. "The Indians brought the seed here and we have the perfect climate for it to grow. I've been growing it for nearly twenty years. This year is one of my best."

"How many farms do you own?" Jerry asked.

"One is enough to keep me busy." He pointed to the workers. "These are good men. They keep good aviation fuel on hand to refuel your plane, not like some of the sites where the fuel is poor. It is dangerous where you go?"

Jerry shrugged. "It's illegal, if that's dangerous. Is it dangerous for you?"

The man returned his shrug. "The police turn their heads except for a few who want to make a name. Sometimes– " His voice trailed off. "Why do they want to stop the poor from making a living? Is it that way in America? My father died from hard work trying to support his family. He could have raised marijuana but chose to be within the law. It killed him."

"How old was he?"

"A few years older than me. Do you smoke the product?" Jerry shook his head. "I mostly use it in tea," the man said. "It takes the pain of the day away. How is it you got started in this flying business."

"I first began by boat and that didn't work out."

The man studied him for a few seconds. "I heard a story about a man who came in a small boat, but I think he drowned in a storm."

"That was probably me," Jerry said.

"But you're not dead." The man laughed. "I will tell them I saw your ghost. We will celebrate by smoking ganja." He yelled at a young man. "This is the ghost of the man in the small boat." The young man smiled. "He didn't believe me. I think you made a wise decision to use a plane." He paused as someone whispered into his ear. Then he motioned the man away. "The man said the police are in the region, but they will be not bother. I would like to go to America sometime. I would like to see Disneyland."

This time it was Jerry who laughed. "You could take your children," he said.

"I could, but perhaps you could return and take them for me. I see enough of them." He lit up a cigar. "Was your father happy?"

"That's hard to say," Jerry said. "I guess we were too busy with our own lives to notice."

"You have brothers and sisters?"

"Brothers, younger. We didn't have much."

"And that's why we're both here on this day. It's fate." He took a deep drag on the cigar and let the smoke curl around his lips. "Rich men don't meet in mountain fields." The men were nearly finished with the loading and were beginning the refueling. The marijuana filled nearly all the plane. "I grow good marijuana. You'll see. Not much trash in the bales."

Jerry watched them refuel and walked over to check the oil. Then, he waved goodbye to the old man and climbed inside. He felt more at ease for some reason and wasn't afraid as he taxied the plane down the hill and gently lifted off into the sky. He glanced back and saw the man get out of the chair and walk to a nearby car. In the distance, he heard the roar of thunder.

After watching the Jamaican coast line disappear, he guided the plane around Cuba, making certain he remained in international airspace, breathing easier as he saw the island behind him. Then, the most difficult part of the trip was in front of him. He had to escape the DEA

Chapter 7

radar that would be searching for him when he approached the coast of Florida. The only way to escape detection was to skim across the water, and that was dangerous for an experienced pilot, much less one like himself.

He dropped down to about twenty feet above the water, not daring to look away for even a second, setting his squawk box to 1200—the frequency of a local airplane just enjoying a nice day – and hoped the clutter reflected off the water would confuse the radar. But one wrong move and he'd be in the ocean, at best waiting for the Coast Guard to pick up and arrest him. Suddenly, the plane was buffeted by a gust of wind, and the plane dipped dangerously close to the water. "Jesus!" he yelled. He climbed a little higher until feeling a little more comfortable.

The gust of wind proved to be the beginning of a steady breeze out of the southeast, and it took him a few minutes to adjust to the change. Soon, he was just flying as he had in east Tennessee when he soared over the majestic mountains and swooped down through the long valleys. The Caribbean was a beautiful aqua in the shallow areas – he marveled at the different colors within the large ocean – and looked much more accommodating from the air than from a boat. He had hoped for good weather and the soft breeze was a good answer.

But he knew that the moment he let down his guard, something was waiting to happen, so as much as he desired he couldn't relax. He concentrated on doing the right things to avoid the attention of those watching for suspicious activities. He knew the DEA had trained eyes looking for any misstep.

He focused on keeping the plane at a low altitude as the Florida coast appeared. When he crossed land, he lifted the plane higher, finally able to breathe normally. He changed the plane's heading to the Marathon Airport and relaxed.

When he landed and taxied to a stop at the refueling station, he was exhausted. It was late in the afternoon and he was tempted to leave the plane and get some sleep at a motel, but the thought of leaving the marijuana alone at night was worrisome. So, he got out and stretched his legs while the plane was refueled.

He took a few minutes to glance around. Marathon was nearly the midway point of the Florida Keys, located about an hour from both Key West and Key Largo. The Bahamians and New England fishermen settled the area in in the early 19th century, growing fruit and fishing the rich water. The name Marathon came from the long hours the workers put in when building the Florida East Coast Railroad.

When the fueling was complete, Jerry checked the oil and climbed back inside. A few minutes later he was on his way home.

He pulled the plane into the hangar, and they unloaded the weed into cars, driving to Ralph's house to store it. Jerry was dismayed by the amount of useless stalks but still thought they'd gross nearly three hundred grand.

He thought that Ralph seemed antsy; not the type of anxiousness someone has when they're hiding something, but the concern that comes when they think of the consequences. If they were caught, it'd be a lot of prison time. Jerry figured he'd get another couple of flights in before Ralph decided to call it quits. But that would by okay. By then he'd be able to find another partner.

Distributing the marijuana was not difficult. Jerry had bootlegger friends who were more than happy to sell weed along with illegal whiskey. They sold the product from Kentucky to Memphis. They packaged it into bags, usually not less than ten pounds, and the clients included a wide range of people. Around Knoxville, the biggest market was with students and teachers. Some of the buyers would buy a pound or two to smoke, and sell the rest so they could then buy more. There was a big demand for pot, and Jerry was on his way to finally making his fortune.

When the pot was sold, Jerry made another flight.

It was his fourth trip when his inexperience got him into trouble. He was flying off the coast of Cuba when dense clouds surrounded his plane. It was so thick he couldn't see more than a few feet. His main concern

Chapter 7

was his proximity to Cuba. His navigation map was marked in bold, red letters: MAINTAIN A MINIMUM OF 20 MILES DISTANCE FROM THE COAST OF CUBA. You could get shot down if you invaded their air space.

He watched closely his navigation indicators and thought he was okay, but when the clouds began to disperse, he looked down and saw that he was too near the coast. He quickly tuned the radio to the military frequency and was relieved, because while there was a lot of chatter none of it sounded as though it was directed at him.

He continued to ease his plane to the right. He didn't want to make an abrupt maneuver, fearing it might draw attention. Then, he saw what looked like a tiny dot of light approaching from in front. The dot grew larger and larger until he saw what it was: a MIG fighter. Son of a bitch! And it was coming directly at him. His first thought was that the MIG was going to shoot him down; his second was that it was going to rip off his wings. In what seemed like the blink of an eye, the MIG soared a few feet over him. It was so close he could see the missiles attached to the wings. The noise was deafening and his small plane felt like it was being ripped apart. He was certain the wings had been damaged.

As the MIG soared miles away, Jerry hoped he was in the clear, but then he saw it make a wide sweeping turn and start toward him again. Jerry knew he had no chance to get into international air space before it was on him, so he braced for whatever was going to occur. It spared under him. *God Almighty!* There was a violent lurch of the plane, a fragile kite in a tornado; he fought to maintain control as the wings began to vibrate. This is it, he thought as he waited for the ringing in his ears to stop. He followed the MIG with his eyes, hoping it would continue moving away from him. "Damn you," he said, as once again it turned.

He again saw the dot of light in front of him. This time the MIG seemed heading directly at him; not under or over – at him. This time he was going to fire a missile. But at the last instant, the MIG turned nearly straight up, the after burners glowing red as it began to climb. Jerry could almost feel the heat. And then it disappeared.

Jerry kept waiting for the jet to show, this time maybe from above, but after a few minutes when nothing happened he allowed himself to think that he was safe. And when he looked at the instruments, he knew he was because he was out of Cuban airspace. And if he could help it, he would never return.

When he landed in Jamaica, he found the plane to be in good condition, at least the parts he could see. The excitement had almost made him forget that he'd promised to bring a 14-year-old on a visit to Tennessee. The boy hung around the landing sites and begged Jerry to take him, and finally Jerry said he would if the parents agreed. There were no parents as the boy lived with a distant relative.

Jerry knew what it was like to be poor, so he would take the boy to east Tennessee and show him a different part of the world. The kid was standing on the runway with a cardboard suitcase by his side. "Boss, after they load gas, we go to America?"

Jerry laughed. "Yeah, we go to America."

But it was not to be. During the refueling, one of workers mistakenly punched a small hole on the left side fuel tank. As the gas was being pumped, it began spilling under the plane. There was no way to get the tank repaired in the jungle, so Jerry had to improvise. Finally, he came up with a plan.

"Okay," he told the boy, "climb in. I got this figured out." He would tilt the wings so the fuel wouldn't spill, then get it fixed in Marathon. It was an easy fix if you had the parts.

The boy looked at the gas and then back to Jerry. "Boss," he said, "I think I wait until the next trip."

Jerry was laughing when the plane left the ground.

In another week, Ralph told Jerry he wanted out. Jerry had grown to like him. After getting to know him, and after pushing through all that rich boy bullshit, he was okay – just another guy trying to make a fast buck.

"It's the airplane that has me worried," Ralph said. "It's in my name. No hard feelings, I hope."

Chapter 7

"Why would there be? Hell, you've helped me make a lot of money. What're you going to do with the plane?"

"I think it'll catch on fire," Ralph said.

"I like the way you think."

Ralph grinned. "If you'd like, I can hook you up with someone that might be interested in helping with a plane."

"Already got someone in mind," Jerry said, "but I could use your help in banking my money."

"That won't change. Don't worry about it."

Jerry watched him run his fingers through his Marlon Brando haircut. It'd be easy to take one look at him and think he was soft, but that'd be a big mistake. He held out his hand. "Pleasure doing business with you."

Larry Jones introduced him to Harold Ward, a gregarious man about Jerry's age with a twinkle in his eye. He was from Atlanta and a car thief, which is how Jones knew him. Jerry took a quick liking to him and they would hang out at local bars and lie to each other about women. One day, Ward mentioned a man named Harold Rosenthal, who had been a bail bondsman in the Atlanta area before he dipped his toes in smuggling cocaine out of Colombia. He hired pilots to fly the dope into the southeast, where it would then be delivered to the buyers. As Ward talked, Jerry listened intently, picking apart the scheme, seeing both its weaknesses and strengths. He wasn't surprised when Ward said Rosenthal had been caught and was serving time in a Memphis federal prison. But he *was* surprised when Ward said that Rosenthal boasted that he was soon going to walk out of the prison a free man.

"We need to meet him," Ward said, shoving the empty bottle aside. "Cocaine is where the big money is."

Jerry smiled. "And how exactly are we going to do that? I'm not going anywhere near a fucking prison."

"When he gets out," Ward said.

Jerry laughed. "Yeah, right."

On Friday, Jerry rubbed the sleep from his eyes and found the rye toast and coffee. He had just completed a flight in his new plane and was enjoying his success until Bonnie sat down across the table and said, "We need to talk."

A few minutes later, he hadn't touched his food. The last thing she had said to him was, "I don't know whether he was local or the FBI. He just said he needed to talk to you about the Jefferson City event."

He was giving her his full attention now. "And that's how he described it – an event?"

She nodded. "When I tried to get answers he just said he'd call back when you were home. He talked nice for a police person."

Jerry resisted the urge to curse. The sons of a bitches hadn't come around to just say hello. He looked around the kitchen and for a moment wondered if he should just pack up and get the hell out of Tennessee. He had enough money to start a new life somewhere, but it wouldn't be good for Bonnie, who liked it here.

Her hand started to shake. "Hon, you didn't do it, did you?"

"No, but it might not make a difference. Franklin's got a lot of enemies who'd like to get revenge on him even if he's dead." Jerry got out of the chair and walked into the living room. The couch was covered with the magazines. He picked up one to glance at the cover, some woman wearing a short skirt and smoking a Camel cigarette.

"If you didn't do it, you'll be okay," she said. "You're telling me the truth, aren't you?"

"What'd I say? And you didn't tell them anything else, other than I was gone."

"What would I tell them? Oh, he's busy flying weed from Jamaica right now. No, I didn't tell them anything else."

"Yeah, but sometimes things get said without meaning to," he said. "They didn't try to ask you anything, did they?"

"Just where you were and when you'd be back."

"That's good," he said, not meaning a word of it.

"I couldn't stand it if you had to go to jail," she said.

Chapter 7

"It's nothing to worry about." He reached over and touched her hand. "They're just cops doing what cops do." He thought for a moment. "Maybe we can take a trip and put this behind us. Think you'd like that."

"Where?"

New Zealand, he thought. "I don't know, Miami is nice."

The story was circulating that Franklin Park had been killed by a man he had hired to kill Waymon Poole, that the man said he was going to kill Park instead and take all the money rather than kill a policeman and get paid a little. When Jerry had heard that, he knew God had a sense of humor.

After the last run, Jerry took time to reflect on the past and future. He was making good money, hell he was making great money, but he sensed it wasn't enough to satisfy him for long. There was no denying that a part of him wanted to make so much money he could rub it in the faces of those who said he wouldn't amount to anything. He also knew this was a dangerous attitude because it made you do stupid things. And he had already done enough of those for a lifetime. He had several things going for him, he thought, but his biggest advantage was that he was a damn good pilot. By his calculation, he had flown nearly fifty thousand miles and landed on terrain more rugged than most pilots ever see. So, he could envision himself selling his skill for a lot more money than he was making smuggling marijuana. And this thought invariably led him back to Harold Rosenthal. If the man really did have connections in Colombia – Jerry let his mind consider the possibilities. But Rosenthal was locked in a federal prison so why even think about it.

Jerry was once more thinking of this when he walked in the front door of his mother's modest house on the outskirts of Maryville. His youngest brother was there and nodded toward Jerry. It was noon and his mother had prepared a lunch of fried chicken and mashed potatoes. They talked little during the meal and when they left the table, Jerry slipped her two hundred dollars. She never asked where the money came from.

Later, he took her for a ride in his truck, going by familiar places where relatives lived. She enjoyed getting outside. He pulled into a service station and filled the truck up with gas, bought both of the soft drinks, and him a pack of peanuts. He still enjoyed pouring the nuts into the bottle. He reached into the glove compartment, past the loaded gun, and found a bottle of aspirin. His leg was hurting bad today for some reason, but aspirin usually took care of that.

They drove through Eagleton Village and into Blount Hills where Jerry would hang out as a teenage boy. No one was around that he knew, and his mother didn't want to stop unannounced at a relative's house, so he kept driving. They talked about everything except what he was doing. She had learned not to nose around in his business. She was interested in his kids, her grand children, and wished Barbara brought them around more.

A few days later, two men from the Tennessee Bureau of Investigation came, wearing bad suits with equally bad haircuts. The tall, slim one did all the talking.

"We'd like to ask you a few questions, Mr. LeQuire. May we come in?"

"I don't know," Jerry said. "What's it about?"

"The bombings in Jefferson City," Slim said.

"Hell, I thought you'd already solved that."

"Just a few questions," Slim said, brushing up against Jerry.

"Not tonight, not here," Jerry said. "How about tomorrow, at Shoney's on Alcoa Highway? Say, eightish?"

Slim gave him an impatient look. "All right, tomorrow it'll be."

The next night, they were waiting when he arrived. As they entered the restaurant, Gerald Russell appeared. Jerry said, "This is my lawyer."

Slim looked pissed. "We want to talk with you, not your lawyer," he said.

"He doesn't bite," Jerry said.

"Fuck this," Slim said, motioning to his partner they were leaving.

"This is not good," Gerald said. "They're planning something."

Jerry nodded. "Get a good lawyer to help you, Gerald."

Chapter 8

The street value of marijuana was increasing, along with its popularity, and since there wasn't much competition in east Tennessee Jerry's prices had increased nearly thirty percent in the last few months. He made as many runs as he could.

The Jamaican said, "I didn't catch your last name."

Jerry said he didn't have one because parents where he came from didn't use them. And the man gave him a confused look before breaking out in a grin. They were standing in a field that had been mowed for a landing strip, with ruts where planes had landed in the mud and rocks were protruding through the ground. But for some reason there were no goats. He thought that it was too bad a place even for them.

"And you think I can land a plane here?" Jerry said. It was pouring down rain and already the ground was starting to look like a swamp bog.

"No problem, mon."

"The hell you say. This is nothing but a mud hole." He would have to come in slow. With one miscalculation, he would be in trouble. Also if something went wrong with the controls he didn't have enough experience to get out of the problem. Because of his inexperience, he'd have nightmares about crashing and wake up in a cold sweat. Small planes crashed frequently, usually because of pilot error, and sometimes there was just one chance.

"Many pilots land here," the Jamaican assured.

'Because they're stupid," Jerry muttered.

The Jamaican grinned. "No problem, mon; you'll see."

Jerry almost laughed because it made him think of all the "bubbas" back in Tennessee whose last words were usually, "watch this, no problem."

He privately admitted that he enjoyed the excitement almost as much as the money. He liked taking chances when the reward was great. When he was flying he felt free, like nothing could touch him. This life was what he had dreamed of when he was working a nine-to-five job at the auto place, which he hated. Some people just weren't cut out to do honest work, he thought.

It was one of the reasons why his marriage hadn't worked, that and his wandering eye. He admitted his ex had made the right decision by leaving him and taking the two kids. If they had tried to stay together nothing good would have come out of it. This way they were still friends. He didn't know if he would ever marry again, though he thought he and Bonnie would do okay together.

For the rest of 1980 and into the spring of 1981, the flights were uneventful, and Jerry's cash was accumulating. But he dreaded when the state would arrest him for the Jefferson City charges.

"It's like I've spent my whole life running from the law," he said to Bonnie, "waiting for the other shoe to drop. I know everything that's goes on in my world but this…" He took a breath. "……this is out of my control and I don't fucking like it."

"Let's take the money and leave, Jerry."

"And do what? You don't think I've considered it? Just about every day…when I land and take off from Jamaica, when I fly so close to the ocean I can smell the salt…every day." He looked away. "One big score, and I might have a chance. How would you like to live in Colombia?"

"South America?" She frowned. "I don't know anybody there."

"Neither do I, but we could start a new life there. Harold's been telling me about a man he knows who might be able to set us up with the cartel."

"The cartel?" she said, almost in a gasp. "I heard something about them on TV. They're bad people. I read they cut out tongues and stick them in people's throats. I don't want any part of them."

Chapter 8

"There's that but there's also the good thing that the cops can't touch me there– no extradition."

"God, Jerry, really? The farthest thing on my mind is living in South America. I'd never know what they were saying."

"You'd learn." He rubbed his head, thinking she looked pretty good in those skinny pajamas. "But it's just something to think about. Right now, the guy's in a federal prison and doesn't look like he'll get out soon."

"But we're talking about it," she said.

"Yeah, I guess we are. Ward says he plans to escape, got some sort of deal going for him."

"And you believe that?" she said.

"I'd like to but that doesn't mean a lot. Still, Ward said he was a straight up guy. What I like is that he has experience smuggling cocaine; that sort of interests me."

"Is that why he's in prison?"

"I could learn from his mistakes."

"You've made up your mind, haven't you?" she said. "Jesus, Jerry."

"Nothing wrong with thinking about it." He moved to his feet. "By the way, Harold's coming by later. I thought we could go out to eat."

"Shit, I was hoping we could get drunk and have a little fun," she said.

"We can eat fast."

In late 1981, Jerry was told that his arrest on the bombing incidents was imminent. It came some days later. At the pre-trial hearing, the judge told the prosecution that he didn't think they had much of a case, other than hearsay, but eventually allowed the trial to continue.

His lawyers said that the trial was strictly political and all the evidence, as skimpy as it was, was circumstantial. Jerry steadfastly proclaimed his innocence.

The courtroom was packed when the trial began. The prosecution trotted out witness after witness to place Jerry at Park's home. Witnesses also testified that Park had made several threats against the intended victims, vowing that "someone was going to get hurt." According to one of the councilmen, John Gibson, Park tried to force him to oust Waymon

Poole as chief of police. He said Park telephoned him several times and cursed, mixed in with threats, before hanging up. Warren Stinson, a former employee of Park, said that he accompanied Park to the Maryville airport to meet with Jerry. Later on, he saw Jerry and two other men at Park's house.

The state's theory was that Jerry and Park acted together in the crime, as evidenced by their multiple meetings just prior to the incident. That they found two of Jerry's fingerprints on one of the clocks used as the bomb triggers further indicated Jerry's involvement.

Demolition experts stated that the blasting caps on the bombs had detonated, but apparently the dynamite was old and wet, so it didn't explode. The experts said the work looked like the hand of the same person. They painted the picture of someone inexperienced at making bombs.

The defense produced a witness saying that she had seen Jerry handle the clocks on several occasions because they were in plain sight. She said she had even picked up the clocks. The defense team meticulously went over the state's evidence. Yes, Jerry was Park's friend, which explained their meetings. Yes, it was reasonable for Jerry's fingerprints to be on the clock because witnesses had testified seeing him around them. But why, they asked, were his prints only on one clock? Wasn't it reasonable for many prints to be found or were they to believe that in all the other instances he took precautions? The state's theory just didn't make sense. The only crime Jerry was guilty of was being friends with a man, now dead, whom the state wanted to persecute. Where was the motive? Had the state shown any transfer of funds to Jerry? What would possess a man to do such a thing for a friend? No, it just didn't make sense.

"The state's case is a sham," the defense lawyer said. "It's just a waste of tax payers money."

And many pundits agreed but it only took the jury a few hours to return with a verdict of guilty. Jerry was sentenced to two 5-year sentences to be served consecutively. And the community felt pleased with itself.

Chapter 8

"When I first came here," Jimbo said, "you walk in the yard and someone would get stabbed, as sure as rain. He might be standing by the fence or leaning against the wall, it made no difference. Somebody would run a shank into his side just to watch him bleed. There didn't have to be no reason other than that. You wouldn't believe how bad it was. You couldn't have a decent conversation without taking the chance of saying something wrong and having to watch your back until something happened. The guards didn't give a shit, either. You want to kill somebody, be their guest. The bastards rather watch a good knife fight than eat, I think. Fucking hillbillies. Every one of them probably married their cousin."

He was talking about Brushy Mountain Prison, situated deep in the east Tennessee hills, which housed some of the state's most dangerous convicts. One day there and he knew that Jimbo was right; it was a dangerous place.

"You met James Earl yet?" Jimbo said.

James Earl was James Earl Ray, sentenced to life for murdering Martin Luther King. "Yeah, he likes to shoot pool," Jerry said. "Pretty good too."

"Son of a bitch wouldn't even speak to me," Jimbo said. "You?"

"We talked a little. I think he just minds his own business."

Jimbo lit a cigarette. "Rumor here is that you knew Jacky Laymon," he said.

"A little."

"We were buddies while he was here," Jimbo said.

"I remember him mentioning you," Jerry said.

"I could've escaped with him, but I didn't." Jimbo telling him that he never thought Laymon would ever make it, but the son of a bitch just walked away while he was outside doing some work for the guards.

"I never figured out how someone in for murder would be allowed outside for anything," Jerry said.

"I told you, the guards are hillbillies," Jimbo said. "Fucking shame what happened to him. I hear he was living at your house."

"I don't know nothing about that," Jerry said.

"Yeah, understand. But I hear you did right by him. Is it true they ran over him until his brains oozed from his head? That's what I hear."

"I'll just say he's dead," Jerry said. "And dead's dead."

Jimbo shrugged. "Well, there's men here who appreciate you trying to help him. Word travels fast."

"Then, If I need something, I know who to ask," Jerry said.

"And there's always something."

Jerry settled in to prison life, keeping his mouth shut and minding his business. But he kept waiting for when he would be released, pending the outcome of his appeal to the state supreme court. Though he held some hope the verdict would be overruled, he understood the politics involved, so he was resigned to prison. Unless he could get connected to the cocaine business in Colombia. He had thought about that a lot after the trial. The law couldn't touch him there.

"You think a man could escape a federal prison?" he said to Jimbo.

"Yeah, if he had enough money to bribe guards, No, it wouldn't surprise me none. Only difference between us and them is they haven't got caught. We talking about anyone in particular or just talking."

"In general but what if I asked if you'd ever heard of a con named Harold Rosenthal?" Jerry said.

"I'd say I might've," Jimbo said. "If he's the one used to be a bail bondsman. He's in for drugs, right?"

"Yeah," Jerry said.

Jimbo paused for a moment. "Heard about him because a guy last year said he was in prison with him once. Conversation was about him liking the coloreds."

"Whatta you mean, liking?" Jerry said.

"Worked with Martin Luther King and his bunch in the Atlanta area."

"Interesting." Jerry leaned back against the wall and thought about this. Harold Ward hadn't mentioned that he was a nigger lover. "Is he pretty smart?"

Chapter 8

"Aren't all cons? All I know he told this guy that when he got out he had a plan that'd make him filthy rich, said he was going to combine politics with business, whatever the hell that meant."

"I'd like to talk to this guy who knows him."

Jimbo grinned. "We'd have to hold a séance, then. He died three months ago – heart attack."

A week later, Jerry received the news that he was being released. "I'm not going back," he told his lawyer.

"Well, your appeal has a chance…"

"You don't understand," Jerry said. "I'm not going back."

Two weeks later, he was smuggling again.

Chapter 9

Jerry's primitive flying skills had evolved to where he now felt he could take on almost anything. No longer did he fear straying into Cuban airspace or of crashing into the ocean from a miscalculation. So, today as he flew through the mountain pass, he enjoyed the spectacular view of the lush green mountainside, smiled as he saw the truck parked to the side of the landing area, the men waving white handkerchiefs at hm. He banked to the left to line up the field and eased back on the throttle. There was a slight bump as the wheels touched down and he coasted to a stop close to the truck.

Jerry's enthusiasm for smuggling marijuana was tempered by the certainty that his appeal would be denied and prison would be waiting. While at Brushy Mountain, he had picked up some useful information about Harold Rosenthal and now was hoping he would actually escape from prison and contact Harold Ward. Ward had been writing him, keeping in close contact, just in case. If he could go to work for the Colombians, h thought that would solve all his problems. Marijuana was just a way to make money until a miracle happened.

"This best marijuana on the island," the man said to him. "You get premium price, mon."

Jerry laughed. Every seller told him the same thing, but most of his customers couldn't tell premium from rags. They just wanted to get high. He'd smoked a little but didn't like it. If he wanted to get drunk, alcohol was the way to go.

"See you next time," Jerry said, after the plane was refueled.

Chapter 9

The man held up his hand. "I need to tell you about police," he said. "They been coming around unexpectedly. Last week, they came and took marijuana from a friend."

"I thought you had that handled," Jerry said.

"I don't know. Just be careful when you land."

What the hell am I supposed to do if I see them, Jerry thought, I have to get fuel.

Larry Jones listened to the story. "Couldn't you go somewhere else to get gas? You're not carrying anything illegal."

Jerry laughed. "I doubt that would make much difference." Jones was working on his ground crew and was surprisingly doing a good job, though Jerry still didn't trust him. "You seen Harold today? I need to talk to him."

"No. What you two up to anyway?"

"We're trying to figure if it was the chicken or that egg that came first," Jerry said. "I'll see you around."

"Don't go off mad."

In September 1981, Harold Rosenthal escaped from the Memphis Federal Prison. "Told you he's a smart one," Ward said as he sucked on a beer in a Maryville tavern. "Just walked out of there like he owned the place."

Jerry marveled at the news. He had been in a couple of prisons, and unless it was a workhouse, he saw no way to do it. And Rosenthal was locked behind walls, multiple doors and strings of barbed wire. "Okay, now let's hope he calls."

"You ready if he does?"

"I think so," Jerry said.

But Thanksgiving came and went with nothing from Rosenthal, and Jerry was beginning to believe his boasts to Ward about Colombia were just hot air. In December, he decided to make one last run for the year. He told Bonnie that when it was over, they'd visit some friends in Kentucky in the new car he had bought her.

He walked around the plane and inspected it. He'd made so many flights he thought he could almost do it blindfolded. He recognized every little noise in the plane like it was a part of his body. He rubbed his hand across the fuselage and climbed inside.

Remembering the earlier warning, he circled the landing area to see that it was clear of police. Seeing nothing, he brought the plane down and glided to a stop. The men began loading the marijuana and refueling the plane. He watched the refueling process closely to make sure everything went well. The only problem he'd ever had with the Beech Baron had been caused by a refueling mistake. He checked the oil, more from habit than anything, then stepped back as an elderly Jamaican approached.

"Hey boss, you're looking fine this day," he said. He had a small tattoo on his left arm. "You been on vacation?"

"Vacation. What's that?"

The man grinned. "Take me to Las Vegas, boss. Plenty lucky."

"Climb in and we'll go," Jerry said.

The man grinned. "No money, boss," he said.

Jerry laughed. He had learned to appreciate the Jamaicans and the beauty of their land. It wasn't too unlike the backwoods of the Smoky Mountains.

He started the engines and prepared for the long trip home. The Jamaican held up his thumb to wish Jerry luck as the plane began moving forward. Overall, the runway was slightly downhill and uneven, but not as bad as some. The plane lurched forward, and he felt the bales of marijuana shift. There was a slight upgrade at the start that blocked his view from the runway end, but as he topped the hill he saw them – two uniformed men walking toward him carrying weapons. The police had arrived, and they meant business. He hesitated for a moment – but just for a moment. He pushed down the throttle and accelerated toward them. They frantically waved their guns, and then puffs of smoke came from their barrels. Instinctively, he ducked.

Chapter 9

The plane surged forward. As he neared the men, one of the bullets hit the plane. There was a loud *thud*, and he cursed. If a bullet penetrated the thin exterior and found the fuel, he would be in big trouble. Then, another t*hud* from underneath the plane. Twenty yards from them, close enough to see their faces, and the bastards kept firing. Young men trying to kill him. He felt the plane lift into the air, the engine straining, as he pulled back the stick. He was airborne but not before more bullets hit the plane. He looked back at the policemen who were still firing at him, but the bullets were now falling harmlessly to the ground.

"Son of a bitch!" he yelled. The last trip of the year and bad luck hits. He pounded his fist on the control panel. Why him? Why today? Anxiously, he began to assess for possible damage. The instruments showed nothing unusual, but there were three things he was worried about – fire, a loss of fuel, and a loss of control. Nothing was burning, and the controls seemed okay. But while he couldn't see any damage, he knew that something had happened because the wind noise from where the landing gear folded up was louder than usual. One of the bullets had done something to the plane, and he frantically tried to think of the danger that might pose.

Had someone betrayed him? The question pounded at him. He was going to have to get answers before the next trip. But this concern was unraveled when the noise from underneath the plane increased. Something was wrong. The worst thought was that the landing gear controls were damaged, and the wheels wouldn't lower. Taking several deep breaths, he began to concentrate on what he could control. He knew his ability; if a plane would fly, he could land it under most conditions. He decided that the chance of a bullet damaging the landing gear was remote but still——

He tested the controls again before skimming the water as he approached the Florida coast. Except for the noise from under the plane, everything was fine. He would fix whatever damage there was once he reached Marathon, and if it was major, he'd rent a truck and drive the marijuana to Tennessee. There was more than one way to skin a cat. A mile inland, he resumed altitude. It was a beautiful, Chamber of Commerce day, with clear skies and a mile of visibility. South Florida was beautiful from the sky and he thought he wouldn't mind living here.

He reached down to secure his .38 to prepare for the landing, then made the slow descent into the Marathon airport. He lowered the landing gear and waited anxiously as the wheels fell into place. Okay, he thought, everything works. The plane bounced slightly before settling down and rolling smoothly toward the end of the runway. He touched the brakes and reversed the props. As the plane slowed, the unexpected happened. The plane crumbled to the pavement, followed by a horrible crunching noise, like scraping something across glass, a screeching sound like nothing he'd ever heard, and plane was careening down the runway on its belly.

The front of the plane pitched down and one of the propellers dug into the runway, throwing him around in the cockpit like a rag doll. There was nothing he could do. He could feel the heat as flames shot up from the bottom of the plane, and he expected the tanks to rupture at any moment. Futilely, he fought the controls. Was this how he was going to die?

The plane swerved toward the side of the runway and he worried that if the propeller dug into soft ground, it would flip over the plane. His head slammed against the side, drawing blood; everything was spinning. Then, abruptly the plane stopped as though hitting something and his body thrust forward, followed by silence. His mind worked feverishly. He had just crashed an airplane filled with over a thousand pounds of marijuana. What the hell was he going to do? Panic crept over him as he heard the siren. Racing down the runway was a pick-up followed by a fire truck. Before he could climb out of the cockpit, a young man said, "You alright, buddy?"

No, Jerry was thinking. I'm anything but alright. "I think I'm having a heart attack," he said. "You need to take me to a hospital." He was opening the truck door before the man could answer. "Right now!"

"Okay," the man said. "Just don't die on me."

CHAPTER 9

"Drive." Jerry leaned back in the seat. He had a splitting headache but that was the least of his worries. Still, there was a glimmer of hope. If the could make it through the locked gate, no matter what happened after that he could get away. But he had to get through the gate.

The man, no more than twenty, floored the gas pedal, and as Jerry glanced back he saw the other men looking inside the plane.

As they arrived at the secured gate, the man's radio squawked and someone said, "Shit, this plane is loaded with marijuana."

Jerry looked at him and said, "Listen to me very carefully. I've got fifty thousand dollars in my pocket that's yours if you drive me through that gate. Just through the gate and that's it." He grabbed the radio and threw it outside, sorry that he'd left the .38 in the plane. "Fifty grand. You need to make up your mind right now."

"There's nothing to think about. Buddy, you got a deal. You kidding me? Fifty fucking grand!"

Jerry's relief was short lived because as soon as the man was outside, he started running and yelling at the top of his lungs.

By the time Jerry exited the truck the others had arrived. He was surrounded and one of them had a gun. Fifteen minutes later, the police arrived and took him to the station, where he was placed in a cell until the DEA came. But before they arrived, he made a phone call to a lawyer he knew in Kentucky. He'd met Larry Allen a few years earlier at a bar. Allen reminded him a little of Franklin Park in that they were both shady characters who liked to party. Allen's nickname was "Lying Larry," for obvious reasons. But he knew a lot of influential people and could get matters handled.

"Sit tight and I'll have someone contact you," Allen said. "How much marijuana?"

"About a thousand pounds."

"Shit. Well, don't say a word until he gets there."

And that's exactly what Jerry did.

The Miami lawyer was there in three hours. "Okay, here's what's going to happen. The DEA doesn't give a shit about you unless you can lead them to bigger fish, and the court is already jammed. So, I'm going to get everything delayed, which I don't think will receive much opposition, then they're going to let you go on bond. If I were you, I'd get out of here as fast as I could and never set foot within a hundred miles of the place again."

That would not be a problem, Jerry thought.

In a few days, he was back in Tennessee. While he was in jail, he learned that one of the bullets had damaged the hydraulic shock absorber cylinder on the landing gear, so when the plane landed it was metal against metal, and the landing gear had disintegrated. He was lucky to be alive, but now he was without a plane.

The next evening, he drove his truck down Highway 411, past the restaurants and motels. He had no destination and was just driving. He could think when he was alone in the truck. He had thought about visiting his mother and brothers, but had just kept going when he reached their house. He stopped at a service station to get gas, and went inside the use the bathroom. His leg was bothering him a little so he used the time to stretch it out. He took a couple of aspirins and washed them down with a Coke. He glanced at the road maps carefully displayed on a rack and thought it would be nice to take a trip. Bonnie had said she was ready anytime, but he had too much on his mind.

He dropped some money into a vending machine and got a candy bar, Baby Ruth, and tore open the wrapping. The man behind the counter gave him a curious look, like he knew him from somewhere, a man who tried his best to look tough, but Jerry had seen his share of tough guys and ignored him.

"Don't I know you?" the man said.

"Could be," Jerry said. "See you."

He got back inside the truck and drove off, thinking the man didn't know how lucky he had been, because Jerry had stuck a 9mm under his shirt and didn't give a damn if he had to use it.

"They're fun people," Bonnie said a few days later. They were just driving into Kentucky after spending a few days with friends outside Cincinnati. "You enjoyed it, right?"

Chapter 9

Jerry didn't respond.

"What's wrong with you?" she said.

"I'm thinking."

"You've been moody since we got in the car," she said.

"Jesus, Bonnie, won't you let me think?"

"About what? I have a right to know."

"Look, I'm looking at prison time, and I don't have a fucking airplane," he said. "Now, is that enough answer for you?"

Yesterday, Jerry had learned of a place in Kentucky where he could probably lease a Piper Navajo. With a Navajo, he could fly without refueling, but the downside was that he wasn't checked out in the plane and would need someone to teach him. But right now smuggling was all he had to hold on to.

His concentration was diverted by an 18-wheeler that ran right on his bumper before passing. Interstate 75 was filled with trucks this evening. He turned on the CB to listen to the chatter, hoping it would get his mind off his troubles. A minute later, he heard a trucker boast, "I blew the doors off that son of a bitch." Jerry felt his rage build, and unable to control it, floored the gas pedal and passed him on a hill. When Jerry slowed down, the truck passed him and the driver hoisted his middle finger. Jerry, now boiling with anger, said on the radio, "You think you're tough, pull your sorry ass over and we'll see how tough you really are."

Bonnie looked at him in disbelief. "What are you doing?" she said.

"Stay out of this."

There was a lot of chatter on the radio as to how that would be a bad idea for Jerry, but he passed the truck and flipped his indicator lights on, easing the car to the shoulder. In his mirror, he saw the truck pull over.

Jerry grabbed his .38 and got out of the car. In the darkness, he saw the man holding something in his right hand. A tire thumper, Jerry thought. He would take it away from him and crack open his head. But as he got close, he saw it wasn't what he thought and before he could react, he felt a sharp pain in his chest as the small caliber bullet ripped through his skin.

He stumbled back, fire raging in his body and squeezed off three shots in succession. The trucker crumbled to the ground.

Jerry managed to make it to the car where Bonnie was standing. "I got to get to a hospital," he said.

She turned on the flashing lights and took off. A mile down the road, Jerry threw the gun out the window. Flashing lights appeared from behind and Jerry told Bonnie to pull over. If he didn't get help he would die. The Kentucky State trooper saw his condition and told her to follow him.

When Jerry opened his eyes a few days later, he had no idea where he was. Bonnie explained that he had been moved to a new hospital for surgery to remove the bullet in his chest. She said he had nearly died. It took him a few moments to regain his senses. What about the cops, he asked. She said she told them she didn't know what happened, and they hadn't pressed. And the trucker? He's alive, she said. Jerry wasn't sure if that was good or bad news.

Later that day, the State Police arrived. "What happened?" a trooper asked.

"I was having a discussion with the driver when someone shot me from a passing car," Jerry said. "That's all I recall."

"They shot both you and the trucker with two different guns, is that your story? Wow, is that the best you got?"

Did he get shot, too? Jerry said. The policeman smiled and said the trucker told a different story, he said you shot him and he fired back in self defense.

"He must be delirious," Jerry said.

"And you must be dumb if you think we're gonna believe that."

"If I shot him, where's the gun?" Jerry said. "Maybe he shot me, everything happened so fast I don't know, but I still say someone else shot. Hell, maybe he had a buddy. He's a son of a bitch is all I know. Tried to run me off the road. Now, if you don't mind, I need to get some rest. I hurt like hell."

Chapter 9

This dialogue continued for a few days until the policeman said Jerry could return home while this got sorted out. Jerry could tell he wasn't much interested in two rednecks shooting each other. Whether in Tennessee or Kentucky, cops were the same.

It took a month for him to heal but he had already made arrangements to lease the Piper Navajo to resume his smuggling flights to Jamaica. He had found a pilot experienced with the plane to go on the first flight with him. The pilot had been in the smuggling business and could be trusted. They flew commercial into Jamaica where they were picked up and taken to the landing site. It was new to Jerry and he needed to be sure it was sufficient for the Navajo. What he found was the shortest runway he'd ever seen.

He turned to the pilot. "Whatta you think? No way, right?"

"It might be doable," the pilot said.

The strip was on a short hillside that bottomed out to a valley a thousand feet below. "You're going have to explain that to me," Jerry said.

"Ground effects," the pilot said. "It'll be close, but I'm pretty sure that with ground effects we can get enough lift before we reach the cliff. Ask him if other planes have made it."

"Sure, boss, plenty planes," the Jamaican said.

"You've seen planes take off from here?"

"Plenty times, boss."

The pilot looked at Jerry and shrugged. "It's up to you."

Jerry closed his eyes and tried to visualize the take-off. He had learned his lesson with the boat about getting in over your head. "How many planes have taken off from this site with marijuana?"

The Jamaican thought for a moment, then held up five fingers. "Many."

Jerry considered it. He would have never thought of ground effects in this instance, but he saw where it made sense. When a plane is near the ground or water, the drag is reduced, and lift is more easily obtained. When the surface is uneven, the lift is even greater. In this instance, once the plane lifts off and sails over the cliff, the detrimental side of ground effects – and there is that side – is gone.

"It would be risky," the pilot said, "but if you want my honest opinion, I think we could do it."

Jerry told the Jamaican they'd be back in four days.

That night, Jerry read about ground effects. He read a lot about airplanes, trying to make up for his lack of training. He underlined what he wanted to see. "I think we'll be okay," he said to Bonnie.

"You sure?"

Was he? "Pretty sure," he said.

The morning started off with trouble. Something was wrong with the starter, and they had to delay the flight. Suddenly feeling discouraged, Jerry told Bonnie that if anything happened to him she should take the money and leave.

The evening showers had passed when they took off the next morning. By the time they reached the ocean, the skies were blue and the sun bright.

"You come," the Jamaican said, sounding surprised.

"Yes, I come," Jerry said. There were over 70 landing sites in Jamaica, but he was willing to bet that this was easily the worst. In fact, it was probably one of the worst in the whole entire fucking world. Just then, a jeep pulled up. Jerry looked anxiously at the man.

"Pull plane up hill, mon. No worry."

"You ever been in a small boat in the middle of the worst storm of the century?" Jerry said. "Don't tell me not to worry."

The man seemed confused but smiled anyway.

The fluffy clouds sailed away and a light mist fell, but soon moved on. The marijuana was loaded and the plane towed to the top of the hill. Jerry looked at the smiling Jamaican and said, "You want to come along, mon? No problem."

The Jamaican smiled and said, "Not this time, boss."

Chapter 9

"Didn't think so. It's not a good day to die." Jerry had once talked with a man so afraid of dying that he wouldn't take anything with him he would be ashamed of someone finding.

"Plenty safe, mon."

Jerry glanced at the pilot. "And you're sure about this?"

"Piece of cake," the pilot said, laughing.

Jerry looked down the hill. From inside the cockpit it looked even shorter. He had seen longer football fields. "Oh, what the hell. Let's do it."

The pilot pushed the throttle forward as Jerry reminded himself that other pilots had used this site and lived to fly another day – if the Jamaican hadn't lied. Which was a distinct possibility. As the speed increased, the pilot began pulling back the stick trying to coax the plane into the air. The stall alarms were blaring because there wasn't nearly enough speed to lift off.

Jerry felt his ass tighten "God damn!"

The plane lifted upward a few feet, but no more. And the runway was coming to an end.

"Come on, come on," the pilot pleaded.

They were no more than ten feet off the ground when the plane soared off the cliff – and fell toward the ground. Jerry's stomach was in his throat. The valley floor came toward them like a fastball from a baseball pitcher. "This isn't good," he yelled. The pilot kept urging the plane to obey. Down and down, faster and faster until…The first hint was when the nose of the place lifted up just a fraction, but there was still doubt if there was enough room. Then, as though caught in an updraft, the plane came parallel to the ground and thrust upward. In a moment they were climbing.

"I'm don't want to do that again," Jerry said.

"I might not either," the pilot said.

It was a nice plane, and with the pilot's instruction, Jerry was getting comfortable with flying. It was more responsive than the Baron and faster, too. As they crossed the coastline, the pilot said, "I think we have company."

Jerry glanced back and saw a small dot. "When?" he said.

"About fifty miles after we hit Florida. I didn't think much of it at the time but now I'm suspicious. Let's see if he can keep up with us."

The plane surged forward as Jerry wondered if it was the DEA tailing them. A few minutes later, the pilot said, "I think we lost him. This baby will really move."

But shortly they learned the bad news, when a voice on the radio said. "This is the Drug Enforcement Agency. Please identify yourself."

"How the hell did they pick us up?" Jerry said. "We did all the right things."

"Must've been that military base near Key West," the pilot said. "I'll take evasive tactics and see if we can shake him."

Ten minutes later, the plane wasn't in sight but Jerry wasn't taking any chances. He called his ground crew and told them what was happening. "Park the truck across the runway after we land," he said.

"What if they keep coming?" Jones said.

"Shoot the fuckers," Jerry said.

When they approached the Madisonville airport, clouds had covered the moon, and it was black when the plane touched down. "Let's get the hell out of here," Jerry said.

But as they reached the ground, Jerry saw the plane approach. It came in fast, too fast to see the truck, and as soon as it landed there was a huge noise as the plane rode up and over the truck, then slumped to the ground on its belly.

"Good god," the pilot said. "Reckon they're dead."

"I don't care. Let's go."

Just then, they were bathed in light from an overhead plane.

"There's fucking two of them," Jerry said. "Let's get the hell out of here."

Two armed men stumbled out of the crashed plane. "DEA!" one of the agents yelled. "Throw down your arms."

Chapter 9

Jerry was already running when his crew began firing at the government agents. Flashes of light punctuated the darkness, forcing the agents to take cover.

The light from the circling plane clearly illuminated the runway, but had not found him. "We can't stop," Jerry said, heading across open ground toward the trees about a hundred yards ahead.

In what was the strangest response Jerry had ever heard, the pilot, panting like a dog, said he needed a smoke.

"You're going to get smoked if you stay here," Jerry said.

As the gun battle raged on, they neared safety. He kept expecting to hear the sound of a bullet whiz over his head, but the only way he was going to get shot was through bad luck. Then, out of nowhere a police car pulled up a few yards from the crashed plane. The cop jumped from the car with a shotgun in his hand. "Drop your guns and get on the ground!" he yelled at the agents.

"We're Drug Enforcement Agents, you idiot," one of them said.

"I'm not going to tell you again. Drop your guns and get on the ground." The car headlights were right in their faces.

The cop was on Jerry's payroll, and the DEA guys weren't going anywhere until everyone had gotten away.

"We're DEA, and those men are getting away," the agent pleaded.

"The only people I see are you two with guns," the cop said. "Now drop your weapons and show your identification."

In a few minutes, Jerry was safe, as were his men. But he wouldn't be safe after they found his fingerprints. He was a dead man walking.

Two days later, he contacted Larry Allen to meet with him in Knoxville. Jerry wanted Allen to see if the authorities were looking at him for the shootout, certain they were because the plane was leased in his name. Allen found that warrants had been issued against him. Jerry cursed his bad luck.

But that all changed a short time later when Harold Ward said he had finally heard from Harold Rosenthal. "He's in Bermuda and says the feds are closing in on him," Ward said. "If you'll fly him to Colombia, he'll get you a job."

"That's nice, but I'm fresh out of airplanes at the moment," Jerry said.

"Fuck," Ward said, "then let's steal one."

Chapter 10

In the quiet moments of his thoughts about past events, Jerry had repeatedly gone over his bad luck. Ward said it happened to lead him to Harold Rosenthal; there could be no other answer. He was simply meant for bigger things than he was experiencing; he was meant for Colombia and cocaine. Jerry accepted this. Although he knew nothing about cocaine smuggling, he knew about airplanes and how to avoid detection. And he already had an efficient operation, so he could be ready as soon as he arrived in the new country. And since there was no extradition from Colombia, he would be safe.

He considered this as he broke into the Sevier County Airport and found the airplane in the unlocked hangar. It was fully fueled as he expected because they usually were, so all he had to do was to paint over the numbers. It was a nice plane he could easily adapt to fly nonstop in his cocaine smuggling. It was fate.

"Has to be," Harold Ward said when Jerry picked him up in Atlanta. "What else could it be?" He laughed. "Damn, Slim, we're going to be rich." He liked to call Jerry, "Slim," because compared to his own physique, it was a fitting name.

After refueling at the DeKalb-Peachtree Airport, they took off for the West End, Bahamas. He thought of the irony; he was heading toward a place where his smuggling had almost ended before it began, and now he was using the country as the doorway to a new life.

"Fate," Ward said, laughing again. "What I could use right now is a drink."

The trip passed quickly, and soon Jerry was shaking Rosenthal's hand. He was at least a decade older than both of them, with a non-descript face. But he seemed like a decent guy, so that made Jerry feel at ease. They went to a motel, where they spent a couple of days waiting for Rosenthal to ensure that everything in Colombia was arranged. But he acted with a sense of urgency because he said the authorities were closing in on him. The only thing he had said about his prison escape was that he was "walked" out of prison, which Jerry took to mean the guards had assisted him. But it would take a lot of money to pull that off, so he still wondered.

"You think the feds were in on this?" he said to Ward.

"To what end?"

"Damn if I know," Jerry said, "but something doesn't add up."

Ward handed him the bottle, now nearly empty, and said, "If that was true, why are the police looking for him?"

"Feds aren't police. I'm talking about the CIA."

"Christ," Ward said, glancing at the purple ceiling.

"Yeah. All that talk about helping the rebels in Colombia makes me wonder."

Ward held up a finger as if a sudden burst of inspiration had come over him. "But why would they dump him here?"

"That's a good question. Let's get another bottle."

Rosenthal talked openly about his experience in Colombia and admitted the mistakes that led to his capture. His new plan would address that, but Jerry saw holes in it. Since he didn't fly himself, he depended on pilots located in America, and that meant he had little control of what they did. If you ran a business, you needed to be more hands-on, especially when that business was smuggling. But Rosenthal was smart, so maybe he could pull it off.

"Richard," Rosenthal said, thinking Jerry's name was Richard Martin, "you will have no trouble getting a job. The Colombians need pilots."

And I have a plane, Jerry thought. "And the Cartel will protect me?"

Chapter 10

Rosenthal smiled. "They will protect all of us," he said. "Just don't get caught in America." He shrugged. "As for me, I'm going to open a business on the side, make myself a regular citizen. I'm even going to bring my daughters to visit."

"Is that easy?" Jerry asked, thinking of his own family.

"It can be done."

Jerry thought that was something to look forward to. Bonnie would love to visit. He had told her he would only be away for a couple of months but knew she didn't believe him.

Rosenthal sipped the drink, not much for alcohol, and said, "I've already told a few people about you and Harold, so you should start immediately. You'll like them and you'll love the area. It's like a picture postcard, a lush green with beautiful flowers."

"How about the Cartel?"

"Business," Rosenthal said, "they're all about business. Don't ever screw them." He stared at Jerry. "Not ever. They'll kill you on the spot."

"I wouldn't blame them," Jerry said. "I'd do the same." He thought about this a moment. "How do you get paid?"

"Any way you want," Rosenthal said. "They'll pay you in any currency you can think of, put it any place you want…all you have to do is tell them. But I suggest you keep it where you can get your hands on it."

It was something Jerry would have to think about. He had calculated that the plane could carry nearly a ton of cocaine, using barrels for in-flight refueling. He had thought about fuel bladders but that made it seem like he would be flying a bomb, so barrels seemed a better idea. He could rig a simple connection process using valves, and Ward could throw out the barrels over the ocean once they were empty.

Jerry closed his eyes for a moment and thought about how much money a ton of cocaine would bring on the market. Maybe twenty million, or thereabouts. It was a staggering number. And he would get his piece of the pie. He finished his drink and told Ward to get another bottle.

The next morning, they took off for Colombia. The plan was to enter Colombian airspace where they would be met by another plane and led to a landing spot. Then, they would be taken to a city called Barranquilla until someone arrived with instructions. It was the Medellin Cartel they would be working for, so they would meet with their representative. Then they would come back for the plane and fly to Medellin. The instructions seemed odd to Jerry but Rosenthal insisted that the Cartel always had good reasons.

As the plane gained altitude, Jerry's hopes soared along with it. His life was changing.

He was leaving behind his girlfriend, his ex-wife and their two children, friends. He was, or soon would be, a fugitive in two states, so he would always be on the run. But that, of course, was his choice. Everything he had done had led him here. He was certain about it. Like Ward said constantly, the journey's aftermath was clearly up to fate. Someday he hoped to understand the grand scheme of fate, but for now he just accepted it.

He let him mind wander to the future. How much money was he going to make delivering cocaine? Rosenthal said he paid his pilots a hundred grand, but Jerry wasn't sure he believed him.

He skirted around Cuba and thought of his brush with their Air Force. It was a reminder to always be vigilant. He told Rosenthal of the event and how he had almost pissed in his pants. Rosenthal nodded and pulled out a stick of gum. He seemed nervous, but Jerry attributed that to his lack of time in an airplane. Ward was the same, though not to the same degree. But flying gave Jerry a respite from thinking about trouble as he concentrated on watching the instruments. He had never flown into Colombia and needed to make certain that he flew into the assigned air corridor. Rosenthal had spent the last day in Bermuda making sure everything was taken care of concerning permission to fly into Colombia. "We have permission," he had said, nodding emphatically. "Someone will be waiting for us when we call on the radio."

"Damn, that's a lot of water," Ward said, looking downward.

Chapter 10

Jerry smiled. He would be seeing a lot more of it if things worked out.

Rosenthal nudged Jerry in the side. "You say you knew James Earl Ray?"

"Yeah, a little."

"He's a redneck racist," Rosenthal said. "Son of a bitch should be shot for what he did to King."

"I don't much care," Jerry said, "one way or the other. Why are you so interested in niggers, anyway?"

"I'm Jewish, and I understand oppression."

"I understand being poor," Jerry said. "Do you?"

Rosenthal shrugged. "I guess we all have our baggage."

"Tell him about the Sandinistas," said Ward, who had for the most part been quiet.

Jerry wasn't the least interested in revolutionary movements but said nothing.

"Well, it's a long story," Rosenthal said, "but it's a group I hope to be able to support because it's another example of how the government officials become wealthy on the backs of the oppressed. The Sandinistas decided to fight back, and I'm going to help."

"What does that have to do with Colombia?" Jerry said.

"It's all South America. Oppression is why Escobar rose to power, it's why there is a Medellin Cartel – and the people adore the Cartel leaders. Oppression doesn't limit itself to one country."

"And what's in it for you?" Jerry said.

"Satisfaction."

Jerry glanced at him, thinking he was an odd one. "It's not for me," he said. "I just want to keep a low profile and make money."

"Lots of money," Ward added.

It was Jerry's theory that Ward was mostly interested in three things – women, booze and money. There was nothing wrong with that unless they were allowed to interfere with good judgment.

"I intend to have a full life in Colombia," Rosenthal said, "and to never return to the states. This will be my home."

Never was a long time, Jerry thought.

"What about you?" Rosenthal said. "What're your plans?"

"Haven't given it much thought."

"To get filthy rich is a good start," Ward said.

"I figure I'll give it a couple of years to see how things pan out," Jerry said. He would wait to see if things cooled down regarding his convictions, how interested the authorities were in finding him. When he got money one of the first things he was going to do was to pay off the bail bondsman so he wouldn't be hunting for him. It was his experience, and one that Rosenthal, himself a former bondsman, verified, because you didn't want one for an enemy. Besides, Bam Webster had been cordial and Jerry wasn't going to rob him of rightfully owed money.

"That makes sense," Rosenthal said. "But you'll like the area and the people."

"I hope you're right." Jerry took the plane higher and checked the readings. They should be seeing the coastline in a few minutes, and he wanted to make sure his coordinates were right. "When we reach Colombian airspace, I'm going to drop down, just in case someone screwed up with the instructions."

"There's no need for that," Rosenthal said. "Everything's been cleared. I told you that."

"Better safe than sorry," Jerry said.

"If we look like we're trying to hide, someone might get curious," Rosenthal said.

"The whole point of flying low is to keep people from getting curious," Jerry said. "It'll be fine. I've done this a hundred times."

"But I haven't, and I don't want to start now," Rosenthal said. "You need to trust me on this. It's rugged terrain that you're unfamiliar with."

The son of a bitch was scared, but he had a point about the terrain. Still, they didn't want to be looking down the wrong end of a military jet's cannon. "I need to think about it."

"He says we're cleared," Ward said.

Chapter 10

"Okay, but if you're wrong our ass will be grass with an angry lawnmower after us," Jerry finally said.

"Good," Rosenthal said, smiling at him. "It'll be fine, you'll see."

Jerry leaned back. This was a good airplane, easy to fly. It was his transportation to wealth because he had thought of ways to make himself invaluable to the Cartel. And he had the feeling they would pay nicely for that. He laced his fingers behind the head and watched Rosenthal squirm when the plane veered slightly to the right.

"What the hell you doing, Slim?" Ward said.

Jerry laughed. "Just having a little fun," he said. Up ahead he saw the coast and was soon flying inland. I'm here, he thought, feeling the urge to yell. He was in goddamn Colombia.

He glanced down, a beautiful sight, lush green mountains interspersed with long valleys. This was going to be his home. And it didn't seem too bad from overhead.

He was going to be the best, most dependable pilot the Cartel had ever seen–a trusted friend. He didn't drink to excess and didn't use dope. He was going to treat this like he'd treated his marijuana days, as a business, except he was going to be better. He was going to learn as much about the Cartel thar he could, befriend the members and gain their trust.

Somebody had told him that the DEA wasn't as involved with cocaine as they were with marijuana. Because of its bulk, marijuana was easier to spot, while you could bring in coke in a shoe box. And Americans in high positions wanted cocaine, not college kids who were easy marks.

Jerry said, "How do they pay off the military? I thought they were trying to get rid of the Cartel."

"I don't know, but my pilots have never complained about interference," Rosenthal said. "Other than that, your guess is as good as mine."

"You ever been shot at in a plane, Harold?" Jerry said.

"I told you, I don't know how to fly."

"Exactly, which is why you should never take anything for granted."

Rosenthal attempted to smile but was unable.

The cloudless sky was bright as Jerry settled in for the rest of the flight. Rosenthal began talking about being in prison, and how it wasn't a hard life. And Jerry thought about Brushy Mountain. There had been nothing easy there.

"Tell me again why can't we just fly to Medellin?" Jerry said.

Rosenthal made a motion with his hands. "I'm just following instructions. Maybe they want to check you and Ward out first."

"Maybe, but it doesn't make any sense," Jerry said. He glanced at his bearings again and picked up the radio transmitter. A few seconds later, he was transmitting on the assigned frequency. A voice in broken English came back shortly. The plane had them in sight.

They were well within Colombian airspace when Jerry spotted it. Then the pilot came back over the radio and told him to follow. Which he did for several miles before the pilot said they were going to land.

"What's he doing?" Jerry said. He didn't see any place to land. All he saw was a dense jungle. "Surely this isn't the place."

"They know what they're doing," Rosenthal said.

But Jerry wondered. He watched as the small plane swooped down, much too fast, he thought. And then he saw it, a small clearing that looked carved out of the forest. The Colombian plane bounced along the terrain and moved to the side of the clearing. The pilot was motioning frantically toward Jerry, who by now was shallowing out his approach. But as Jerry looked up he saw the jet approaching from the north. "Son of a bitch." It was maybe ten miles away and closing fast. He looked at Rosenthal. "We're in trouble." It was an all too familiar sight. Knowing he had to get down as quickly as possible, he dropped the plane to a few feet from the ground before leveling off. They hit with a *thud* and he jammed on the brakes. They had barely stopped before Rosenthal and Ward were out and running toward the jungle.

Jerry wanted to secure the plane, but the jet was getting closer. "Let's get the hell out of here, Slim!" Ward yelled. The Colombians were shouting at them, but Jerry didn't want to leave the plane. It was his ticket to wealth.

Chapter 10

"What are you doing?" Rosenthal said. "Forget the goddamn plane."

Finally, Jerry ran as fast a he could, as the noise from the jet became nearly deafening. Just as he reached cover, he heard the machine gun fire, and when he looked back his plane was a ball of fire.

The Colombians ushered them to a truck after it was clear the jet had left. "What the hell happened back there?" Jerry said.

"Military," one of the Colombians said. "I don't know why they come."

Jerry looked at Ward as to say, 'What were they supposed to do now?'

The ride to Barranquilla was along a dusty trail that eventually turned into a road and finally a highway. By the time they reached the city, it was dusk; yet the driver still hadn't turned on his headlights. They stopped at a small apartment building and were told to wait inside until someone came in the morning.

"And do what?" Jerry said.

"Wait," he was told again.

Rosenthal had gotten over his initial shock and was reassuring them that everything would be okay. It was just a mistake. Jerry wanted to wring his neck but for now sleep would have to do. He whispered to Ward that they had just lost their meal ticket.

The next morning, a powerfully-built young man arrived and said he was taking them to Medellin. His name was "Little Al," simply named because his father was "Big Al." He spoke acceptable English and conducted himself professionally. "We're going to ride a bus to Medellin. You are not to speak to anyone and if anyone asks you questions, let me answer. Understood?"

Jerry nodded.

"Understood?" he repeated.

Jerry was pretty sure that if they were difficult, the man would kill them on the spot. They had entered a far different world.

The bus smelled of dirty bodies, the seats were cracked, and exhaust fumes leaked through the rusty floorboard. The three of them were the only white faces there and drew curious stares from the other passengers. Jerry saw one man staring at him with eyes that said he would kill him for his shoes and think nothing about it. Jerry understood what desperation would drive a person to, so he turned away to avoid any confrontation. This wasn't his country or his problem.

He looked out the window, and what he saw was poverty, much like what he had seen in Jamaica. Jamaicans fought through poverty with marijuana, and Colombians had cocaine. When he was a young boy in east Tennessee, mountain people did the same with moonshine. He closed his eyes and tried to rest.

Colombia, and Medellin in particular, had achieved international notoriety as a major drug trafficking center. It began modestly in the 1960s, with exiled Cubans living in Miami. They began cultivating the coca plant in Colombia and smuggling small amounts into the United States where it would be changed into cocaine, an elaborate process involving laboratories. Then, in the 1970s, the Colombians began importing coca paste from Peru and Bolivia and refining it in Colombian laboratories. The paste was dissolved in a small amount of diluted sulfuric acid, with potassium permanganate added to cause oxidation. The process created the white coloring cocaine was known for. The product was dried to convert it into cocaine hydrochloride, which is the white, crystalline powder used on the street. In this form, it has a bitter taste, so it is usually cut with other products to make it more acceptable. This also increases the amount of cocaine for sale.

About this time, a group of Colombians, including Pablo Escobar, Carlos Lehder, the Ochoa brothers, and Gonzalo Gacha, formed a drug network to orchestrate the delivery of the cocaine to the United States, as well as to insulate the traffickers from the government and others wishing them harm. The Cartel was intelligent and brutal – massacres were reported involving the use of chainsaws.

The Cartel's level of violence was high by any historical standard. They bribed government officials, and if that didn't work they killed them. Many Colombians fled the country in a self-imposed exile. As the United States' thirst for cocaine increased, so did the Cartel's power.

Chapter 10

Within a short time, they gained significant political power and began exerting their influence on an international scale.

They used a sophisticated means of laundering their vast wealth, much of the laundering done through U.S. banks in Panama. Like most of their illegal activities, much of the laundering was accommodated through significant bribes and threats. Some, however – and this was according to Rosenthal – was as simple as handing someone a suitcase filled with millions of dollars. The man would then phone someone in Europe, and money would be transferred to a Swiss bank. The Cartel had the best lawyers and more money that most people could fathom. When the son of one of the richest dealers was caught by the United States, the father offered to pay off the $2 billion Bolivian national debt if his son was released.

From the moment the bus left Barranquilla, it climbed and weaved up long stretches of broken asphalt. Shimmering in the distance was the mountain range that towered into the clouds, and below those clouds was the mysterious city of Medellin.

Little Al spoke to some of the passengers in Spanish and then smiled to indicate everything was okay. Jerry had been told it was nearly 500 miles to Medellin; a long time on a bus without air conditioning. He tried to sleep but Ward kept mumbling to him. "I need a beer. My ass is sore. My legs hurt." He went on and on with the complaints. Rosenthal sat with Little Al, not by choice but because no one else would sit with him.

A small squatty man would catch Jerry's attention from time to time and say, "Hello." As the sunlight caught the old man's face, Jerry noticed the deep cracks and hints of yellow in his skin. And every couple of minutes he would lean back and cough. Then, he would force a smile and say again, "Hello."

"What's his problem?" Ward whispered. "Is he touched in the head?"

Jerry laughed. "We're sitting in a third world bus with nothing in our pockets but our balls, and you're asking if *he's* crazy?"

Thirteen hours later, they finally arrived in Medellin, exhausted and in a foul mood. They took a cab across town to an apartment complex where they were given a room. It wasn't bad.

"Now what?" Jerry asked.

Little Al smiled. "Soon, others will come to talk," he said. "You will wait right here." He went to a nearby store and brought back food and beer. "Tonight we get drunk."

Chapter 11

Jerry felt like a piece of furniture being shoved from room to room. When he and Ward walked around the area, Rosenthal would remain in the apartment. He warned that Medellin was a dangerous place if you weren't under the protection of the Mafia, which is how the Cartel was known.

The first ripples of his new life were beginning to sink in. In some ways, it was as though he had awoke from a long night's sleep to find himself in a strange county where he didn't understand the language and faced an uncertain future. Although there was noise everywhere, he was surrounded by a wall of silence. Looking back, he could see how it would have been better if he had known what he was walking into. He knew he should have asked more questions. But it was too late for regrets. He was just going to have to survive. And he was a survivor.

The police seemed to be everywhere. Medellin had progressed from a coffee exporter to cocaine, and those who dealt with the powder were significantly more violent than coffee growers.

"Is okay, though," a skinny, emaciated Colombian told him. He wore thick glasses and his pants were much too short to hide his paisley socks. "Cocaine creates many jobs." He rubbed his hand together. "Many jobs." He looked around. "No police, see? Is okay?" And indeed it seemed there was a hands-off relationship between the police, just as long as trouble didn't spill over to the streets.

"We must be crazy as loons," Jerry said to Ward. "Look where we're at." He had expected the Cartel to rush to him with outstretched arms – and maybe they would have if his airplane was intact—but nothing was happening. Every time he thought about his plane, he got pissed at Rosenthal. No matter how many times Ward tried to defend him, he was going to get mad. It was a perfectly good airplane that with a little precaution could be sitting out there ready to fly. He could still see the bullets rip through it.

"I'm sane as a judge," Ward said.

"You mean sober as a judge."

He heard Ward whisper, "Yeah, well most of them are sane, too. And I'm not crazy."

Jerry laughed. "You're crazier than me. You know why? You could have stayed. Nobody was looking for you, like they were me." He knew what Ward would say, that they were buddies, and he believed Jerry was going to make both of them a lot of money. He would say, "Well, you wouldn't be here if it wasn't for me." And he would be right. They were joined at the hip in this venture, and he knew that Ward didn't like to be called crazy because he had heard it enough growing up. "Well, I guess you had your reasons, too. But look at us now; two hillbillies walking around in a city where they'll shoot you just to take your shoes." Ward looked him and said nobody was getting his shoes because the moment he saw the gun he was running with the wind. It was one of their jokes. Jerry had brought up the idea of maybe getting caught and that the smart thing to do was to stay alive and use their money to stay out of jail. But Ward said, not him; he was running with the wind. Anyway, he said he trusted Jerry to keep him out of trouble. Even if something bad happened, Jerry would be there to help. I'm putting myself in your hands, Slim. Jerry liked that.

Rosenthal also was getting impatient. Finally, he said, "Richard, if your friend was here I'd hire him to kill someone. This isn't right." He was talking about a contract killer Jerry had known. He had told Rosenthal the story of the man trying to kill a whore with poison, but he put in too much arsenic and the meat began to smell. When she refused to eat it, he shot her with a .22 caliber pistol, but still she lived, prompting him to say that whores are tough to kill.

Chapter 11

But a day later, Rosenthal left with a Cartel member who promised they would come for Jerry shortly.

Jerry spent some of the time doing what he was good at, which was observing people. You could learn a lot by observing, he had found. He had already concluded that the Colombians were basically friendly, but if you crossed them that could quickly change. The women seemed soft and warm, like Southern women, and they liked gringos. When he ate out, the waiters went out of their way to be kind to him. Since he was a gringo, they would explain what he shouldn't eat, mostly those foods with a lot of spices. Jerry liked the food and found it not much different from what he had eaten in Tennessee. They had a barbeque dish called fritanga, consisting of meat and sausage, with small potatoes. They also served a wide variety of fruits that Jerry enjoyed.

The city was about 5000 feet above sea level, hot and humid but better than most parts of the country. Medellin was filled with both poverty and extreme wealth. Those with wealth lived in the well-protected neighborhood of El Problado, and while there were other prosperous neighborhoods, none were like El Problado.

One night at a nearby bar, Jerry asked about the neighborhood. The bartender said, "You have friends there?"

"Maybe," Jerry said.

The bartender gave him a cautious look and walked away.

Medellin was within the Aburra Valley and was Colombia's second largest city. It was surrounded on each side by majestic mountain ranges Because of its elevation and proximity to the equator, the climate didn't vary significantly, although Jerry could attest that it got both hot and humid.

He liked what he had seen thus far, friendly people, beautiful women, good food, but the delay was getting to him.

"It's beginning to look like we're on the outside looking in," Ward said, as he sucked on his bottle of beer. "What're we going to do?"

"Wait," Jerry said.

He and Ward would take taxis almost everywhere they went. The Medellin highways were mostly two lanes, much wider than in Tennessee, and if a car wanted to pass, the oncoming car would move to the left and the car being passed would move to the right. This practice was unsettling to Ward. "We are fucking going to get killed, Slim," he said.

Ward's sexual appetite seemed insatiable, so they went to a lot of bars to pick up women. They would either go to a motel or bring them back to the apartment. It was a routine Jerry liked, but it wasn't why he had come to Colombia. He wanted to go to work, but more and more he was sharing Ward's pessimism.

But then it happened. As Ward lay sleeping, his pants still on from the night before, a bottle of whiskey on the nightstand, and music playing on a portable radio, Jerry sat across a table in a nearby restaurant from Humberto Herrera. He had arrived with a large man, who even though it was hot wore a jacket that bulged at the side. He introduced himself as a member of the Medellin Cartel. He looked to weigh about two hundred pounds, in his early forties, with a rugged handsomeness. One of the first things he said was that Jerry should call him Humberto with a silent H.

The waiter approached and spoke softly to him in Spanish. "He wanted to know if you'll be coming here often," Humberto said. "I said you would."

Jerry knew what was being transmitted. He would now receive the same respect as Humberto, who was an important member of the Medellin Cartel. He allowed his hopes to soar.

"You had excitement arriving here, right?" Humberto said. His English was excellent, though he spoke with a heavy accent. "I'm sorry about your airplane. The problem has been resolved, too late for you of course, but it will not happen again. And don't worry about your airplane. We have mucho planes." He winked at Jerry. "You're a good pilot, si?"

"Yes, a very good pilot," Jerry said.

"Good. And your organization, is it intact?"

Chapter 11

"I'll use the one I had when smuggling marijuana," Jerry said. Herrera seemed to know a lot about him. "They're good at doing what they're told and at keeping their mouths shut."

Humberto smiled daringly. "You had trouble with the officials but managed to get away," he said. "I like that. You remind me of an outlaw. We have lots of outlaws in Colombia. Many of them are my best friends."

"That's what people call me," Jerry said. As he looked toward the entrance, a man and woman entered and were quickly escorted out by two of Humberto's men.

Humberto said, "You don't drink much or use the powder."

Jerry realized they had been watching him. "No, I don't." He had mostly limited his drinking to beer.

"But your friend, he drinks a little too much. What does he do for you?"

"He helps me fly, to keep things settled in the back. And he really doesn't drink that much. I'll make sure of that."

"In the back? What does that mean?"

"I'll have to have extra fuel, so I've come up with a plan to use 40 gallon barrels. I can rig up a delivery system, but when the fuel is empty someone will have to throw the barrels out. I don't want them sliding around."

"Ahh, you don't use the bladder?"

"No, I'll use the barrels."

"Good, that seems smart," Herrera said. "I like you already, Ricardo."

"What plane would I be flying?"

"I think it's called a Piper Chieftain," Humberto said.

Jerry was familiar with the plane. It was a larger version of the plane that had been confiscated at the Monroe County Airport.

Humberto folded his hands across his chest and studied Jerry for several moments before saying, "So, you think you'd like to fly for us?"

There it was – the offer. Jerry could barely contain his excitement. "I think I'd like that very much. It'll take me a few days to set something up."

Humberto looked at him a moment. "I think we have a good relationship, Ricardo. Now, any questions, my friend?"

"How much will I make?"

"We start at $3500 a kilo."

Jerry tried not to gulp. "How many kilos will I fly?" he said.

About 450, sometimes more. We have many kilos in the warehouse. I will arrange the loads from the other members and each one will be carefully marked. I will tell you where to deliver in Miami, and you will be paid immediately."

"Did you say $3500 a kilo?" His math wasn't that good but it sounded like they were going to pay him nearly two million dollars.

"Even more if we like you," Herrera said, smiling. "Like I said, we have many kilos to ship. Now, tell me your plan."

Jerry had given this a lot of thought. He would fly into the small airport in Madisonville, offload into several cars, and head toward Miami. A wrecker, along with an excellent mechanic, would accompany the caravan in case there was car trouble. Also, there would be a driver behind to divert the police if one of the cars was pulled over. The driver would do something to draw the police attention and then the pulled over car would leave. Hererra liked the plan.

"Very smart, Ricardo." He finished his drink. "Soon we meet Pablo. You will like him."

Jerry assumed he was talking about Pablo Escobar. "I know who he is."

"He is a great man," Herrera said. "He likes airplanes. You will see."

Moving much too fast, Jerry took a deep breath. "How many trips a week will I take?"

Herrera shrugged. "How many will you want to make?" he said. "The others will want you to fly as much as possible." He sized Jerry up. "You are in good shape, si?"

Jerry nodded, thinking he had fallen into the mother lode of riches "And I will always report only to you?"

Chapter 11

"Yes, the other families will communicate through me. And I will be responsible for your payment. Now, about your living arrangements. I have arranged a nice house for you to have. Bodyguards will be provided to protect you from kidnappers, many kidnappers in Medellin. You will enjoy the house." He gave Jerry a wink. "It is free."

Kidnapping Cartel associates, especially pilots, and holding them for ransom was common, so Jerry was glad to hear he'd be protected.

"Free?"

Humberto laughed. "Your money is no good in Colombia, Ricardo. Now, you are one of us." He patted Jerry on the shoulder. "Let me show you what that means." He motioned to the waiter. "When he comes, tell him you'd like the best cigar in the house."

The waiter arrived, and Jerry did as requested. In a minute, the waiter arrived with a complete box of Cuban cigars. "My gift, Senor," he said.

Humberto looked at Jerry and laughed.

Jerry ordered a Coke, though about then he would have liked something stronger. Herrera ordered a Coke, too, but his was mixed with bourbon. "So now you can relax, Ricardo," he said. "You are one of us, and that doesn't come easily. Most of our pilots are employees, but you are an independent contractor. We admire that you came with your own plane even though it is now gone." He sipped the drink. "Now tell me about crash landing your plane in Florida."

Jerry told him the story. When he was finished, Herrera smiled. "I bet the man now has second thoughts about refusing your money. But if I may, let me offer advice: when you bribe someone, make it at least twice what you think he will accept."

Jerry nodded. "I'll remember that," he said.

"You do not need to worry about past transgressions," Humberto said. "You are safe here."

"I sure hope so."

Herrera smiled; he always had one available, it seemed. "Can you fly the jets?"

"No, but I guess I could learn. I think they're dangerous for smuggling, though. They draw too much attention."

"In America, perhaps," Herrera said. Another smile. "But that is a conversation for another time." He finished his drink. "My man will take you back, Ricardo." He took Jerry's hand. "We are going to be good friends; you will see."

When Jerry told Ward about the conversation, Ward was ecstatic. "You're a frigging millionaire. How much do I get?"

"We'll work something out," Jerry said, "but you need to watch your drinking. The Colombians are watching us."

"I don't drink that much."

"Listen, Harold. We're working for the Colombians now, and these are dangerous people. You don't cheat them, lie to them, or fuck their wives." He stared at him. "Understand? You don't fuck their wives. This is a business where we can make a lot of money, but if you screw it up you don't get fired, you get killed."

Jerry kicked off his shoes and flopped on the couch. He needed a little quiet time to let it all soak in. He thought it was imperative to understand all the little nuances of the Colombians. He didn't want to do or say something that might offend them, so he had watched Herrera's expression closely when they talked. He sure didn't want to get on the wrong side. Herrera didn't have to kill him; just say something to the police and have him thrown into jail. He had heard stories of people rotting in Mexican jails, and this didn't seem a lot different from Mexico to him.

Jerry called Larry Jones to set up the organization. The load cars would be driven to a motel, and Jones was to wait until Jerry called with instructions on where to take the cars. The cars would be left in a parking lot, and Jones and the others would then return to Tennessee.

"You have any questions?" Jerry said.

"Well, when you fly in the first load, maybe we should go over it again."

Jerry sighed. "All right." He had some misgivings about the confidence in Jones' voice, and thought that perhaps he should send Ward

Chapter 11

back to oversee the ground operation. But he enjoyed having him in Colombia.

"How is it there?" Jones asked. "Colombia pussy as good as I hear?"

"So far, so good." He wasn't going to tell him much more than that because Jones was careless with his talk. "I'll get back with you in a week. Get it done this time, Larry."

"Oh, he'll be okay," Ward said that evening. He picked up a fork and stuck it in a piece of steak. "He just doesn't think real fast on his feet. But he's a helluva mechanic, so you won't be having any mechanical trouble with the load cars." He chewed on the steak and washed it down with a beer. "I'd say that's pretty damn important, Slim."

"I just hope he can follow instructions," he said. "I don't want him to suddenly think he has a better idea."

"I don't think he'd do that," Ward said. "See, he'd be too scared to cross you."

Jerry disagreed. Jones might not be the brightest star in the universe, but he wasn't scared of much. He could change his moods with the blink of an eye.

"You want me to talk to him?" Ward said. "You know, make sure he understands how important this is."

"I'm paying the man $35,000; he sure better know how important it is. That's more than he'd make in three months chopping cars and selling parts, and it's a helluva lot easier. You would think he would make sure everything went just as he was told. But yeah, make sure he understands."

The next day, Jerry met with Rosenthal to tell him the good news, not mentioning what he was getting paid because he thought his deal was probably better than Rosenthal's. Rosenthal seemed happy for him.

"You're here at the right time," Rosenthal said. "When I came here before it was kind of hit or miss, a bunch of small traffickers trying to get the product out of Colombia any way they could. And if a load was confiscated by the DEA, they were out of financial luck. It was inefficient. So, Escobar and the others saw an opportunity. Rather than be bothered by these small smugglers, they would let them join them. The Cartel would ship as small a quantity that anyone had, including it in one of the loads of the Cartel members. And – here's where it gets interesting – the Cartel insures the load. If it gets captured by the DEA or anyone else, the Cartel provides an identical amount to replace it. And by dividing up the loads on the planes, the exposure is reduced. Of course, this doesn't come free. The Cartel gets a percentage of the profits. These people are smart businessmen."

He paused for a moment. "When I was in prison I gave this a lot of thought, what makes the Cartel tick. Yeah, it's all about drugs but in order for the business to thrive you have to have juice with the government, and not just this government but those of the surrounding countries. I'm telling you this, Richard, it's all about politics. Politics is the way of power in this place. Hell, Escobar is running for Congress. Christ – can you imagine that? You walk around parts of Medellin, and they talk about him like he's a god. Won't be long before they build a statue of him. And now he's going to Congress. So, yeah, if you want to make it here you got to find a way to worm yourself into politics. I can see that clear as day."

Jerry frowned but said nothing, thinking it sounded like a one-way ticket to a place you would never return from – the great bullet hole in the head. "Well, I plan to stick to my business, Harold, and I suggest you do the same."

When Herrera met with him a few days later, Jerry told him he was ready to begin the flights, but he wanted to be assured he would not be flying marijuana at any time. Marijuana had hexed him. Herrera laughed and said he understood and not to worry, there would be no marijuana.

A cool breeze was blowing in from the mountains as they dined on the patio. Three men, each wearing a large purse that housed an automatic weapon, were watching them. Herrera said his people would weigh the cocaine, load it and then weigh it again when it was delivered, emphasizing the latter. Jerry said if the weight came up short he would pay the

Chapter 11

difference. "I like that," Herrera said. "Do you have good men you can trust?"

"I think so."

"And you take care of them, right?"

Jerry nodded.

"Good. Remember this, Ricardo: worry about people first, then merchandise, then the equipment. Okay? You do that and everything will be okay."

Jerry liked the man already. They might be different people but they shared a lot of the same values.

"Know what I think?" Ward said, later. "I think we've fell into the mother lode of money."

"Fallen," Jerry said. He didn't want the Cartel to think they were just a couple of ignorant hillbillies. "We've fallen into the mother lode of money."

"Hell, Slim, it's the same thing." Ward laughed. "When we going to make the first run?"

"Friday," Jerry said.

But it was the next week before it happened. Herrera was embarrassed by the delay, explaining that the Cartel had a few things to understand before allowing the flight. "In these times we must be careful."

"These times" Jerry had learned, meant that the DEA was increasing its attacks on cocaine smuggling. Agents were attempting to infiltrate the Cartel.

The route he planned to take was through the Yucatan Passage and crossing land somewhere near southwest Alabama. From there, he would fly to one of several destinations he chose. He would begin by flying to the airport in Monroe County because that was convenient to Larry Jones and the other members of the ground crew.

The Colombians liked the idea of having their "own" pilot better than their arrangement with Rosenthal. Rosenthal was actually buying the cocaine from the Colombians and taking it to the States to sell. He was acting as an independent businessman and that wasn't making the

Colombians as much money. Besides, the number of "moving parts" in his organization was a source of worry. They much preferred keeping it simple. No matter what Rosenthal might think, he wasn't going to make as much money as Jerry.

Jerry heard a rumor that Rosenthal had hit up the Colombians for $60,000 for the destruction of "his" airplane, arguing that it was their fault it had been destroyed. And supposedly they had paid him.

Jerry's first flight was a load from Herrera and the Ochoa family, a little over 400 kilos. Jerry called Tennessee to make final arrangements. His plan was to fly into the Monroe County Airport, arriving soon after darkness, where the cocaine would be off-loaded into cars and the plane would be refueled, including adding new fuel barrels inside the plane. Then, Jones would lead the cars into south Florida where they would wait for Jerry's instructions.

A small plane took Jerry and Ward a few hundred miles from Medellin, to where the cocaine plane was waiting at a crude airstrip in the jungle. When he arrived, the cocaine was brought out in duffel bags and loaded onto the plane.

The excitement was intoxicating and his heart was racing as he carefully counted the bags, not wanting to exceed the plane's weight capacity. He attempted conversation with the men but they spoke little English, and the men carrying automatic weapons didn't seem the type to make small talk. One of them had the eyes of a stone cold killer, the type who would kill a man, then drag him through town tied to the back of a car.

The forty-gallon fuel barrels inside the plane were individually tied down to prevent any movement. With the added weight, the plane struggled to get airborne. It was a crude arrangement. A hose was stuck in the barrel, and an electric pump sent it to the engines. When the barrel was nearly empty, the hose would be moved to the next barrel. Jerry would use the fuel in the barrels first, so as each barrel was emptied, it would be thrown out over the water. This was necessary to help with the off-loading of the cocaine.

Chapter 11

"Make sure you drop it straight down," Jerry said to Ward. "I don't want it to hit the plane."

The trip would take about 11 hours, so Jerry told Ward to try to relax. It was something he wouldn't be able to do because this was his first flight of such a great distance. One miscalculation, and God only knows where he would end up. He adjusted the VHF Omnidirectional Range Navigation System to the first destination signal and hoped he was right. He checked the cross winds and adjusted the plane's direction until it tracked the VOR signal. His plan was to follow the signals from Barranquilla to Cancun to Key West to Mobile and then to Tennessee. The actual route would be from Barranquilla to Cancun and to Mobile, but he would use the Tampa and Key West VOR signals to make sure he was heading the right direction. His flight instructor had taught him that trick.

When it was daylight, he could see landmarks to make him feel comfortable, but through the night he would be flying blind, except for the navigation system. And he already wished he had more flying experience.

The Caribbean was beautiful from above, and he told himself to enjoy the flight. "Nice, huh?" he said to Ward.

"It'll be a helluva lot nicer when we're through."

Jerry looked at the chart again. At some point, he would be entering the zone where authorities would be watching and become curious about his intentions. He banked the plane sharply to the right and the navigation needle jumped. Then, he moved back and needle settled down.

"What was that all about?"

"Just checking something," Jerry said.

"Well, give me a warning next time. For god's sake, Slim, I'm nervous enough as it is."

Jerry leaned back and smiled. He was becoming more confident. Down below he spotted a cruise ship. He had never been on a cruise and thought that one day he would buy his own ship, maybe sail around the world. With the money he was making, he could afford his own crew.

A sudden experience with turbulence shook him out of his reverie, as the plane lurched upward. He had no idea of the cause but in a moment it had passed.

"Christ!" he said.

"You playing again with me again?" Ward said.

"Not this time." He decided not to relax even if it wore him out. He had too much money at risk.

Once he reached the VOR destination, he switched to another frequency. It was like the game "connecting the dots," as the navigation system led him along his path. When the first barrel was empty, Ward walked to the back and connected the hose to another barrel. Then, he dumped the empty into the water. "I hope to hell I don't hit someone."

"It's a big ocean," Jerry said, laughing.

Jerry was pleased that the fuel system was working so well. As it was, he wasn't going to have much margin for error. Loaded with this account of cocaine, the plane went through fuel quickly.

Eventually he approached the VOR where the authorities could spot him. He dropped the plane to a low altitude, about a thousand feet, and looked for the coastline of the United States. Darkness was fast approaching, but he would get to Tennessee on time.

"There it is," Ward said, his voice pitched in excitement.

Jerry saw the lights of the coast and breathed a sigh of relief. After another altitude adjustment, he checked the fuel gauge and saw that he had enough to make it. He passed over Alabama and resumed altitude, hoping those looking at him would think he was just another airplane. Glancing at his watch he said, "We're on time."

He made a call into an airport to ask a question. His ground crew would be listening and would know the call meant he was nearby. It was the same tactic they had used when he was flying in marijuana. In a few minutes, he spotted the airport. No one manned the remote site during this time. The only exception was that on weekends there was one man who came to watch only because he was an aviation fanatic and that was his only free time.

Chapter 11

The plane touched down smoothly and coasted to a stop where Jones and the rest of the ground crew were waiting. Jerry and Ward climbed out. Jerry's legs were stiff from the long flight, so he watched as they unloaded the cocaine.

Jerry repeated the instructions. They were to take the merchandise to South Florida and wait in a motel for his instructions. They were not to stop except for gas, and they were not to touch the cocaine. Once they received the instructions on where to take the cars, they were to lock them and return to Tennessee. Only after the transaction was complete would they get paid.

Jones said he understood. "Don't worry," he said.

"I get paid to worry," Jerry said. "Now, put the barrels in the plane and make sure each one is secured."

The barrels were loaded and filled. They had worked out fine on the first leg of the trip. Jerry watched Jones tie each barrel down. It was critical; otherwise the barrels could shift in the plane and turn over. And that would not be good.

"Did I do right?" Jones said.

Jerry answered with a stare. The man was starting to piss him off. He waited until the cars had left before climbing back into the plane. In a minute, they were heading for Colombia.

"We're going to be rich," Ward said, slapping his hands together. "Damn, this is fun."

Jerry wouldn't exactly describe flying a round trip from Colombia to Tennessee as fun, but it was exciting.

Empty, the plane was a lot more responsive. He set the navigation system again and headed into the darkness. One deep breath, then mentally preparing for eleven more hours of flying. He glanced toward the rear of the plane. "How's the barrels?"

Ward turned his head. "We got some time left." He was quiet for a moment. "What kind of gun you think was on the jet that shot us up when we landed."

"Probably a 60 caliber," Jerry said. "It was something to watch, I tell you that. I bet he was having fun with us. I could almost see him laughing."

"I never mentioned it before," Ward said, "but I pissed in my pants. I couldn't help it."

Jerry looked at him and laughed. "It'll be our secret, Harold."

Although the Cartel had paid the authorities for a safe flight corridor to fly in and out of Colombia the day of the flight, Jerry still flew low into the country. It was daylight when they arrived and he was exhausted. He had spent nearly 23 hours of straight flying, a full day, and all he wanted to do was sleep. The pilot flew them back to the city and Jerry slept for nearly twelve hours.

The next day, he thought about the money – $1,500,000. He paid Ward about $90,000. "Don't gripe," he said. "That's a damn good wage for a glorified gas station attendant."

He had already called Jones with instructions on where to take the cars. Once the cars were parked, Jones called him back. The whole operation was over in minutes, and the crew was on its way back to Tennessee. He had again warned Jones that if he had any funny thoughts, he should remember who owned the cocaine. They would kill him and his family.

"How much did you make?" Rosenthal asked a few days later.

Jerry just smiled. "Enough," he said. A lot more than you make, he thought. Already the Colombians wanted him to make another delivery.

"They liked the promptness of the delivery, Ricardo," Humberto said. "Now, let's discuss the next load."

Jerry had to tell Humberto that he needed a few days off between flights. The emotional drain was as high as the physical toll, and he didn't want to be so tired he became careless. He tried to limit the flights to twice a week. As usual, Herrera understood and didn't insist on a change.

"You can take a break, Ricardo," he said. "We are ready to move you into your new house. You can furnish it anyway you like."

Jerry eventually settled into a routine. He would fly, sleep, and fly again. And taking some time off to furnish his house was a welcome break. He had never had a real house before.

Chapter 11

It was a large villa – Mediterranean style – surrounded by a high wall, with a gate at the front manned by a guard. The small house in the back where four bodyguards lived was larger than the house where he had been raised. The bodyguards were instructed to follow him everywhere because he was now a member of the Cartel, a pilot who was an important cog in their money making machine.

The main house was about 5000 square feet, with four bedrooms and three baths, and a beautiful garden in the back. Ward, who was living with him, looked around and said, "Christ, this is fucking mansion. We can get all the women we can handle."

Jerry wasted no expense in getting the house just like he wanted, because the Cartel paid for everything. He bought new furniture and hired a decorator. When he was finished, it was like what he saw in magazines.

"How the hell did you wrangle a new house?" Rosenthal said. "What kind of deal do you have with the Cartel, Richard?" It was the kind of question Jerry would usually find offensive but he owed Rosenthal a pass, so he shrugged and said it was because he was a pilot. Rosenthal seemed to understand and said that his operation was going okay, but not without a few problems. As they talked, Jerry was tempted to again warn him about becoming involved in Colombian politics but they had gone down that road before. So, he just wished him good luck, thinking he was going to need it because South American politics was a grenade that could explode anytime.

Chapter 12

The house became his sanctuary, where he could bring people in for social events, including Herrera who liked to party. He had not yet asked Escobar to visit but Humberto said that might be a possibility. Sometimes he would invite the bodyguards in for a drink but as a rule they didn't speak English so the Cartel was about all they had in common. They were loyal to a fault and ready to give their lives for him. Ward called them guard dogs, but Jerry had never seen an animal as quick to kill. Once he was staring at the front gate when a young man walked by and did nothing but gaze toward the house. One of the guards ran toward him with a gun and yelled in Spanish. The man fell to his knees with his hands knitted behind his head. A few moments later, the guard said something to him and the man left in a hurry. It was apparent that no one was getting to the house unless they were approved, so Jerry felt secure leaving his considerable money in the house.

Herrera took him under his wing and tried to make him feel at home in this strange land. Once, when they were riding in the mountains he said, "Most of us are from bad places, Ricardo. We tell you our stories, and they sound the same. Escobar is building housing for the poor. Many call it a publicity stunt, but they don't understand his – our – story. Our parents worked with their hands, simple people who only wanted the best for their family. But they were helpless against those with money and guns. They lived in fear that one night the mobs would come." He shook his head. "We don't forget the injustice. Escobar, as were all of us, was molded by that fear. Each of us knew that we had to do something

Chapter 12

to get out from the control of unjust men. But he would never forget the injustice. We could not be at the mercy of those filled with hate."

"Humberto, do you ever consider quitting?"

Humberto gave him a curious look. "Quitting? And doing what, Ricardo? No, this is my life. Will I retire one day?" He thought about it a moment. "Perhaps, but not soon."

"Well, I guess I could quit all right," Ward said, when Jerry recounted the conversation.

He didn't sound certain. "And walk away from the money?" Jerry said.

"It's not easy, is it? I see what you're saying, but I've really never given it much thought." Ward was quiet for a moment. "Goddamn, Slim. Now I'll worry since you've put it in my mind. Live here the rest of my life? I don't know about that. You really know how to fuck up my mind, don't you?"

It was something to think about. Jerry knew that if they stayed in Colombia long enough they might start looking like a threat to someone. It was just a feeling. "Well, we're from the south and we want to get back one day when it's safe, right?'

"Right."

"Well, I'll be thinking about how to do that and still make our money."

"Yeah, I like the sound of that," Ward said.

Living in Medellin was like living in the Wagon Wheel, one wayward look and all hell might break out. The murders were increasing weekly and no one seemed to give a damn.

"Hey, guess what," Ward said. "I got a letter from Jones yesterday. He and his old lady are thinking about buying a house."

"Long as he doesn't pay cash," Jerry said. Jones was continuing to worry him, nothing he could place his finger on, but just a bad feeling. He glanced out the window as the sun was beginning to set. Sunsets were beautiful here. "You want to go into town, maybe have a drink? You might be able to pick up a couple of women."

"Shit, I'm all for twofers," Ward said. "Maybe we could go to the Ochoa's and have dinner. I like their tamales."

Jerry grinned. What he really liked was the young waitress with the big tits and pouty lips.

Making two, sometimes three, weekly flights was taking its toll, but the money was so outrageous he couldn't bring himself to slow down. Escobar liked him, which meant his services were always in demand. He could make $10 million a week if his body could hold up. His ground crew was complaining, but they too liked the money.

"I'm worn out, Slim," Ward said over a hamburger and beer. "Last night I couldn't even get it up."

Jerry was not having that problem, at least not yet. He was seeing a beautiful young woman named Maria. She worked as the international operator for the telephone company, and he had liked the sound of her voice so he asked if they could meet. She agreed, though reluctantly. She spoke several languages and was helping him learn Spanish.

She didn't mind that he worked for the Cartel or that bodyguards accompanied them everywhere. She was Catholic but had no difficulty rationalizing their sex. "Pablo is a hero here, Ricardo," she said. "Perhaps one day you can take me to one of the parties."

Jerry nodded, though he doubted that would ever happen. He didn't want to involve her with the Cartel. At his last party with some of the leaders, women walked around naked and were there for the asking.

The last time he talked with Escobar was at a social event at Escobar's house, with heavily armed guards everywhere. He was looking at an aviation magazine when Escobar walked over and asked him what he thought of the airplane pictured. Jerry said there were much better and at the same price. Escobar had slapped him on the back and laughed. "I like one who speaks his mind, Senor Martin."

Jerry had met most of the leaders and ate at some of their restaurants, always remembering that he was just an employee. He kept his head down and his mouth shut. He understood little of what was being said, but the food was always good and the women were beautiful.

Things were going good. His flights had gone without any problems and the cocaine was delivered on time. He had gained the reputation of one who could be depended on.

Chapter 12

"You know why Pablo and the others like you, Ricardo," Herrera said. They were riding in the back seat of Herrera's car. "Unlike your friend, Senor Rosenthal, you have not lost any product." Jerry had heard that one of Rosenthal's shipments had been captured by the DEA. "I have many families pleading for your services. Griselda says she wants no one but you." Griselda was Griselda Blanco, known as the black widow because it was rumored that she killed her husbands. She was in Miami, and her sons handled the cocaine in Medellin. "You will be rich, my friend." He leaned back in the seat. "Someday we will rent a big boat and take a trip to all the islands, fucking all the beautiful women on each. On that you have my word."

Herrera told Jerry to buy the finest suit he could buy because they were going to party. Herrera liked to party and the Cartel members liked Herrera, but Jerry felt uncomfortable around them when it was for a long length of time. He was afraid he would say something offensive because he didn't know or understand their customs, so mostly he just remained in the background. He would much rather be with Ward or Maria.

Surprisingly, he hadn't experienced any close calls with the DEA during his flights. Although Herrera said they were trying to infiltrate the Cartel to gain information on smuggling activities, he hadn't seen anything resembling a plane following him. And his ground crew had not had any problems as well. It was strange considering what he was hearing about other smugglers. Ward said it was what he had told Jerry many times: fate. Fate was dictating their success.

But on one of the flights, it seemed that fate had other plans for them. It was overcast as they neared the coast with a deep fog rolling in like ocean waves. Jerry finished his bottle of water and checked his instruments.

"Slim, I hope the hell you can see," Ward said.

Jerry nodded and decreased the plane's altitude. "You just keep an eye out for the coastline."

"Fuck that, I'm looking for the water. Jesus!"

Jerry smiled as he leveled out the plane fifty feet above the ocean. Danger exhilarated him. A hitman had once told him the same thing. It was the way of the outlaw. He glanced at Ward and studied the symptoms of concern on his face; the jaw muscles tightened, a nervous twitch in his right eye. When Jerry got concerned, fearful of his life, he could feel his shoulders tighten, like a spring coiling to release its energy at just the right moment.

"Shit, I see it," Ward said. "There's the coast."

Jerry was skeptical. He checked the instruments again. They were still too far out. "Don't think so."

"I see the fucking lights," Ward said.

So did Jerry and for a moment he doubted the instruments. "God damn," he muttered.

"What?"

"It's not the lights; something else." He was in a no-win situation. If he pulled the plane up, he would probably be caught by radar, and if he didn't – well, what the hell were those lights?

"Hang on," he said, as they neared them.

"Oh, shit. Oh, fucking shit." Ward's face had turned an ashen color as the plane skimmed the masts of the anchored sailboats.

"I bet they're pissing in their pants," Jerry said. But he knew the possibility of being reported so he began taking evasive actions. He turned to his left and searched for the small airport he had previously seen. Then he dove down as though to land, flew a few feet above the runway, and took off again, hoping this would fool any prying eyes. When, a few minutes later he didn't see a chase plane, he breathed easier. But all the events had left him with a questionable amount of fuel to get to Tennessee, so he found what looked like a deserted airstrip and hoped it had a fuel tank. It did. After refueling, he headed for Tennessee.

"Well, I'll be damn," Larry Jones said when he heard the story. He was putting in the fuel barrels and securing them to the plane. "I guess on this trip you earned your money."

Jerry said to him, "Larry, you got something on your mind, say it."

Chapter 12

"What could I have on my mind?" Jones said. "I'm just a hired hand."

"Who's paid well. Anyway, that's not the way to say it. If you're pissed, you should say, 'I'm just a lowly hired hand.' That way you'd place emphasis on how pissed you are."

Jones stepped away from the barrels and looked at him. "What the fuck you talking about? If I was pissed I'd tell you. It was just fuckin' comment."

"One thing I'm good at," Jerry said, "is reading people. It's an art form in Colombia. You look at a man's eyes, the way his mouth twitches, what he does with his hands, and you get to know a lot more than what he says. For instance, when you said it was just a comment, you turned your eyes away. Why? Because you were lying. So, I'll ask you again, why are you pissed?"

"Okay," Jones said, checking the last barrel to see if it was secured, "you want to know. You and Harold have a high time in Colombia, making all that money, while me and the others risk our butts driving to Florida. And for that we ain't getting paid enough."

Jerry stared at him. "And if I ask the others, they'll say the same thing?"

"They're probably too scared to say anything, but it's the truth," Jones said.

"Well, just for the sake of conversation, how much should I pay you?"

Jones closed his eyes a moment. "A hundred grand a load," he said.

Jerry waited. "Yeah?"

"All right, maybe eighty," Jones said. "Anyway, that's piddling money to you."

"Do you know how much I make, Larry?"

"I got an idea," Jones said.

"An idea is not a fact, just an idea, right?" Jerry kept staring at him. "You could be wrong as sin. You agree on that?"

"Yeah, but–"

"So you have this idea and now you think I'm taking advantage of you. Am I getting this straight? What you want to do, form a fucking union?

Is that it? Well, hell, Larry, nobody's making you do this. If you think it's unfair, just leave."

"I didn't say I wanted to leave," Jones said. "You asked if I was pissed, and I told you why."

"You remember when you hung me out to dry in the Bahamas?" Jerry said. "Even then you complained about the money. If you'd just said, 'Okay, Jerry, I'll risk my ass in that boat and try to make this successful,' I might be more likely to be sympathetic to your complaint, but as it is now, you can kiss my rosy red ass. Now, tell Harold to get ready to leave."

The path from coca leaves to cocaine goes through many steps. Cocaine is produced from the leaves of the coca plant that grows almost exclusively in South America. For small amounts of cocaine, the leaves are soaked in gasoline and other chemicals to extract the coca base, which is then poured into molds where the water is pressed out. This leaves a brick-sized mold that is almost fifty percent cocaine. The laboratories were scattered across the regions to produce copious amounts of the drug. The cocaine that Jerry smuggled would be cut by drug distributors, sold and then cut again before reaching the streets.

Hererra tried to take Jerry to one of the largest labs in Colombia, but Jerry politely refused. He only wanted to understand the business that directly affected him. That way, if something went wrong, they wouldn't come looking for him.

He had seen how justice was administered in Medellin. It was silver or lead; you either agreed to help the cartel for a price or were shot. He had seen a man gunned down on the street by a Cartel assassin on a scooter. Murders were routine in the city. *Silver or lead.*

On one occasion, his bodyguards whisked him away from the city and took him to a remote place in the mountains. Not much was said on the harrowing ride through the narrow passes, only that the Cartel had been warned that some of their members were designated to be killed. Jerry remained in the safe house for a day before being allowed to return to his home.

Chapter 12

Herrera said it was becoming worse because the CIA and DEA were bribing people to assassinate the Cartel members. Jerry wasn't sure he believed this because Herrera suspected the organizations of everything, especially the CIA. Later, Rosenthal told Jerry he had been approached to work with the CIA. While on the surface this seemed outrageous, Jerry had seen enough funny business in Medellin to know that anything was possible.

Within a few months, Jerry had become wealthy and Ward had made more money than in his entire life, but was becoming more and more anxious to go home. It was easy for him because he wasn't facing prison time, something Jerry reminded him off, so Ward asked it he could take a few days to visit his family. Jerry said it would have to wait until the Cartel had a slack time for deliveries. Meanwhile, Jerry had been in discussions with Herrera about the possibility of moving to Florida, if that could be safely arranged. Herrera said it might be possible if Jerry could expand his organization so he could increase flights for the Cartel. With Herrera, it was always about delivering the product.

Maria saw Jerry's anxiousness to return and did her best to change his mind, teaching him Spanish, introducing him to friends, even having her parents cook meals for them. They liked him and thought she had a nice boyfriend. "Where else could you go where you have more respect, Richard?" she said. Soon, Jerry discovered just how true that was.

During conversations had and conversations overheard with Cartel leaders, Jerry had learned that the Central Intelligence Agency was a big part of the drug culture in Colombia. For reasons Jerry hadn't quite figured out, they dealt with cocaine. The Cartel feared the DEA, but not the CIA–except as a competitor. There was an unwritten agreement between Escobar and the CIA: they left each other alone. So it was a surprise when Herrera approached Jerry and said that the CIA, through a revolutionary front called M-19 wanted to discuss business with him. Jerry asked about the group but Herrera shrugged and only said they were just another organization with a bee in their pants. Colombia was filled with such groups. Christ! Jerry thought. The CIA knew about him? What was that about? Herrera told him to calm down because he was alright. They're not after anyone; they just have heard good things about you and want to see if you might be interested in their offer, and no, he didn't know what that was. But it had been cleared and things were fine. And that's all he knew, except it was a lot of money.

Jerry couldn't get over the fact that the CIA knew he was smuggling. What else did they know? This was the goddamn CIA, not some moronic state agency. He thought this changed everything. Herrera assured him that it changed nothing. The CIA could be a valuable ally if used properly and if you never forgot that you could never completely trust them. He said there were agendas and then there were CIA agendas.

It was a few days later when Jerry listened in the sanctuary of his living room as the tall, well-dressed man introduced himself and began talking. He spoke with little or no accent but from his features Jerry thought he was from South America. He said he wanted Jerry to fly cocaine to Europe and return with heroin. His safety would be assured and all he had to do was take off and land. All details would be taken care of, safe airports provided—all he had to do was to fly the plane and keep his mouth shut.

Jerry said, "And for that you'll pay me twenty million a flight?" He lifted his glass of bourbon and looked at the man in disbelief. "What's the catch?"

"No catch, Senor Martin. I can see your thinking, but this is a legitimate business deal. Cocaine over and heroin back. We'll provide the flight training, assist with the airplane, and deposit the money wherever you desire. Initially, you will fly it to Medellin, but later you may be required to deposit it elsewhere. In all cases, you will be protected."

"Yeah, how?"

"By the highest order," the man said, smiling.

"Why me?"

The man shrugged. "Why not you? You're an excellent pilot, dependable, and come highly recommended." He sighed. "I know you are skeptical, which is why I will give you some time to think about it. But one

Chapter 12

thing I can't overemphasize – You will be safe. There will be no threat from authorities of any kind."

Jerry thought about the money. Twenty fucking million dollars! "How long do I have to think about it?"

"Two days."

Jerry said, "And if I say no? Will I have to worry all the time?"

"Of course not. Then, this conversation never happened, and we won't see each other again."

A few hours later, Jerry was sharing a drink with Herrera. "What was that all about, Humberto? It doesn't make sense they would pay me that kind of money when they could hire someone for a fraction of the cost."

"Well, they are not fucking with you, if that's your concern," Herrera said. "As for why such a large sum, when you consider the profit they will make, it is not that much money. And the Ochoa's vouched for you, as did Griselda."

"So, you're saying I should accept the offer?"

Herrera shrugged. "That is up to you. It's a big decision. Did he say how many flights you would make?"

Jerry shook his head. "No, only that it wouldn't interfere with my business with you."

Herrera scratched his head. "That might be possible, but–"

"That's what I wondered, too," Jerry said. "Right now, I'm leaning toward refusing it. Twenty million makes me a big target. And if they ever decide to cut their losses – well, it's a lot of money."

"Yes, it is," Herrera said. "But if it is the CIA, rejecting them might–"

"What are you saying? They might want to kill me? Jesus, Humberto!"

"I didn't say that," Herrera said. "Let's just say they want to make you an asset, but you turn them down. Maybe they think you need to be taught a lesson. As I said before, there are agendas and then there are CIA agendas."

"And that's supposed to make me feel better?"

"What I'm saying, Ricardo, is that I need to make a few calls before you make a decision," Herrera said.

That seemed like a good idea to Jerry. He said, "I feel like I'm being set up; you know, damned if I do and damned if I don't. Jesus Christ, this is a fucking mess. If I take the deal, they–"

"The CIA has ways to make you disappear – I understand," Herrera said. "But if it is them, perhaps I can take care of it if you decide to reject the offer."

"Would you take it, if it was offered to you?" Jerry said.

"I would not work for the CIA under any circumstance," Herrera said. "But my circumstance is different from yours."

Jerry was feeling sick to his stomach. He had gotten into something way over his head, and he saw that Herrera agreed. He watched Herrera put his hand into his pocket and bring out a pen and write something down. "A reminder to make the call," he said.

The way the safety deposit box in the bank worked was you showed identification and walked inside with a clerk. He then took your key and opened a door where the box was hidden. Then, he took his key and yours and placed them into two locks to get access to the deposit box. He then left you alone.

Jerry thumbed through the money, several million dollars, and put an unknown amount in his briefcase. He'd been surprised at how much money you could put in a large box. He made sure he had enough money on him if he had to leave the country in a hurry. The next thing he did was to call Ward and tell him to pack his suitcase and not to ask any questions. Then he drove over to Maria's and had sex.

"This was a pleasant surprise," she said, rolling on her side.

"Surprises can be good," he said. He rolled over and grabbed the drink on the bed table. "I might have to go away for a while."

She stared at him. "Where?"

A damn good question, he thought. "Somewhere. I'll let you know."

"Are you in trouble?"

"I don't know," he said, being honest. He had decided that if Herrera couldn't assure him he'd be safe if he refused the offer, he was going to take it. He didn't want to spend his time looking over his shoulder. If

Chapter 12

the assurance came, he was going to refuse the offer. There was too much baggage that came with the CIA. How much money did he need, after all? "Do any of your friends know I work for the Cartel?" He had told her to say he was a pilot for one of the oil companies in Medellin.

"If they do, I didn't tell them," she said.

He believed her. Anyway, if it was the CIA they had their ways to know all about him. And like the man had said, why wouldn't they contact him? They wanted someone dependable who could keep his mouth shut. Their problem was that he didn't trust the law, and no matter what their initials were, they were still the law. He finished his drink and reached over to caress her breasts. Maybe just one more time before he left.

Chapter 13

"I don't want you to worry about it," Herrera said as they flew to where the shipment was being loaded on the plane. "I heard from high authority that your refusal will have no consequences."

Still seeing the look in the man's eyes when he gave his answer, Jerry wasn't so certain. But he didn't trust anyone associated with the law, and you could double that if they were associated with the government. What had they ever done for him except cause trouble? He once heard a man say that the government was so bad he wondered if the founding fathers would do it again, if they had the chance.

"I love the river," he said. "Summer afternoons we used to fix baloney sandwiches and go down to the water and fish for catfish. Sometimes we would take off everything except our underwear and jump in, even if it was muddy. That's what I thought about when I made my decision. I know it sounds crazy but I didn't want to do something where I might never get that chance again."

Herrera waited a moment before saying, "When you finish this run I think we should get away for a while, have some fun. Does that sound okay?"

"Honestly, I'm so worn out from all this," Jerry said, "all I want is to sleep for three days."

Herrera laughed. "Okay, maybe some other time," he said.

The delivery and return went like clockwork and Herrera gave him the good news that the Cartel was going to increase the payment. So, he and Ward celebrated, and when Jerry awoke the next morning, he saw a young woman lying on top of Ward, wearing nothing but panties.

Chapter 13

Jerry walked out to his patio and sat under an umbrella. The Colombian gardener was digging around a bush, his short legs like tree trunks growing out of his khaki work pants. Jerry motioned to him and said to change clothes because he wanted to go into the city. The man's name was Jorge, and his uncle had been involved in the cocaine business for more than ten years. According to his story, Pablo Escobar's vision had made them all rich because he revolutionized the drug business. Escobar had made it easier for the Cartel members to get cocaine to ship, though there was a price to be paid to him. Then he had gotten rid of the old smugglers who wouldn't go along with the new way. Griselda Blanco had been forced to leave Colombia because she balked at paying so much for her cocaine. The early days of Escobar had been bloody but for those who survived, the money was worth it.

An hour later, Jerry went into a shop to buy flowers for Maria, accompanied by Jorge and another man, both heavily armed. When he left, he told Jorge he was going to meet his uncle and he and the other guards should stay outside the restaurant.

In a few minutes, he sat down opposite the heavyset man wearing a panama hat. Jerry told him about the CIA offer. He was a friend, an older man, who Jerry had met at a Cartel social event.

The man folded his arms across his chest and said, "Heroin. I myself want no part of it, but many within the Cartel see it as another promising product to maintain their revenues. Did they say who they represented?"

"Something called M-19."

The man nodded. "And you did not tell this to Herrera?"

"He knows about. He said they represented the CIA."

"And he was probably right. After M-19 seized the Dominican diplomats, things went wrong for them, the CIA interceded and made an alliance with them." He waved away the waiter. "M-19 was born after a fraudulent election on April 19, 1970, when the National Popular Alliance was denied an electoral victory. Their mixture of socialism and populism appealed to many, so their ranks soon increased, but for a long time they seemed to struggle with their true identity. Were they thieves or idealists?

"On Christmas Eve of 1979, the group dug a tunnel into the arms depot of the Colombian Army and stole over 5000 weapons that they used in bank robberies and other means of urban warfare against the privileged. In 1980, guerrillas seized 15 diplomats at the Dominican Republic Embassy in Bogota. It took over two months, and the CIA's help, to negotiate an end to the siege." He took a drink of the bourbon and carefully set it down, as though it was liquid gold. "The group had a few early run-ins with the Medellin Cartel. In a misguided effort to raise money, they kidnapped drug traffickers and their families for ransom. Recently they even attempted to kidnap Carlos Lehder when Lehder thought he had an alliance with them. It was madness but kidnapping seemed an easy path to riches. They were wrong. It was brought to a boiling point when the same month, M-19 kidnapped the sister of Jorge Ochoa and demanded $15 million in ransom. Escobar let it be known around the country that the Cartel would not tolerate kidnappings by guerilla groups attempting to finance their revolution through ransom money. An organization known as Muete a Secuestradores – Death to Kidnappers, was formed. Soon, the M-19 guerrilla militants were being killed at random, along with anyone harboring them. M-19 leaders were killed and the police just watched. Eventually, they decided that kidnaping drug traffickers and their families was bad business, and the Cartel and M-19 formed a hand's-off peace agreement. Despite their grievances against the guerrilla group, Escobar and the other Cartel leaders understood revolutions and allowed them to continue, as long as they didn't interfere with Cartel business."

"The million dollar question is, do you think I'm safe?" Jerry said.

"Well, if Herrera said you were, your chances are pretty good. He doesn't speak alone."

"Just pretty good?," Jerry said. "I was hoping for something better.'

The man smiled. "While the Cartel might think they have everything under control, they don't, especially concerning either the CIA or DEA.

Chapter 13

Don't let anyone tell you otherwise." He shrugged. "But you're probably okay. I doubt they see you as a threat to them."

"How about if they're just pissed off?" Jerry said.

"Better not to think about it. In this war between the Cartel and the authorities, it's difficult to tell who is who." He laughed and spread his hands. "We believe it was the CIA who paid M-19 to kidnap Ochoa's sister and Lehder."

"Why was the CIA interested? It doesn't make sense to me."

"Richard, the CIA plays every angle in Colombia. If they thought they could force the Cartel to negotiate for a piece of the cocaine trade—" He paused for a moment. "But there is more to the story, as there usually is with your intelligence agency. They used Colonel Noriega of Panama to pay for the woman's release, for which he was paid several million dollars. They hoped this money would grease the way to doing drug business with the Sandinistas. At that time, Nicaragua was beginning to increase their drug production. The CIA would buy drugs from the Sandinistas and use the profit to buy guns for the Contras." He laughed again. "Like I said, you can't tell the enemy from the friend."

Jerry finally concluded that in Medellin everyone had their own agendas, no black and white just various shades in between.

"You made the right decision for you, that's what you have to believe. But understand that when you deal with the CIA, there is always more than the obvious, which is to say that if an offer happens again, you need to look closely before making a decision. Another offer means they see you as an asset on one hand, but rejection means you could also be a liability."

When the man left, Jerry finished the bottle and ordered another. What the hell had he gotten himself into?

In late summer 1982, Rosenthal lost another load of cocaine when the plane crashed on takeoff. Neither passenger was badly hurt, but the plane was destroyed. It was the second cocaine load he had lost since his arrival in Medellin. In his defense, both the landing and takeoff sites were barely adequate, and you always had to watch the maintenance people to see that they did what needed done. On one flight, the mechanic had left the oil cap off, and when Jerry took off, oil began spewing across the engine. He was able to land before the engine imploded, but it was too close. And the planes were too old, something he had repeatedly complained about to Herrera.

Jerry dreamed about having his own plane, maybe a couple that he could properly maintain. "I'd add a panther conversion kit," he said to Ward, as though that meant anything to him. He had read about the kit in an aviation magazine. It would not only make the plane faster, it would boost fuel economy to reduce the number of fuel barrels required. The cost of $180,000 was not a problem. He would have the best looking planes of any smuggler.

The kit put in new starters, redesigned propellers, additions to the wings, more efficient vacuum and fuel pumps, and other significant improvements. With the new power the kit provides, he would be able to increase the amount of cocaine per load, which would make him a lot more money, as well as pleasing the Cartel.

"Let's do it," Ward said, willing to go along with almost anything Jerry suggested.

Increasing demand became a problem because there was always more coke ready to be shipped than the plane could handle. This caused trouble with a few clients who wanted to overload the plane, especially those shipping for Griselda Blanco. Finally, Herrera had to call her to straighten that out. Jerry was already filling the plane over its recommended weight, but her shippers wanted even more shipped. But she intervened and said that when he said it was enough, they should honor his word.

"I do not like speaking to her," Herrera said. "She has no conscience. She is more brutal than Escobar, and there are those in Medellin who would like to see her dead." He slapped Jerry on the shoulder. "But I think she likes you. You are making a lot of money for her."

A week later, Jerry told Herrera that sometime in the near future Ward was going to stay behind in Tennessee to visit family but he thought he

Chapter 13

could handle the flight by himself. "I will go with you, Ricardo," Herrera had said, but Jerry didn't think that was a good idea. They discussed this as they rode around Medellin the back of Herrera's car.

Herrera said, "You have opened many eyes among the members, Ricardo. Of all the American pilots, you have the best record. You are not crazy like many of them." He laughed. "Perhaps it is because we pay you so well." Jerry didn't know what others were making and didn't want to. "But there is talk about giving you more loads. Or had you already heard?"

"I'm already doing all I can do," Jerry said.

Herrera shrugged. "But if you had more planes and pilots?"

Jerry looked at him. "You mean set up my own operation?"

"Do you think you could find pilots?" Herrera said.

Jerry thought about for most of the night. Could he find them? Finally, he decided that from here he couldn't. But the opportunity nagged at him. However, the thought of the CIA in his life nagged even more. Since his last meeting with them, rumors began flying about their activity in Colombia. While he knew they were active, he hadn't been aware to what extent. When he questioned Herrera about it, the Cartel leader said that the CIA had helped with the formation of the Medellin Cartel because they would rather deal with one organization that many small operations.

"What are we doing, Harold?" Jerry wondered aloud. "Cops, robbers – what the hell is the difference? This is one fucked up country."

"Shit, let's go back home then," Ward said. "The CIA, Israeli intelligence, DEA – I say we get out of Dodge while we can." Jerry agreed completely, but with so many people looking for him, he didn't know if it was possible.

Another rumor going around was that the CIA, with the help of the Colombian government, was "kidnapping" drug smugglers from the country and taking them back to the States to stand trial. Mostly these were those who had angered Colombian officials, or who had gotten in the CIA's way. But there was also the story that the CIA was waging a war against anyone who might be a danger to their drug smuggling program, including those who knew too much, for the first time making Jerry glad he had refused to go along with M-19's CIA offer.

Medellin violence increased as the rumors about the CIA escalated. It seemed to Jerry that there was a murder a day on Medellin streets. Even with bodyguards, it was a crapshoot. Demographically, if you looked at it through the eyes of a gringo, it was fifty percent criminals and fifty percent victims. As beautiful as it was, Medellin was looking more and more like a death trap.

"If we're going to stay here, what we need is a vacation," Ward said. "You, me, Maria just taking a few days off. We could fly to Bogota."

"Yeah, well try explaining that to the Cartel," Jerry said. He knew that the production of cocaine never took time off, so the supplies were building up faster than the deliveries could accommodate. And the Colombians in Miami were constantly pressuring for more supply. And why not? By the time they cut the product a few times, their profits quadrupled. Cocaine use was growing and had supplanted heroin as the drug of the day.

"Humberto said something about flying to Miami soon," Jerry said.

"Did he say when?"

Jerry shook his head. "He said we could party, do a little gambling, but he didn't give a date. Don't look so disappointed. I'll ask him again."

"We've earned it," Ward said.

As Jerry's flights continued to go without any problems, more and more Cartel members were lining up for his services. The Tennessee pipeline, as it was called, was the most efficient within the smuggling operation. Not one kilo of cocaine had been lost. But the success came with a price as now he was turning the flights around in two days, and it had caught up with him. Sometimes during the flights he had to fight from falling asleep. He was tempted to take some of the product up his nose to stay awake but his strict policy was simple: no drugs. Cocaine was poison and he would fire any of his men caught using. If the money

Chapter 13

he was paying them was burning a hole in their pockets, they needed to find another way to blow off steam.

As for his own money, he was giving thought to purchasing real estate in Medellin. Herrera said it was a good idea. Both Ochoa and Escobar were buying property, so it was a safe investment. But he knew nothing about real estate, and that gave him hesitation. In fact, he realized that he knew little about finances at all. He had always made money and spent it immediately, never having that much to save. Enjoy life and worry about tomorrow later. But now, later had arrived and he knew he needed to do something with his millions.

"Maybe gold," Ward said.

"Maybe a townhouse in Miami," Jerry countered.

"Now, that sounds like a winner," Ward said.

Maria liked the idea of buying something in Miami. She said she wanted the experience of staying there. What the hell did that mean, he wondered. *Experience?* She acted like it was an amusement park. But he'd heard that Miami was a lot like Medellin. You could get killed just for looking the wrong way.

They stopped at a bar where she drank two rum drinks with cute names and he had bourbon on the rocks. Before she ordered a third, she said, "Richard, my parents want us over this weekend. It'd be a chance to tell them about the real estate possibility. They'll think you're prosperous."

"Maybe," he said.

"Let's leave it to God," Ward said, a few days later. He was sloshed to the gills and leaning back in the chair in Jerry's living room. "That's what the preacher used to say, 'Just leave it to God.' Anyway, you don't know a damn thing about real estate, so stop fretting about it."

"So I just leave it to God to make the decision for me? Is that what you're saying?" Jerry had attended church a little as a child, but had never bought into what they were selling. It seemed too easy and his experience said not much worthwhile was easy. But he liked the thought of a God; he had just never met Him.

"Well, if you want my advice, I say you keep everything you own within reach so if the lights go out, you can pick it up and run."

It was a pleasant October day when they took off from the jungle airstrip. The plane lumbered slightly before lifting off. Once they were airborne, Ward winked at him and said, "1982 has been a good year, Slim. You ever think about how it was in Tennessee? Jesus, it's so good, sometimes I think something must be wrong with us."

"Wrong?"

"Yeah, you know, doing something that will come back and bite us in the ass. Surely, there has to be a catch."

"Just don't get caught," Jerry said. "And there's not a damn thing wrong with me. I'm just getting payback for all the shit I've endured over the years." He glanced at Ward. "Maybe deep down, you want to get caught."

"Fucking no, Slim, not me. I'm just saying how good things are, that's all."

Jerry agreed. He would probably be the richest man in Maryville should he ever return. Ward was happy because he was going to visit family, and Jerry was happy because he'd received a nice letter from Bonnie saying how much she missed him. It was good to be missed.

"I feel guilty at making you handle the barrels by yourself, Slim," Ward said.

Jerry smiled at him. "I'm a big boy," he said. Ward had been talking about this trip nonstop for a week. "Have a good time."

"I'm going to spend some of my money."

Jerry put the plane on autopilot and walked to the back to make sure the barrels were properly restrained, though the only issue they'd ever had with the barrels was when Ward almost hit the tail section when he threw out an empty.

He returned to his seat and took back control of the plane. "Just don't get mugged," he said to Ward.

"Shit, I heard that."

Chapter 13

The flight went without a hitch, and when they touched down in Tennessee, Ward nearly jumped from the plane. The ground crew had brought a car for him to drive to Georgia.

Jerry ate something and made small talk with his crew as they loaded the duffel bags of cocaine into cars. Clouds were rolling in, and rain was in the air. He spoke briefly to Larry Jones, who was loading the fuel barrels and tying them securely to the anchors.

"I'm guessing you're still having fun in Colombia," Jones said.

"I'm working my ass off, if that's what you're saying," Jerry said.

"You don't think I am? Driving to Florida twice a week wears on you."

"Yeah, you already said that."

"Not to mention the worry about getting caught," Jones said. "There's times when I wonder when we park the cars if someone's going o run out and start shooting."

"Nobody's going to fuck with the Colombians. Don't worry about it."

"You think so?" Jones said. "Man could take that coke and sell it to a dozen people."

"And he'd be dead in a week, too—him, his dog, cat and kids. Then just for good measure, they'd cut off his dick and rape his wife with it."

"I hear they get ripped off all the time," Jones said, "but I guess you know more than me. Anyway, I might like to come down there sometime. You know, see what it's like."

Waiting on Jerry to say something, while he stood there grinning. "Yeah, you should do that when we have a work break. And speaking of work, you'd better finish tying down the barrels. I'd like to leave in thirty."

"Right away, boss," Jones said. "Yes sir."

"What was that?"

Jones grinned at him. "You know why Baptists don't fuck standing up? Somebody might think they're dancing."

A few minutes later, Jerry taxied down the runway and lifted into the yellowing sky. About 700 feet into the climb he heard a popping noise toward the rear and as he cocked his head to look, the plane suddenly tilted back and the engine stall warning horn started blaring.

And he knew that something was terribly wrong.

The plane was nearing vertical and the message was clear: the plane's center of gravity had shifted. All he could think of was, *You can't mess this up, Jerry.* But it was difficult to think when alarms were blasting in his ear. There was no way he could ever explain to others what he was feeling. The plane was going to tip over. He pushed the plane forward, urging it to respond. *Come on, you son of a bitch. Level out.* He could hear the engines straining as the plane began to vibrate. More loud noises came from the back of the plane, cables snapping, barrels turning over. The plane turned to the right and he prepared for the nose to spiral downward, but just when he was ready to accept his fate, the nose turned back to the right and began to level. *Come on, baby,* he urged.

In a few moments, it was over and he was in control of the plane again. After waiting until his heart stopped racing, he engaged the autopilot and leaned back. He was bathed in sweat. Then, he walked to the rear to assess the damage. Two barrels had broken loose and had covered the floor with fuel.. The plane reeked of gasoline. It took only a few seconds to see the cause, the barrels hadn't been properly secured. How could Jones be so careless?

He did what he could to secure the other barrels before returning to his seat, wondering what he was going to do? The loss of fuel ruled out any chance of flying to Colombia and the Colombian markings on his plane ruled out landing at a strange airport, which meant he had to return to Madisonville, but that was going to be dicey because by the time he got there, a worker would be present, a volunteer with a fascination and curiosity about aviation, according to Jerry's crew, and would probably come out to see who was landing at such a late hour. And then he would see the markings.

But there was no other choice than to take the chance. If he got lucky, no one would be there and he could find more fuel and leave in the early

Chapter 13

morning. The spilled fuel in the plane wouldn't go away so easily, however. One spark and the whole thing might go up in flames.

Keep your mind on what you can control. He made a checklist of what he would do once he landed safely. He would find a telephone and call one of Jones' relatives who lived in Madisonville, explain who he was and that he needed a place to stay the night. Then, he would sort things out with Jones.

His cynicism began rising to the surface. Was it a coincidence that the only time there was a problem with the barrels was when he was flying solo? He knew Ward would never hurt him, but Jones – he wasn't so certain. He closed his eyes for a moment. Jesus, what was he going to do?

It was pitch black when he approached the small airport. He touched down the wheels, anxious, his butt so tight it hurt, and waited to see what happened. But it was one of the best landings he had ever made. Taking a large breath, he brought the plane to a stop at the end of the runway. But just as he was beginning to feel safe he saw the headlights coming down the runway and knew it was the worker. He climbed out of the plane and made his way to the safety of the trees.

When finally the person arrived to pick him up, Jerry's anger had vented. All he wanted now was a place to sleep; morning would be time to sort things out. "Larry isn't home," the man said, but Jerry knew that. By now, he and the others should be well on the way to Florida with the cocaine.

But when he walked upstairs, expecting to strip down and collapse into the bed, he saw what he wouldn't expect in a million years. The room was filled with duffel bags of cocaine.

Chapter 14

There was no hiding Jones' surprise when Jerry finally contacted him. He had gone to Maryville for what he said was personal business. An hour later, he had returned to Madisonville. He made the excuse that he was planning on taking the cocaine to Miami the next morning, and had told the others to come to his house at eight.

"What are you saying, Larry? You unload $20 million of coke in your house! I've got a notion to scatter your brains all over these walls. You're either the dumbest person I've ever known or–" He pointed his finger at him. "You tried to kill me, didn't you? Kill me and then tell the others they might as well sell the coke to the Colombians themselves. Is that it?"

"God damn, Jerry, you know me better than that."

"I know you, all right. Well, this is what's going to happen. I'm getting the others here, and we're going to deliver the product. Then I'm going to decide whether to take care of you personally or turn you over to the Colombians."

"Shit, Jerry, it was just a mistake."

Jerry motioned with his hand. "Get the hell out of my sight."

Jerry called Ward the next morning to tell him what had happened. Ward said, "The barrels had turned over? You mean he didn't secure them the right way? And you're sure there wasn't a chance he just screwed up?"

Jerry stared at the phone in disbelief. "You expect snags from time to time," he said, "but you tell me how the barrels could come loose. You know how it works, so go ahead and tell me."

Chapter 14

"Yeah, it doesn't make sense. Do you believe his story about the cocaine?"

"No. I don't know the truth but he was lying. Maybe he saw a way to get rich, I don't know. Maybe he thought that with me dead he could make his own deal with Herrera to get my share of the money. Hell, he might even try to set up something like Rosenthal has in Medellin."

"Slim, is he dead?"

"Jones?"

"Yeah, did you kill him?"

"I scattered him all over the bedroom," Jerry said.

"Oh, shit."

"Naw, I'm just talking," Jerry said. "But I wanted to. I don't know what I'm going to do about him."

"I would've thought you would've killed him."

"Maybe I'm getting soft," Jerry said. "I told Humberto we had lost the plane but he didn't seem upset."

"They've got a boatload of planes, Slim."

"I know. Listen, I've been doing some thinking. How would you like living in Miami?"

"You mean permanently?"

"Yeah."

"Deal me in, baby. Would we ever go back, though? I've got stuff there I want to keep."

"Yeah, I need to talk to a few people and get my money," Jerry said. He certainly owed it to Maria to tell her he was leaving, and the Cartel leaders would take it as a sign of respect if he explained his plans face to face. "I need to see if it's doable, but I think it is. I called Larry Allen this morning to see if he knew where I could get another plane. He's agreed to meet me in Atlanta later this week. I'd like you to be there with me."

"With bells on, Slim. Fucking Miami, I can't believe it."

Allen said he knew a pilot who might be able to help with the problem. The pilot had previous dealings with a man living in Fort Lauderdale who was known as the fixer because he could find anything and get anything done. If it had anything to do with planes, he was the man. "He has a funny name, German I think," Allen had said.

When he asked if the business was illegal, Jerry told him it didn't make any difference as long as the money was right. Allen agreed.

The first thing Jerry noticed about Bonnie was that her hair was shorter, maybe a little fuller, too. He had purchased her an airplane ticket to Atlanta and paid for cab fare to his hotel. She said, "I nearly had a heart attack when you called," as her arms wrapped around him, her body pressed against him, making him think of things they could do later. She pulled away slightly and looked him over, as he did her. "Are you here to stay? I don't think anyone's looking for you now."

He shook his head. "Not here," he said, "but I might move to Florida." The more he said it, the better it sounded. He missed seeing his family. He looked at her again, seeing the outline of her white panties under the nightgown. "You know what I'd like to do right now?"

She grabbed his hand. "You're reading my mind," she said.

An hour later, he rolled out of bed and found the bottle, pouring a drink and downing it in one gulp. He had missed Bonnie more than he realized. When he had called her on the phone and asked her to meet him, the excitement in her voice had turned him on like he hadn't experienced in a long time.

"That was nice," she said from the bathroom.

"Yeah, it was." But the sound of the shower drowned him out. He fixed another drink and propped his feet on a table. He asked if the police had been asking about him and she said that other than a bail bondsman, no one had.

"I went to Miami once," she said. "I saw a man pull out his dick and pee on a palm tree at the beach." She ran her fingers through her hair as it blew upward, then turned off the dryer. "I think he was gay. There seems to be a lot of gay people there."

Jerry smiled. She was the only person he knew who didn't call them queers. "You should see Medellin," he said.

Chapter 14

"Would I come there with you, Miami?" she said, after a few seconds of silence.

"Maybe after things settle down." He couldn't see that happening because he didn't want anything tying him down. Besides, it might be dangerous.

"I'm not stupid, Jerry. I know you like seeing other women, and that's okay because maybe I like seeing other men. What? You think I don't have needs too. I'm not saying I sleep around but you told me yourself you'd understand if I went out. So me going to Florida won't change what you do."

He was surprised by her candor, and for a moment it made him angry, but she was right. He would never make a long-term commitment, so why shouldn't she enjoy herself.

"You're not going to say something?" she said a few moments later

"We both do what we think is best," he said.

She stared at him, then said, "Thanks for the money. It comes in real handy."

He'd been sending her cash, sometimes a lot, without explaining where it came from. He had a natural distrust of women keeping secrets. "Put some of it in the bank for a rainy day. Just make sure it's under ten grand. They have to report ten grand."

"That's a lot of money," she said, turning on the blower again.

He grinned. "You might be looking at one of the richest men in Maryville." He saw her skeptical look. "It's the truth. I've got so much money I could walk into the police station and say 'Hey, I'm Jerry LeQuire, but if you won't tell anyone I'll make you rich.' And I'd get away with it." He knew the power of money in a small town. And while money didn't make you invincible, it increased your odds of surviving. "If something goes wrong, the first person I'm going to call is F. Lee Bailey."

"I've heard of him," Bonnie said, beginning to grasp what he had just said. She put the blower on the table and poured a small drink. "You think if he'd been your lawyer in Jefferson City, things would be different?"

"Well, that was a crooked case, so maybe it would've been the same," he said. "But he might have been able to get the charges dropped just because of his reputation. You ever read anything about the sheriff?"

She shook her head. "I read something about Franklin's estate, though. Something about back taxes, but I could be wrong." She sat down and stretched out her legs. "I ran into Gerald Russell once. He was coming out of a bank. He looked good. He was a good basketball player, wasn't he?"

"Real good," Jerry said. "Played in college."

"Well, he's tall enough for it."

"Did he ask about me?"

"I said you were away but I wasn't sure where," she said. "I don't think he was that interested, really."

"Lawyers don't want to know my business," Jerry said. He placed his hand in her lap. "I got time for some more, then I have to make some telephone calls."

An hour later, he was talking with Herrera again. "Did you think over what we talked about?" Jerry said.

"I think it's a good idea," Herrera said. "You'd have more planes for the product. The others agree as well. And you would have a bigger plane?"

"Yeah, and I could interface with your people in Miami when there's a problem," Jerry said. "That way there'd be no misunderstandings."

"Good, good. I like it already. When will you begin?"

"I've got a meeting set up with some people," Jerry said.

"So, we're talking about a couple of weeks?"

That would be pressing it but Jerry knew Herrera had a schedule. "I think I could do that." In the worst case he could lease a plane until his operation was set up in Florida. "I need you to make sure my money gets here. I'll tell the bank that you're my representative." He trusted Herrera

Chapter 14

to always do the right thing. Cartel leaders had a strict code they lived by.

"Just let me know. Maybe when you come down, I can give it to you. Or I could just have one of my people in Miami contact you— we could swap, si?"

Actually, that sounded like a good idea to Jerry. "I'll let you know when I get to Florida," he said.

Herrera said, "When I come to Miami, perhaps you and I could get a couple of cars and party. You will like Miami. There is a sex club – I can't recall the name—that is mucho fun. Rich women with exotic desires."

"You're beginning to sound horny, Humberto."

"I am always horny, Ricardo. You know that."

Jerry instinctively nodded. "One thing, Humberto, I don't want to have to deal with Griselda."

Herrera laughed. "The black widow won't harm you, Ricardo. She likes you."

"All the same, I'd rather not."

"I understand. I'll put out the word – no Griselda for Ricardo." He laughed again. "Anyway, she might want to fuck you. She likes to fuck, either men or women."

"And if you have any juice in south Florida with the cops, I'd like for them to leave me alone, too," Jerry said.

"I'll see what I can do." Herrera paused a moment. "You might be leaving at the right time, Ricardo. Another person was taken in the middle of the night and returned to America for trial. This extradition treaty is worrying us. Pablo vows to punish Colombian officials who cooperate with America."

"Do I know him?"

"I don't think so. He didn't live in Medellin," Herrera said. "It has us worried. This is looking bad, Ricardo."

"Are you taking precautions?"

"Of course. I have men outside my house when I sleep. And I've increased my security alarms." He paused for a moment. "There will be much blood spilled over this. When Pablo gets angry, there is always blood."

The news made Jerry even more determined to make the move to south Florida work out. After telling Herrera he would fly to Medellin once he got a plane, he hung up the phone and found Bonnie.

He said, "I'm almost certain about Florida. When I get there, I'll see about bringing you down for a vacation."

She leaned her head back and winked. "Would it be okay if I brought a boyfriend?"

He patted her butt and laughed. "Only if he brings another girl."

That evening, he placed a phone call to a Maryville businessman he had known for several years.

"I want you to find anyone in Maryville that has a grudge against me and see what it would take to make it go away," Jerry said. "I'd like to think I could visit my family without always looking over my shoulder. And that includes the police."

"We might be talking about a lot of money," the man said.

"Whatever it takes."

Larry Allen came over to the bar in Jerry's room and refilled his glass. "Like I said, David says there's a man in Fort Lauderdale named Hank Maierhoffer who can get you an airplane. David wants to know how you'll buy it? You need a middle man or what?"

"I'll pay cash," Jerry said. He looked Allen over. He looked like he'd gained a little weight since their last meeting.

"You know, you still owe me ten grand for the Marathon lawyer. I'm not being pushy, but money is money."

Jerry walked over to the desk drawer and opened it. He counted out ten thousand in hundreds and handed it to Allen.

Allen said, "That's a lot of money you have in there. You rob a bank?"

"Look at me, Larry. Do I look like a bank robber?"

Allen stuck the money in his pockets. Then his gaze moved to Ward who had been sitting quietly in the corner of the room. "Okay, you say you want a plane, so I'm guessing it has something to do with drugs.

Chapter 14

That's fine with me but I want you to know that as a lawyer, it's best I don't know any details."

Jerry almost laughed, this coming from a man who'd probably steal from a preacher if the reward was high enough. And he knew that Allen would take any dope he could snort or stick in his arm. But if acting self-righteous made him feel better, that was okay.

"This Maierhoffer, tell me about him," Jerry said.

"I've never met him but Dave says he can get things done fast. I think he's retired military and has a lot of connections."

"And he's from south Florida?"

"Owns a fixed base operation at the Fort Lauderdale International Airport," Allen said. "Works on airplanes, maintenance stuff, and rents space for airplanes – that kind of stuff. He might be a few years older than you."

Jerry would check him out. "Okay, sounds good so far. Now, tell me about what's going on in the Marathon case. Are they still hot to get me down there or is it forgotten?"

"I don't think they want to do anything," Allen said. "The DEA's after cocaine now, not marijuana." He took another drink. "Meet me in Lexington in three days and we'll work things out. Meanwhile, I could use a little cocaine if you have any handy."

Jerry made a few calls to his Miami friends to check on Maierhoffer. They didn't seem to know much about him but they were glad Jerry was considering moving his operation. "I'll take you deep sea fishing," one of them said.

"Well, it'd better be a goddamn big boat," Jerry said.

Chapter 15

Jerry was impressed with Hank Maierhoffer, not because he had a commanding appearance – he was an ordinary looking man, with weight to spare – but because of his attitude. He seemed the type to be undaunted by any task. "Jesus, Richard," he said, "I can get you a plane tomorrow. What else do you need? Give me something more difficult than an airplane."

"You know anything about real estate?" Jerry said.

"You looking for a place to stay, you've come to the right person. I'll even throw in my housekeeper for good measure. My wife's getting suspicious of her, if you know what I mean."

They sat around for a couple of hours, sharing drinks and stories. Maierhoffer had retired from the military and worked with airplanes most of his life. He was married, with a boy about to enter his teen years.

"Sometimes I worry about him," he said.

"Does he like to fly?"

Maierhoffer nodded. He stared at Jerry a moment. "Okay, I'm going to come right out and say it. What this meeting's really about is more than just a plane, right?"

"What makes you think that?"

"Richard, I've been around the block a few times so when someone who I barely remember calls and says it's urgent that I find an airplane for a guy he doesn't know, I get curious. So I say, okay but I need to know his name, and when he tells me I call a few people to look you up.

Chapter 15

And I hear you got a first rate reputation with people who – well, let's just say who I respect. And that says a lot about both of us."

"You might know too much about my business," Jerry said.

"Yes, and if you didn't need my help, I'm pretty sure this conversation would end right here. But you do and I can accommodate you."

"I'm listening."

"You come to Fort Lauderdale and I can make it safe for you. Make a list of who or what is worrisome and I'll take care of it. Now, I know that sounds like bullshit from a man you've just met but once you get to know me, you'll understand I don't lie. I've been at the same place long enough to make a few connections and–" He hesitated a moment–"and to tell the truth I've been waiting for someone like you to come along."

"What does that mean?"

"I don't believe you want a small operation," Maierhoffer said. "You're a businessman. So, in that regard I can get you excellent pilots, pilots you'll be able to trust. You take care of the others, and I'll handle the pilots," always a step ahead of Jerry. He let his hand slide down over his belly. "There's one I know, they call him 'The Hat.' You'll like him, I guarantee. He's dependable and keeps his mouth shut. And then I know a man who lives in the Bahamas – well, over the years I've come to know many people who can help you. I've got good organizational skills from my military training and perhaps more importantly I've got a place at Fort Lauderdale International where you can keep your planes and know they will be properly maintained."

Just like they'd known each other for years, Jerry thought. But that was okay. He had watched him closely as he talked, studied his features. Not bad looking, out of shape a little, but Jerry could see him getting into trouble with women. Maybe when he was younger, a bit of a rounder.

"We're already talking about planes when I don't even have one," Jerry said.

"Jesus, Richard, tomorrow. You don't believe me, watch." He walked to the telephone and made a call. When he returned he said, "I was wrong. We can pick it up the day after tomorrow."

"How much?"

Maierhoffer smiled. "Do you really care?"

"It'll be in cash."

Maierhoffer shrugged. "Cash is all I deal in. You'll cut me a percentage."

Like that was a given. Jerry almost laughed. "I'll pay you a decent finders fee, Hank. I'm not a bank."

"Oh, okay," Maierhoffer said.

Jerry liked the way he handled it, not showing that he was pissed, if he was.

"If you know where to look, you can find real bargains on planes," Maierhoffer said. "And nobody says a word about who bought them or why. It's like picking up something at a flea market."

"I would need to feel safe. You say you can fix that but I need to be sure."

"You pay me enough and it'll be like you're locked up in Fort Knox. Like I said, you just tell me who's worrying you and I'll take care of it."

"It's really that easy?"

"It is for me, and I told you I don't lie."

"Everybody lies," Jerry said, refilling his glass with the cheap bourbon Allen had provided. What the hell was he thinking? You live in Kentucky and you don't buy good bourbon? Said a lot about the man. "Okay, I'll make a list."

Larry Allen came into the room and said, "You making good?"

"It'd be better if you had some good booze," Jerry said. "How about running down to the liquor store and getting some Jack Daniel's?" He flipped him a twenty. "And you can keep the change."

"You know him well?" Maierhoffer asked when they were alone.

"Not that good. Now, about the pilots – where do you get them?"

"Wherever they're hiding out at the time," Maierhoffer said. "They're usually broke and on the run from something, but they'll work hard and you won't have to worry about them. I'll see to that."

Chapter 15

Jerry smiled. "You understand I can smell bullshit from a hundred paces. You might be good but there's nobody *that* good." Jerry paused. "I'm talking about protection, pilot services and all the other stuff. I'll be satisfied if you can do half of that. Now, you have any connections in Miami?"

There was a slow gleam in Maierhoffer's eyes. "I know people you don't want to know," he said. "And then I know some you might."

"How about Colombians?"

"I see all kinds of people in all kinds of planes flying through, so it's possible I might have done business with a few of them. But that's not my business, you understand. I serve to help those who make it their business."

"You know Humberto Herrera?"

"I've heard of him," Maierhoffer said. "I've also heard of Pablo Escobar. Jesus, Richard, sure I know who he is."

"I work for him."

"The hell you say."

Jerry laughed. "No, I report directly to Herrera." He watched Maierhoffer's expression change from disbelief to respect. "I know them all – Escobar, Lehder, Blanco – all of them."

Maierhoffer swirled his drink for a moment. "You don't seem the kind of man to tell me this to impress, so I'm wondering why."

"I just want you to know not to mess with me," Jerry said. "If we're doing business together, you need to know who I am."

"It's funny, but I knew that was what you would say. Just looking at you, it seems appropriate. That certain tone you can't have unless you mean it. But you don't have to worry about me because we have the same interests. You want to make money, and I want to grow your business." He winked as Jerry. "For a percentage."

"More like a salary, maybe," Jerry said.

"Can I ask you something? You ever thought about owning your own airport? You know, a place where you can do your business without worry about interference?"

The question was amusing—his own airport? Nevertheless, he saw the look in his face, the way his jaw was set and the earnest tone of his voice. "No, never crossed my mind, but it might be worthwhile to consider."

Maierhoffer perked up. "You find this airport in a godforsaken part of the county where no one gives a shit what goes on as long as they have a job, then you fix it up to make it look legal…" Maierhoffer paused a moment. "…say, you put in a flying school, nothing fancy, just a couple of small planes and an instructor a couple days a week. See, you're legit now and no one takes a second look. How's that sound?"

"Like a movie script," Jerry said.

"But this one's real. See, things like that is what I can do for you." He looked up as Allen returned and handed Jerry the bottle.

"Had one in the garage for special occasions. Just slipped my mind."

"We're still talking business, Larry," Jerry said, nodding toward the door, noticing that Allen kept the twenty. "But thanks for your help." He refilled the glasses and slid one over to Maierhoffer. "He doesn't need to hear this."

"Agreed. Where did you say you met him?"

"I didn't," Jerry said.

"Yeah, I got it. But you trust him, right?"

"He's afraid of me," Jerry said.

"Sometimes that's the best kind of trust. Now, you really interested in an airport or are we just talking?"

Jerry grinned. "I'm open to new ideas," he said.

Maierhoffer leaned close as if to share a secret. "I know this place near Slyvania, Georgia, that might be interesting. I've heard a few pilots mention it, but I've never been there to look it over. Maybe after you get settled in we could fly down and take a look."

"How would you go about buying an airport?" Jerry said.

"Okay, you'd have to have a dummy corporation, but that's not a big problem." He nodded toward the door. "I bet he knows how to do it. If not, I know people who do. And all the transactions would be in cash so there's no easy way to tie it back to you."

Chapter 15

"Maybe. Once I get the plane, I want to put a panther conversion kit in. Where can we do that?"

"There's a place in Nashville that does it – I think. I'll look into it to make sure." He moved to his feet. "I need to get back to the hotel. How about us meeting in the morning right here around noon? Is that okay?"

"Yeah."

Maierhoffer extended his hand. "I can't tell you how glad I am to meet you, Richard."

"That was fun," she said, pulling up her panties, black like her hair, silk with lace around the bottoms. She had a good body and nice legs.

He agreed. Karla Espinal was skilled in bed, more than most prostitutes he had known. Though it made no difference to him, she confessed that she had only sold herself a few times, when she worked for a small airline whose boss wanted to curry favors from his clients. She had the looks to do just that, a white Cuban with a nice figure and pretty face, a man's type of woman. She was not the prettiest of the pretty, but well above average, and her smile lit up the room. She said she had used drugs and sometimes had sold cocaine on the street. In regard to that activity, she admitted her weakness to cocaine but said she was fighting to control her desire and had been clean for almost a year. She was nervous around him at first because she said he had an overpowering presence, but after the second go with sex, she relaxed. She had been around drugs most of her life, knew people who distributed cocaine, and had observed its malice firsthand. Jerry found her intelligent, well-spoken, and dangerous. She was not by any stretch a mild woman. As he looked into her eyes, he saw the same look when he looked in the eyes of others he had known, a willingness to kill if necessary.

Ordinarily, this would have sent him running, she was in some way a loose cannon, but she had a magnetism that wouldn't allow him such an easy dismissal.

"You must think I'm awful," she said, running her fingers across his chest, "telling you my life story, but I figured Larry would tell you if I didn't. My god, I can't believe what I just said." She said something in Spanish and laughed.

"What was that?" he said.

"I called myself a dumb ass."

"Why did you take such a big chance selling drugs for a small amount of money?" he said, sitting up in bed.

"It seemed so easy."

"If you don't know who you're selling to, it's never easy," he said.

"You're right, of course, but I told you I'm a dumb ass." She wrapped a sheet around her nakedness, barely covering the top of her breasts, shaped like small melons, perfectly formed. "Now, what do you do in the coal business, Richard?"

"This and that. We speculate in coal options and buying old mines."

"Sounds impressive." She moved to her feet, letting the sheet fall to the floor. "When you move to Fort Lauderdale, will you invite me to visit? I love south Florida."

"Maybe," he said.

She walked to the mirror and ran a brush through her dark hair. Then she slipped into her faded blue jeans that hugged her like skin. "I can come anytime, if you're wondering. I don't have any commitments."

It was her eyes, set wide apart, dark, mysterious, like deep pools of water at dusk, that drew him to her.

"I'll give you a call when I get everything arranged."

Two days later, he and Maierhoffer flew to Nashville in his new plane and arranged for the conversion kit installation.

"Didn't I tell you everything would work out?" Maierhoffer said. "A cinch, Richard." He rapped his knuckles against the fuselage. "And the plane is a beauty."

"Yes, it's nice. Now, what about pilots?"

"I'll have one within a week of you getting to Fort Lauderdale."

"That'll be in two days," Jerry said.

Chapter 15

It was closer to five when he finally settled in. He called Herrera and said he was flying down on Saturday. When he arrived, his friend seemed worried.

"More blood in the street, Richard," he said. "Escobar is out of control."

Jerry wondered if this was a good time to make a change. "Do I need to be careful with my words?"

"Just convince them you'll have more pilots to move their product," Herrera said.

Jerry need not worry because the Colombians urged him to establish his operation as soon as possible. They would provide as much load as he could handle and wanted to begin shipping in a week. So, after explaining his departure to Maria, promising to fly her to Fort Lauderdale soon, and picking up his and Ward's personal belongings, he returned to Fort Lauderdale where, as promised, Maierhoffer provided a pilot, Maurice 'The Hat' Roundy. He was in business again.

He arranged for Karla to come to Fort Lauderdale and move into the house Maierhoffer had found. He had given it a lot of thought, weighing the pros and cons, but her sexual prowess and fluency in Spanish were too good to pass up. He gave her the ground rules, which were no running around, no drugs, and keeping her mouth shut about his business. He warned there would be a stiff price if she broke them.

In the weeks that followed, he added more planes and pilots, and soon was flying multiple trips a week to Colombia. He was using a couple of small airports to land and offload the cocaine. The cartel was pleased with the efficiency of his operation and began increasing his payment. In turn, he paid more to his men. Karla was an asset since some of the Colombians spoke little English, and she could be the interpreter. They liked her being around because she was both pretty and smart.

"Jesus, Richard, you need at least one more pilot. You're working their butts off." Maierhoffer replaced the oil cap and climbed off the ladder. "I know one in the Bahamas, if you want me to arrange something."

He enjoyed Maierhoffer's companionship and dry wit. He brought a valuable asset to the organization, always coming up with ideas and getting things done. But he knew Maierhoffer had selfish reasons foe wanting more pilots: he charged a fee from each pilot.

"OK, but he's the last. Now, what about that airport you talked about?"

"Plantation Air in Sylvania – yeah it has possibilities," Maierhoffer said. "You still interested?"

Sylvania, Georgia, was west of Savannah, in a remote, rural area. Jerry had checked it on the map when Maierhoffer said they might be able to buy or lease it. "We need to check it out. How about Monday?"

That afternoon, Herrera and Alberto Arrango flew into Florida to visit. Arrango spoke no English and spent most of the time either talking through Herrera or Karla. He was a man with a reputation of doing bad things when he became angry, so Jerry treaded carefully around him. He was there because, as one of Jerry's largest clients, he wanted to make sure everything was still good. At least that was his excuse. Jerry thought the real reason was that he liked to screw beautiful American women. Along with a new house on the intercoastal waterway, Jerry had purchased several boats, one a 70-foot yacht he named the *Bituminous*, carrying on the façade of being a coal baron. Herrera and Arrango used the yacht to party in a grand style.

Jerry set up several dummy corporations for laundering his money but still had a closet stacked high with hundred dollar bills. At one time, he calculated it totaled over $20 million. And the money kept rolling in. He would drive to Miami on Sundays in his pickup truck and meet with the Colombians, who would dump bags of money into the back of the truck. He would then bring it to his house where they would use a machine to count it. What to do with it all?

He controlled several houses, one that he used for his ground crew and another that he used for the women he brought in on the weekends. Maria came, as did Bonnie, along with others. When Karla found out about this, she was enraged. And when Jerry told her it was none of

Chapter 15

her business, she used some of the money her father had given her and purchased her own house, which came to be known as the *pouting house*.

Even though she didn't know Jerry's true name, she knew his business because she was present when he met with the Colombians. It was a necessary evil, Jerry thought, but when he thought she was using drugs again, he worried that she might talk a little too much. So, he whacked her in the face to teach her a lesson. He knew it was wrong but he had warned her of the consequences. When she said she was sorry, he felt guilty.

"Am I wrong to let her know so much?" he said to Maierhoffer.

"Richard, sometimes you have no choice but to trust people. You trust me and we're not even sleeping together."

This brought a laugh from them both.

Jerry leased the Sylvania airport, which had everything he needed, including long runways. Maierhoffer hired a few locals, mostly retired folks, to help, thinking they would be less suspicious than the younger crowd. He had become Jerry's right-hand man.

Jerry often had his brothers visit, something he hadn't been able to do for a couple of years. His son, who had gotten into trouble in Tennessee, moved in with him, and Jerry spoiled him with nice cars and the use of a boat. But Jerry's main emphasis was his smuggling activity. He kept reminding his pilots how to avoid detection, what to do if they became suspicious, and to always remain sober. They were the lifeblood of the organization. And they were good.

"Are they better pilots than you, Richard?" Karla said.

He didn't think so.

He brought a new face to the organization, a woman from Kentucky named Bonnie Anders. She was like him when he was younger, a country person who had hustled for money most of her life. He brought her in for two main reasons: her skill at wiretapping and to monitor Karla, who was privy to so much information he couldn't bring himself to completely trust her. He made his intentions clear to Bonnie. "Report back to me and to me alone."

Jerry had difficulty in cutting loose from his past and kept in contact with some of his friends, even though he knew it was dangerous. He would invite them down and take them to Miami where they would visit sex clubs, a far different experience than what they found at home. He was living a life so extravagant it was difficult for the ordinary person to fathom. But it was not without problems. Through Bonnie's wiretapping of telephones he found that some employees were smoking marijuana. He reluctantly fired them. One of his houses was broken into and ransacked, and he believed they were looking for his money. This prompted him to load several suitcases with cash and have Karla and Bonnie accompany them on a private jet to Tennessee.

"You need a contingency plan if things go wrong," Karla said.

He smiled. "If I get caught, call F. Lee Bailey."

He carried a gun at all times but the only occasion he thought he might have to use it was when he was traveling in Miami and was pulled over by a local cop. But the cop gave him a traffic warning and moved on, unaware of how close he had come to death.

He and Maierhoffer often flew to various places to look at airplanes, just in case there was one that interested him. Jerry enjoyed collecting planes, thinking that one day he would find one that could carry double the load at the same speed. Money was never far from his thoughts. Herrera wanted Jerry to expand his operation by hiring more pilots and flying loads five times a week, but the logistics of that were daunting. It would mean more ground crews and he already was having difficulty in keeping up.

"I could help," Maierhoffer said. "Hell, we could fly every day if that's what they want. It's just more men."

Jerry missed flying the Colombian route but resisted the temptation and contented himself by sometimes helping with the offloading. It provided the opportunity to observe his crews. He was certain that his was the most efficient operation within the Medellin cartel. Herrera agreed and said they were considering increasing the money paid to him because he had not lost a single load. And this was uncommon.

Chapter 15

Meanwhile, back in Medellin, people were still being killed. While Escobar was no longer the killer, he had plenty of help to carry out his revenge. And according to Herrera, he had a list of those who had wronged him over the years and was just waiting for the right time to strike. Jerry wondered if this had been told to him as a reminder that loyalty was still demanded even though he was no longer in Medellin.

One of Jerry's laundering schemes was to establish many bank accounts to deposit money, all under $10,000 in order not to report to the IRS. Then, he could write checks where checks were required. Surprisingly, Karla knew a lot about money laundering, as did Maierhoffer, who seemed to have some knowledge about everything.

Women were everywhere in south Florida and Jerry, with his money, was like a kid in a candy store. It was his weakness. For the most part he was able to be discreet and hide it from Karla, but not always. And she would leave and snort some cocaine as her way of pouting, but there was nothing she could do about it. He would fuck who he wanted to fuck. He suspected she was also sleeping around but was never able to prove it. If he ever did, he would make her pay. In his mind, she was held to a different standard than him.

He enjoyed his home, living on the Waterway, and sometimes would take the cigarette boat to a nice restaurant frequented by the rich and famous. He felt at home; after all, he was a coal baron. He found this amusing because when he was young, coal was associated with poverty. When the trains came through, they would dump coal for the poor to pick up. But there was no poverty in his neighborhood; this was Fort Lauderdale with all the glitz and glamor of a Hollywood lifestyle. Here, no one cared how you got your money or whether it was old or new. Money made you invisible because you simply blended in with everything. And he loved it. Life was good in south Florida.

He and Maierhoffer sat in the latter's cramped office and drank beer. The room smelled of oil stained rags, and the battered desk was covered with papers.

"You ever think of cleaning this place, Hank?"

"Not a lot. When's the next flight?"

"Tomorrow," Jerry said. He paused a moment. "You know, with all our talk I really don't know much about you."

"Jesus, Richard, with me you get what you see."

"You said something about working in the Middle East. What did you do?"

Maierhoffer shrugged. "Same as I've always done, work on airplanes. And I've told you a hundred times I don't like to talk about the past. What's done is done." He smiled at Jerry. "You want to talk about yours? No, didn't think so."

Jerry nodded, something odd about the way he always moved from the subject, but maybe, like himself, there were secrets that needed to remain secrets.

Maierhoffer said, "I appreciate what you did for my son. He had a great time."

Jerry had taken the boy flying, letting him handle the controls, and flew him to an airport in Broward County to fly a remote controlled J-3 Cub.

"But you shouldn't have given old Red a bottle of Vodka for Christmas. Jesus, Richard, he's a fucking alcoholic."

"He might as well get drunk on good stuff than that rotgut he buys," Jerry said. "Why don't you come to the house this weekend. Bring the wife." He knew she wouldn't come. She was aloof and always seemed guarded around him. Karla thought she acted scared.

"I'll let you know."

But Jerry had to cancel the invitation. On Friday he was visited by the CIA.

Chapter 16

Jerry knew they were Feds the moment they walked up to where he was inspecting one of his planes. They wore cheap suits with thin, black belts, white shirts and solid ties, and they walked arrogantly, like there wasn't a damn thing anyone could do about it. They flashed their badges and said they wanted to talk.

"We'd like to offer you a deal, Mr. Martin," one of them said.

Jerry wondered what kind of shit he was in. This wasn't the corrupt filled city of Medellin where almost everyone was on the take one way or the other, this was Florida in the land of the free.

"We know your business," the agent said, "so let's dismiss any protest. But we're here to help, not to cause trouble."

Jerry tried to hide his smile. "I really don't know what you're talking about so why don't you humor me?"

The agent, tall and slender, with a New England accent, said, "Are you familiar with the Contra rebels, Mr. Martin?"

"I read the papers," Jerry said.

"Then you're aware of our situation."

"I know that Congress cut out the funding for their war," Jerry said. He knew a lot more than that but wanted them to talk. Living in Colombia made him acutely aware of the politics of the Contra and Sandinista fight.

The agents looked at each other for a moment. "I'll be honest with you, Mr. Martin, we need pilots with the kind of skills your pilots have."

"Let me see if I have this right. You're asking me to fly for the CIA? Is that what you're saying?"

"In a word, yes. We would like you to, from time to time, fly material to Costa Rico, for which you will be adequately paid. In addition, we will provide you the use of several of the airfields we control, from which you can enter the United States without fear of the DEA or other authorities."

"You want me to fly weapons," Jerry said.

"Some of the material will be weapons, yes."

"You're asking me to break the law."

"To break–?" The agent laughed. "You'll be working under the authority of the Central Intelligence Agency."

"That is acting in opposition to Congress," Jerry said. "Hell, men, let's be honest here. You want me to do your dirty work." He took a deep breath. "How do I know what you said about safe airfields is true?"

"Try them out and see for yourself," the agent said. "You'll find the arrangement better than what you now have."

Jerry looked at the smug son of a bitch, the kind of look under normal circumstances he might want to push in the ground, and again wondered what kind of trouble he was in. He understood what they were doing – first he would fly weapons to the Contras, then later they would *ask* him to fly drugs from South America. He had heard the Contras were dealing drugs and he was certain the CIA was, so it made sense. The thought of having safe airfields was encouraging but his enthusiasm was dampened when he considered the CIA could decide to end the relationship by shooting him in the head, or by placing explosives in his planes. Nothing like a cold dose of reality to ruin the moment.

"I'll have to think about it," he said.

"We'd like your answer today."

"And you just got it," Jerry said.

"Okay, call me at this number when you decide, but no more than two days."

Jerry looked at the card and shoved it in his pocket. "What happens if I refuse the offer?"

Chapter 16

The agents turned to leave. "Then this conversation never happened," one of them said.

"That's all?"

"We're the CIA, Mr. Martin, not the fucking DEA."

"Jesus, Richard," Maierhoffer said. "How the hell did they know?"

"Probably from my time in Colombia. The question is, what to do about the offer?"

"You've got to take it, no doubt about it."

Jerry looked at him. "It's not fair to my pilots to put them in that situation."

"Then you fly the plane."

This stopped him. He hadn't thought of that possibility.

"See, that would work," Maierhoffer said. "But insist on ceryain conditions."

"Such as?"

"Such as us inspecting the cargo. No C5, no explosives, nothing that could go bang in the night," Maierhoffer said. "And two hours to inspect the plane before takeoff."

Jerry's mind started wandering all over the place and he fought to rein it in. "How much money should I ask?"

"A hundred grand a trip – maybe a hundred fifty, fifty for the use of your plane."

Jerry said, "I heard stories about CIA handlers when I was in Medellin. Some of them had bad endings."

"You could make it work, Richard."

"You think so? Would you fly with me when I go?"

Maierhoffer stared at him a moment. "Hell, yes, I would."

Jerry moved toward the door. "I'm going to decide tonight," he said.

"I'd go with you," Maierhoffer repeated as Jerry walked into the oppressive heat.

The next day, Jerry called with his answer: no. He gave no reason and the agent simply said, 'Goodbye, Mr. Martin.' Jerry wasn't sure why he had turned down the offer. It was just a feeling in his gut, but he couldn't see himself working for the feds. When he told Maierhoffer his decision, his friend seemed disappointed and said he hoped it didn't come back to hurt him.

But as the weeks passed, Jerry pushed his CIA worries aside. Business was good and he and Karla were having fun. He even shared some secrets with her, but not his real name. Bonnie's reports were encouraging. *She's trying, Richard.*

Each conversation with Herrera further enforced the good decision he made to leave Medellin. The extradition treaty Colombia had signed with the United States had become a nightmare. People were disappearing in the middle of the night, taken to America to stand trial. When Jerry asked about the status of Harold Rosenthal, Herrera said he had heard nothing.

Jerry told Bonnie and Karla to make another trip to Tennessee with suitcases filled with money. They didn't ask why. He thought Bonnie was a good influence on Karla, and he liked that she was a country girl. She had a daughter who Jerry thought was getting into trouble in Kentucky, making wrong choices, much like he did at her age.

As the money poured in, he gave more thought to retiring. He had all the money he would ever need and he could go to a place where extradition was difficult, bring his entire family, and live the good life. But walking away from so much money was difficult to accept. It was like having a pipe spilling out hundred dollar bills and you controlled the valve.

"Don't get me wrong," he said to Maierhoffer. "I'm not saying I'd never retire, but it won't be an easy decision. If the right opportunity came up, then maybe I would."

"It might not be a bad idea. You're my friend, and I'd hate to see something happen to you. I'm thinking about hanging it up myself. Maybe we could move to the Mediterranean."

"You might love parts of Colombia," Jerry said.

In May 1983, Jerry had to cancel a flight because of military maneuvers in the Caribbean. He had planned to fly Karla to the Sylvania airport to

Chapter 16

watch the plane land and be offloaded, but there were no need to take the risk. Then, at the last minute, Herrera called and said he really needed to move the product, so Jerry put the flight in operation again. However, he decided to stay in Fort Lauderdale. So, on May 23, Jose Pine left the jungles of Medellin with $20 million of cocaine and flew to Sylvania, Georgia.

It was a cloudless night, starlit sky, with winds out of the east when he saw the runway. Jose was excited because his brother, recently hired, was supposed to be on the ground crew. Jose was a skilled pilot and landed the plane smoothly, the wheels rolling true down the pavement. He watched as the ground crew pulled up and began picking up the duffel bags the co-pilot was dumping from the plane. He strained to see his brother but the darkness wouldn't allow it. He could hear Harold Ward barking orders to the men, urging them to work faster. He could see that there were two cars.

"Okay, let's go," the co-pilot said, and Jose gunned the engine and began rolling down the tarmac. Soon, he was on his way to Fort Lauderdale.

On the ground, Harold Ward was slamming the trunk of the Oldsmobile, anxious to get back to Susan, who was with him in Sylvania, when Peanut Abner said, "What the hell is this?" Ward looked up to see two cars speeding toward them. They had flashing lights but he didn't think they were police. "We need to get the hell out of here!" he yelled.

"Cops!" Mike Sweeton said.

The cars screeched to a stop and men wearing police uniforms jumped out with drawn guns and began shooting. Ward ran toward the woods, felt something hit him in the back, but kept going. As he briefly turned, he saw another of his crew shoved against the car and shot. There were more shots, a cry of pain, before the cars raced into the darkness.

"What the hell am I going to do?" he wondered aloud.

He heard a noise and saw Sweeton stumbling toward him. He was bleeding. "We've got to get to a hospital," Ward said. "Jesus!"

Thirty minutes later,, his girlfriend picked them up and drove to the nearest hospital. He and Sweeton came up with what they would tell the authorities. Ward would say that he worked at the airport for Hank Maierhoffer. He had been at a bar with Sweeton, and after a few drinks invited him to the airport to show him around. That was where both of them were jumped by two men, robbed and shot.

"What about Peanut?" Sweeton said.

Ward shook his head. "I don't know.

But Peanut Abner had escaped unharmed and found a pilot to fly him to Fort Lauderdale. He told Jerry how they had lost $20 million of cocaine. "It looked like an inside job," he said.

Jerry was stunned and felt betrayed. "What about the others?"

"I don't know," Abner said. "I'm sorry."

Jerry handed him another drink. "It's not your fault."

After a fruitless attempt to learn the condition of his men, more bad news arrived; someone had again broken into his rental house, this time kicking in the door, as though they were looking for someone. Now, Jerry feared he was being hunted.

Humberto Herrera was in Miami, and along with another man, arrived an hour later. They were fully armed. "How the hell could something like this happen, Richard?" he said. Jerry explained that he had no idea but had suspected he was being watched. He told about the door being kicked in at the house.

Herrera scowled. "Who would want to kill you, Richard?"

"It's either my people or yours," Jerry replied, knowing that Herrera had enemies.

Herrera shook his head. "My enemies know where you sleep," he said. He paused for a moment. "I am going to send someone down here to question your men. His name is Terry Cornell, Sr. I will vouch for him."

And Jerry wondered what was going to happen. Would torture be involved? And what happened to Herrera's earlier statement that the men were the most important, not the product? But betrayal was a hot

Chapter 16

button among Cartel leaders, which made him worry even more about the fate of his men.

"I can handle this, Humberto," he said.

"That won't be good enough. The man who will come is trusted by the Cartel. He will find the truth."

It took Jerry a few days to learn who was caught, who was shot, and who escaped. And he was pleased that they all denied drugs were involved. But just to make sure, he had Bonnie wiretap telephones to see if anyone was talking.

In another conversation with Herrera, he asked who would be dumb enough to steal from the Cartel.

"It was an efficient operation, right?" Herrera said. "Well planned?"

"Yes."

"Then perhaps they didn't act alone."

And Jerry immediately wondered if his CIA friends were involved. Had they decided that if he didn't want to be an ally, he was no longer of any use to them? But they must have acted with someone's help. Had they approached one of his men with a generous offer? Who could be the mole?

"Jesus, Richard," Maierhoffer said. "I'm sorry for what happened but relieved that you weren't there." He looked away for a moment before finishing the beer. "What we were talking about recently; this might be sign you need to retire."

The man sent by the Cartel was Terry Cornell, Sr., a retired cop from Chicago. He brought along his son, Terry, Jr, who was in his twenties and claimed to be an ex-Miami policeman, but Jerry had his doubts.

The Colombian intervention got everyone unhinged. What kind of torture would be involved? Jerry told them he wouldn't let that happen and told this to Herrera, but the Colombian gave him a look that said there was nothing he could do about it. But his words gave Jerry the assurance that things would be good.

He was right, for Cornell put the men through a series of sophisticated lie detector tests and interrogations, but there was no torture. He appeared to know what he was doing and when it was over he said they all passed.. So, Herrera gave Jerry the okay to continue the shipments.

Jerry leaned back in his desk chair and watched as Cornell, Jr. crossed his legs. He said, "What did you do on the police force?"

The question brought Cornell to an upright position. "I was a cop."

"No, I mean, what did you do? Were you working drugs, walking a beat, things like that."

"I was in a patrol car. Just routine stuff, mainly."

"But you know people there, right?" Jerry said.

"Yeah, sure I know a lot of people, if you're asking if I have any juice."

Juice. It sounded like something you might say if you were playing a big shot, instead of actually being one. It convinced him that he needed to do a more complete background check on the man. He'd have Bonnie make a few calls.

"I can be a big help to your organization, Richard. I've got good organizational skills."

"Maybe later," Jerry said. "Right now I need you to help with the ground crews."

"I didn't come here to be a flunky."

"You came here because you tagged along with your daddy," Jerry said, "and he's gone. Now, if you want to work for me, you'll do exactly as I say, and if you disobey I'll kill you. We got that straight? I want to make sure there's no misunderstanding here. I'm the boss and you're the employee. You might not like it, and from the expression on your face I can tell you don't, but that's the way it is."

"Yeah, I get it."

Sitting there like he wanted to kill him, not knowing that if the Colombians hadn't told him he was one of them, meaning they owned him, he'd already have a gun across his face.

"Pass it on to your friend, DeFranco," Jerry said. DeFranco had tagged along with them; the Chicago connection, Karla called them. Herrera said they did a few jobs for the Colombians in Chicago, not going into detail.

Chapter 16

The guy started to smile, then let it go. "I'll be sure to tell him."

"Let me tell you something, Terry, something I've not told any of my people. There's a man who works for me who all I have to say is somebody's causing me trouble, and you know what he'd do? He'd walk right up to him and shoot him between the eyes, Pop, pop, then he'd walk away and never give it a second thought. Is that the way they do it in Chicago? Now, I got work to do."

Cornell and DeFranco were always outsiders because their attitudes were different. Not many within Jerry's organization trusted either of them. Cornell, especially, wasn't trusted. Perhaps it was the way he was so presumptuous with people he barely knew, acting like they had been friends forever. His father, on the other hand, was well liked.

"He's an asshole," Karla said as they shared a booth in a local diner. Jerry had polished off a hamburger and she was dabbling with the remnants of french fries.

"You ever get tired of saying that?" Jerry said. "Hell, Karla, you don't think I know what he is?"

"Then why keep him around? He gives me the creeps. Tell Humberto to send him back to Chicago."

"He can be useful. Has he said anything to you? I can kill him if that'll make you feel better."

"Why do you say things like that, Richard? No, he hasn't said anything to me, but it's just that–Like when Humberto was here other day, Terry starts talking to him like they're old friends, like he knows all about Humberto's business, throwing around names. I could tell it made Humberto angry but did that stop Terry? No, he kept at it. It's just not right. and I don't think we can trust him."

"Then I'll kill him or have Humberto do it for me. Look, I don't like this any better than you, but I'm not in a position to negotiate with the Colombians. I'm lucky they haven't killed all of us.. We got robbed, and they probably think somebody he was in on it; I don't care what the lie detector tests showed, I know how they think. So I put up with jerks like Cornell until things get back to normal."

"Well, I don't trust any of them," Karla said.

"I told Bonnie to check on Cornell. I think he's lying about the police work."

She covered her mouth. "I'm in shock that you think he would lie," she said.

"Fuck you." He ordered another hamburger and beer.

She was quiet for a minute, then, "What does Hank say about this?"

"Wants me to retire," Jerry said, "like it was a sign from God."

"Maybe he's right."

"Not you, too."

Karla said, "You could've been killed, Richard."

"But I wasn't." He finished the beer just as another arrived. "I heard yesterday that the men are going to be okay. They were lucky."

"You have any idea how they knew about the shipment?"

"I have a million ideas but none I can prove," he said. "It wasn't a coincidence that on the same night we were robbed, somebody broke into the house. This wasn't a redneck operation." The hamburger arrived. He smiled at the waitress, young with big tits, and saw the slight wink. "I'm thinking it was the CIA, but when I mentioned this to Hank, he said I was crazy."

"Christ, Richard, the CIA?"

"I know, but I'm wondering how the robbers planned to get rid of the coke. They couldn't sell it on the street; they'd be caught in a heartbeat. But what if they had a buyer – the CIA? It makes sense when you look at it that way."

Karla shook her head. "Let's leave this business, Richard. All this worry is driving me crazy."

"It's not rocking me to sleep either," he said. "Now, there's something we need to talk about. I've said this before but if anything happens – I mean if I get arrested, I want you to take the money off the boat and hire F. Lee Bailey to be my lawyer. I don't care what it costs."

"All the money?"

Chapter 16

He had several million stashed on the yacht. He nodded and said, "All of it. Tell him it's for…" He paused, wondering if now was the time to tell her his real name. "Tell him there's more where that came from."

"Richard, if you think–"

"And do what, Karla?" It irritated him for people to think it was that easy. He was the head of an organization. Could the head of General Electric just up and leave anytime he felt like it? A boss had responsibilities. "Don't say that again."

She looked at him and shook her head in frustration. "Me and Bonnie were thinking of going into Miami this weekend. Did she mention it to you?"

He put down his drink and stared at her. "Miami. What for?"

"Maybe do a little shopping," she said.

Jerry waited, took a drink, wiped his mouth, and carefully framed his words. "Is that all you're going there for? Karla, this isn't the time for drugs, I don't care how worried you are."

"We're just going shopping, for Christ sake," she said. "I'm in control, so don't worry."

Life settled in and soon it was business as usual. Hank Maierhoffer sat behind his desk with his feet propped up and poured a shot of bourbon into a glass he had just wiped down.

"I can get you more men, Richard," he said, "but what do you want me to do about the airport?"

"What I wanted you to do was to keep fucking hijackers away," Jerry said. "Why was I paying you, Hank? Fucking tell me that?" Jerry had waited until the dust settled before telling Maierhoffer how angry he really was, thinking that he had let his guard down. "You were supposed to have safeguards in place to prevent this from happening."

Maierhoffer cleared his throat. "Look, the people screwed up. They thought it was the police."

"No one was to come there, not even the police," Jerry said.

Maierhoffer took a deep breath. "They screwed up, Richard. I'm sorry." He took a drink. "Look, I've got some money so I'll pay you for the airplane you lost."

Jerry looked at him for a moment. He had been one of the first to be examined by Cornell and passed the test without difficulty. "I don't want your money, Hank. As for the airport, burn the son of a bitch to the ground for all I care. What good is it now?"

He was now forced to land in other small airports in places like Evergreen, Alabama, away from the security of his own airport.

"You know the Colombians are still looking at you for this, Hank," he said.

"I figured as much but I've got nothing to hide. Do I need to talk to Humberto?"

"Is it possible you let the shipment date slip out in a casual conversation?"

"What casual conversation? Jesus, Richard, first the CIA and now me."

"Then don't talk to Humberto because his questions are going to be much tougher," Jerry said.

Jerry wanted to believe him. More than anyone else, he depended on Maierhoffer. And he kept telling himself that if Maierhoffer wanted to steal cocaine, he would have done it in a more professional way than to have men rush in blindly shooting anything that moved. Yet, there was something that didn't allow him that comfort of certainty.

"It might've been an assassination attempt," Jerry said. "The man shot in the back had a striking resemblance to me, especially at night."

"What? This is the first time I'm hearing this, Richard."

Karla had come up with the theory. With him dead and out of the way, it would be much easier to move the cocaine – maybe even step into his role as boss. And Maierhoffer would be the logical choice. So, he watched him closely when he revealed his thoughts.

Chapter 16

"And you still don't think the CIA had anything to do with it, do you?" Jerry said. "They hire people to do the dirty work, pay them off in pennies, then sell the product themselves."

"Jesus, Richard, that sounds like movie stuff,"

"And if the Colombians found the CIA was involved, they'd be reluctant to do anything," Jerry said.

"Your imagination is running good today, Richard; I'll say that for you."

"Yeah, you think so? I'm not so sure. I don't know what the hell is going on, so anything is possible."

Maierhoffer said, "Then you should just hang it up and walk away"

That afternoon, Jerry drove into Miami. Through the back windshield, he spotted the black car, the two men, one smoking. He took the next freeway exit and looked back to see if they were following. They weren't. Ten minutes later, he was talking to one of his Colombian friends.

"What are you hearing about the heist?"

The dark man said, "They're blaming you. They think you've got so big you got careless."

"Herrera?"

The man shook his head. "He supports you, but he's under pressure. They think they know who took it."

News to Jerry. "Who?"

"The cops near Sylvania picked up some good old boys with a lot of cocaine in their possession is what I hear."

"No way they could do it alone," Jerry said.

"I guess we'll know soon enough."

"The Colombians are going to question them?"

"When the police are finished."

Jerry talked some more, then handed him the thousand bucks and left. When he got home, he opened a bottle of Jack and walked out to the patio overlooking the water. Karla came a few minutes later, wearing a bikini, looking damn good, and sat down beside him.

"Did you put all the papers on the boat?" he said. He had asked her to take the important stuff and put it in one place where he could get it in a hurry.

"Yes, just like you said. And I took the money out of the banks."

He nodded. "They might have a lead on the hijackers," he said. "Rednecks."

She laughed. "And who believes that?"

"Right." He ran his hand up her thigh, letting his fingers enter the bikini bottom. "You want to fuck?"

"Thought you'd never ask."

Chapter 17

Omar Mahdi had come to work for Jerry in June, introduced to him by Maierhoffer, who assured Jerry he was an excellent pilot. Maurice Roundy checked him out on the airplane and confirmed Maierhoffer's statement. His first flight was soon after than. Maierhoffer called him in the Bahamas and told him to fly to Fort Lauderdale, where he would pick him up. Maierhoffer drove him to a nearby Days Inn and a few days later took him to the airfield. Maierhoffer gave him a chart showing the route he was to take. Mahdi was impressed by the plane and its sophisticated equipment. It had Loran radar and a Hotchkins Fuel Management kit to extend the flying time. The plane was able to fly 16 hours without refueling.

Mahdi left Florida at 9 AM and flew straight to Colombia. When he neared the coast, he called on a designated frequency and was met by a small plane that guided him to the manmade dirt and gravel landing strip. He spent the night and left the next morning. He flew around Cuba, through the Gulf of Mexico before descending to below sixty feet, where he flew for about a hundred miles, out of sight of radar. He landed at the airport and waited while the cocaine was offloaded. Then he flew to Fort Lauderdale and the safety of Maierhoffer's hangar.

Omar enjoyed working for Jerry and especially liked making good money for doing nothing but flying. He loved flying and didn't mind that he was carrying cocaine. Though he had been brought up in the Moslem faith, he had long ago decided that breaking rules was something he had to do to survive. But after hearing about the problem at the Sylvania airport, he began having second thoughts about his job Jerry had explained the possibility of getting caught, assuring him that he would take care of his legal fees, but nothing had been said about getting shot. So, he was thinking that maybe the next run would be his last. He would explain to Maierhoffer that he had another job, or perhaps had family matters that needed his attention. Maierhoffer could tell Jerry.

The next flight was on August 2, 1983. Jerry arrived early and handed him the flight charts. Omar was upset because Jerry's tardiness meant he barely had time to study them before taking off. He needed at least an hour to review the charts and fully understand the instructions. His co-pilot was a man he knew only as Mike.

He flew into Colombia and spent the night while the plane was loaded and refueled. The next day the winds were against him and the flight to the States was bumpy. There was a problem at the landing area so he was told to fly around while they determined if it was okay to land. Finally he was instructed to proceed to another landing strip but was told again that it wasn't safe to land. By this time, he was getting low on fuel and said that he had no choice but to land at the next strip they chose. They told him to fly to a Montgomery, Alabama airport to refuel and they would meet him there.

Omar landed and taxied to the fueling station. He was concerned that none of the ground crew had yet arrived, leaving him alone with a plane filled with cocaine. Seeing no need to put Mike, who was in his early twenties, in danger, he told him to take a cab to a hotel and he would contact him when the ground crew had finished.

As he waited in the vicinity, the man refueling the plane became curious why a black man would be piloting such an expensive airplane. He decided to get a ladder and look inside. When he peered through the darkened windows, he saw the duffel bags. Then, he called his supervisor.

At first, they thought it was marijuana but once the authorities got inside and saw it was actually cocaine, the whole atmosphere changed. Colombians! Just the thought sent fear through many of them. Colombians killed people, especially when you had millions of dollars of co-

Chapter 17

caine. They immediately got away from the plane and placed a call to the DEA.

Omar, unaware of what was transpiring, had been waiting for the ground crew for nearly an hour when the State Trooper arrived. He was placed under arrest and taken to jail. By the next morning, he was joined by Bones Ziegler, Lee Curry, Bill Cox, Ron DeFranco and another guy he didn't know. They quietly discussed their situation and decided it was better for their health if they didn't mention Jerry. So when the DEA arrived, they didn't admit to anything.

When Jerry heard of the arrest, he went into the survival mode. He removed incriminating evidence from his houses, tossed beepers into the canal, and took Karla to a hotel where they would hide while he decided what to do. He knew he could fly anywhere he desired or take the boat and find safety. He had money stashed, so that wasn't a problem, but yet something kept him from running. He felt an obligation to his people. For most of his life, his thoughts had been about him and surviving, but now that his back was against the wall he was thinking of others.

He needed to arrange for his employees to have good lawyers. They would serve some time and he would look after their families – if they didn't talk. And he didn't think they would. But DeFranco worried him. Maybe he would have Lee whisper in his ear.

He warned his son and brothers what was happening, and tried to assure them they were out of harm's way – but he wasn't certain. He also warned Maierhoffer but the man didn't seem worried. His reaction was, "Jesus, Richard, what're you going to do?"

It was a good question. What the hell *was* he going to do? He looked at Maierhoffer and said, "The fucking CIA," noticing just a little concern suddenly appearing on his friend's face.

Jerry continued to destroy incriminating evidence and took steps to make him harder to find. He bought a new car with cash and left his old car where he hoped it would be stolen. It was a bad time in his life, and he had to force himself to think reasonably. He still had time to run and that was more and more entering his thoughts. It was becoming clear

A Species of Insanity

that someone was out to get him, to either shut him up permanently or to put him in prison for the rest of his life. But he was certain it wasn't the Colombians; what would be their point? And his thoughts returned to Maierhoffer; there was something odd about the man. He seemed to have disappeared in the last few days. Maybe he had taken his family and skipped town. Maybe he had cut a deal, maybe he hadn't, but Jerry knew he couldn't be trusted. He wasn't sure who could. At one time, he thought he should throw Karla off the balcony; everyone seemed an enemy.

Finally, he was able to contact Maierhoffer over a payphone. "Jesus, Richard, this place is crawling with cops. Are you okay?"

"Where the hell have you been? I've tried to contact you for days."

"We were visiting some friends in Palm Beach. I thought I told you."

"What are they asking?" Jerry said.

"They want to know where you are."

That meant someone had talked. Jerry cursed. "Don't say a thing, Hank – you hear me, not a damn thing."

"Jesus, Richard, this is Hank. You don't have to worry about me."

With the hot sun pressing against his face, Jerry again thought about getting his money and running, leaving everyone behind, including Karla. He'd have to get lucky to get away clean, but if he went to Colombia, he might be safe until everything blew over. He leaned against his car and thought about it some more. Why the hell not? But there were things he needed to do first.

In the morning, he and Karla went to his yacht to retrieve documents. He was feeling a little more settled now. They would trace the plane and find out who owned it, and more checking would bring out all the other charges, but they would still have to catch him.

"Remember the bank account in Kentucky?" he said. "If I'm not around, clean it out. It's yours." He handed her a key. "And there's a safety deposit box. It's yours, too."

"Will they let me do that?'

"Yeah, your name's on it," he said.

Chapter 17

She was nodding, thoughtful. "How much?"

"More than you need," he said. "And go to Maryville with my brothers until I contact you."

"Are you leaving?"

"Just in case," he said.

"Your brother's don't like me."

"They don't have to as long as I do," he said.

He poured a drink, downed it in two gulps and said, "I'm going back to the hotel. I'll be back in an hour." He kissed her on the cheek and left.

She watched him from the small window. Two men approached as he walked along the dock. She saw one of them flash a badge and knew that Jerry was being arrested. When they climbed into a black sedan, she knew what she had to do. She took the money from the yacht and made preparations to visit F. Lee Bailey.

The bag of money was heavy as she climbed aboard the chartered jet. She flew to New York City only to learn that Bailey was in his Boston office. So it was the next day when she made arrangements for him to represent Jerry. She was still uncomfortable with calling him Jerry. Jerry LeQuire – she repeated the words over and over.

Flying back to Florida, she wondered what the future held. Jerry had told her that he was wanted in several states so she expected he would have to serve some prison time, but perhaps Bailey could keep him from serving any time for cocaine smuggling.

"He's the best," Jerry told her from his jail cell.

Bailey went to work on the cases in Marathon, Jefferson City, and Madisonville, Tennessee. He managed to get the marijuana charges in Marathon reduced to 20 years, served concurrent with any other time. He worked to get the Madisonville marijuana sentence adjusted to concurrent time as well. If, as he suspected, Jerry received federal time for cocaine importation, all the other sentences would run with that time, so it was possible that he would only have to serve 10 or 15 years. Jerry was pleased with his effort.

For a time, it looked like the feds didn't have enough evidence to indict him for cocaine importation, but that changed when he heard that both DeFranco and Terry Cornell, Jr. were going to testify against him. He had paid DeFranco's lawyer, Ken Del Valle, over $500,000 to convince him not to testify, but it proved to be wasted money. He had folded like a cheap tent once the feds applied heat to him.

"I told you not to trust them," Karla said. "He wasn't even a cop."

She was referring to Cornell who was kicked off the Miami police force six months into his employment. The verdict was he just couldn't cut it.

Jerry turned his head toward the wall and cursed that he hadn't listened to her before and sent both of them back to Chicago. Bailey warned that the feds would probably indict Jerry if they testified.

"What about you?" he said, turning around.

Karla said, "You know I'd never say anything." She took him by the arm and smiled. "It's not me you need to worry about. But something has to be done about DeFranco and Terry. They're going to spill their guts, Richard."

"Okay, you're right. Pressure Herrera to take care of them. But–" He paused. "The feds can come after you to make you talk."

"There's nothing they can do."

"Yes, there is," he said. "If they think you're privy to information about the business, you can be charged."

She shook her head. "They can't make me testify, Richard."

When she was gone, he lay back in his bunk and thought about it. The only safe way to keep her from the feds was if they were married. Why not? he thought.

"I want to marry you, Jerry," she said, a few days later. "I've always loved you."

She came up with a plan. She contacted Bonnie Anders and asked for her help, knowing that Bonnie had a lot of contacts in Kentucky. Bonnie said she would take care of it. She visited a local doctor and convinced him he could make a lot of money if he would sign an affidavit stating

Chapter 17

that Karla was pregnant, which was the only way the court would grant the marriage. In less than a week, Karla handed the signed document to a judge, and she and Jerry became man and wife.

Having money made life easy in jail for Jerry. He was able to bribe guards to bring him nearly anything he desired. It helped that he was known as a drug kingpin with close Colombian ties. He was treated so well that he thought he could easily escape if he decided to run.

It amused him to read the Maryville newspaper accounts of his arrest. They were calling him the largest drug kingpin in the Southeast. People he had grown up with expressed shock that he had accumulated so much money. Ironic because it took his capture to finally get the recognition he wanted. No longer was he just someone who worked at the Wagon Wheel tavern, he had become important, with more wealth than they could ever imagine. He was Jerry Allen LeQuire, a drug kingpin!

When he appeared at the Madisonville Courthouse to plead guilty to the marijuana charges, the area was flooded with protection. Men with rifles were on rooftops to make certain that he didn't try to escape. He walked inside wearing his expensive suit and imported shoes, his hair neatly cut and sleeked down, and felt like he was in charge because he was certain what was going to happen. Jerry LeQuire fixed things.

When the proceedings were over, he walked outside feeling satisfied. The judge had slapped him with a stiff sentence, but it was concurrent time and would mean nothing to what he already faced. So, when photographers wondered why he looked so smug, they didn't know that everything had been prearranged. Money talks, he thought, and a lot of money screams.

But the problem with DeFranco and Cornell remained. He once again attempted to get Herrera to convince him to keep his mouth shut, but the Cartel had their own problems and didn't seem very interested.

Bailey had been working with the prosecution on a plea agreement where Jerry would plead guilty to two counts, with an assurance of no further prosecution on any of the charges. When Jerry questioned how much time he would face, Bailey said that since Jerry's employees were getting anywhere from 10 to 13 years, it was likely he would face double that time. And Jerry was sorry he hadn't escaped when he had the chance.

When the indictment came, Jerry took the plea and was sentenced to 26 years. The date was April 23, 1984. On that morning, as Karla was having breakfast at the courthouse café, one of Bailey's lawyers approached and said that he hoped she was proud of herself for what she did. When she expressed surprise, he explained that Terry Cornell's apartment had been shot up by machine guns, killing his mother.

When she was alone, Karla began calling Jerry's family members, warning them that they might be in danger. Then, she made a beeline to her new husband.

Jerry was sent to Marion Federal Penitentiary, a maximum security prison that housed the worst of the worst, where inmates would kill just to get out for a few days to stand trial. The prison was originally constructed to hold 500 of the most dangerous federal inmates, mostly transfers from Alcatraz. Prison administrators aimed to maintain a safe and orderly environment and rehabilitate the inmates while avoiding the high-profile abuses that occurred at Alcatraz. Inmates spent most of their time in "group therapy" sessions where they were berated for their deviant behavior and urged to change. In 1973, the first blocks of "control unit" cells were created. Inmates assigned to the control-unit would spend from 23 to 24 hours a day in one-man cells that were specifically designed to severely limit or eliminate the inmate's contact with other people inside the prison and the outside world.

In 1983, members of the Ayran Brotherhood killed two prison guards. The incident resulted in a 23-year lockdown, and Marion was made a "super maximum" security prison where inmates were in solitary confinement for 23 hours a day, and communal dining, exercising and religious services were disallowed.

Jerry was there because he refused to testify against the Colombians. Their punishment was to send him to this hellhole. But his salvation came, not because of reason, but because they needed the space, so he

Chapter 17

was transferred to a prison in Minnesota. It was bitterly cold in winter but far better than Marion.

Meanwhile, Karla's move to Tennessee wasn't working for her. She was an outsider now that Jerry was in prison, an unwanted interloper, and they didn't try to hide it from her. But she was Jerry's wife, so like it or not, she was there. Along with his brothers, she visited Jerry at the prison. One of his brothers would purchase the plane tickets from the money Jerry had hidden, but she sensed they didn't want her along. She held out hope for the appeal, but when it didn't come, she sank into a deep depression. She began using cocaine again. Sometimes she would dissolve it in water and shoot it into her veins; that way she would be high in a few minutes. And her depression would vanish.

She also began drinking heavily when she was alone, away from the prying eyes of his family. Sometimes she would slip off to taverns and pick up men. Facing twenty years without a man was never going to work. Drugs and alcohol began affecting her mind. She started imagining that her every move was being watched, telephones bugged, followed by spies. She became fearful of Jerry, afraid that he might have her killed. When he arranged for her to have a house, she suspected he had bugged it. When the phone rang, she thought it was him checking to see if she was at home.

And to some extent, her paranoia was justified. As Jerry began hearing the stories, he tried to control her from prison. She had to get permission to have her hair cut, any change to her appearance had to be approved. He thought that the only way to save her was to make her a prisoner until she could adapt to life without him.

But it drove her farther to the dark side. She imagined people talking about her, thinking they didn't believe it was right for her to enjoy life while her husband was behind bars. She was just an ungrateful drug-laden whore. His brothers would look at her with disgust and when she went out, maybe to get a drink at a tavern, she knew they would find out and report it to Jerry. She tried to survive, but how could she without a man? She was a woman in the prime of her life and had never gone for long without a man in her life. Cocaine was her way to cope.

Jerry sensed her despair but didn't know anything to do except warn her to get her life in order. He had no sympathy for weakness, especially from women. "Goddamn it, Karla, I swear if you keep using drugs, I'll reach out to you. You hear me? I'll find you."

Things got a little better when a friend from Los Angeles asked if she would take care of her young daughter, not yet 10. The woman was strung out on drugs and unable to care for the child, whose name was Allyse. Jerry thought it was a good idea, so she took the girl in. She was a beautiful child, but Jerry saw she was in need of medical attention so he told Karla to get whatever money she needed to see that the girl had good health and fine clothes. Each time they visited, Jerry could see the change in them both. Karla enjoyed having the responsibility of a child. Being a stand-in mother gave her self-respect, status.

But the cocaine kept calling to her, and finally she relented. First it was just enough to make her feel good, but that wasn't enough. And as the cocaine increased, so did her affairs. She even went to bed with one of Jerry's friends. In the solitude of the night, she knew her life was spiraling out of control, but there was nothing that could be done. She thought about suicide but lacked the courage. In desperation, she told Jerry she couldn't handle it. She needed out.

"You bitch," he said. "You been screwing every man in Maryville. And my brothers say you've been taking the money and buying drugs. I'm warning you, Karla. You understand me? This is not going to happen."

She didn't need his money, she thought. She already had the money he had given her and if that wasn't enough, she and Bonnie had set up their own cocaine operation, using the prick's own Colombian contacts. Wouldn't he piss in his pants if he knew what she was doing? The bastard was rotting in prison, and she was taking over his operation. Yes, it was small, but she had bigger plans.

"He'll kill both of us," Bonnie said. "He can't find out."

"I'm dying anyway," Karla said.

Chapter 17

The next time she saw Jerry, he told her to pack up and get the hell out of his house. He was going to divorce her sorry ass. And that was fine with her. She was tired of him and his entire family. She was going to return to Kentucky.

Chapter 18

Karla later told the authorities that she left Jerry because he treated her like she was a prisoner. She wasn't allowed to cut her hair, have long fingernails, or wear makeup. She had to be home when he called her two or three times a day and she was certain that he was bugging her house. She admitted that her cocaine use made her paranoid but also said she wasn't making it up.

To support her habit, which grew to over a thousand dollars a day – she had already gone through Jerry's money – Karla expanded her cocaine business in Kentucky. By this time, she and Bonnie had parted ways but that was fine because Bonne was just excess baggage. After all, she was the one with contacts, not Bonnie. Soon, she was one of the biggest cocaine dealers in Kentucky. And Bonnie had taken her cocaine profits to build a new house for her family. Things were going well and everyone was a winner.

But inevitably the drug consumed Karla's life, gnawing at her every hour like a hungry dog. By August 1987, she was mainlining about every fifteen minutes, almost an ounce daily. Unable to function normally, she considered suicide. She traveled to the Kentucky Horse Park in Lexington, armed with cocaine, several syringes, a bottle of vodka, and a .38 revolver. She sat down, drank the vodka, shot up with the cocaine, but couldn't bring herself to the final act, suicide. Instead, she walked to a payphone and tried to call the F.B.I. She was approached by a security guard and after admitting to having cocaine, he took her to his office and contacted the Drug Enforcement Agency. She was eventually charged with possession with intent to distribute seven ounces of cocaine.

Chapter 18

Faced with a long prison sentence, Karla went into the survival mode, using her trump cards – her association with Jerry and her knowledge of the cocaine trade in Kentucky. While the federal prosecutors thought they were dealing with a simple drug case, what they really had found was the mother lode of prosecutorial riches. Karla began cutting deals and telling stories, not just about her but anyone else that could benefit her. She quickly implicated Bonnie, who had no leverage now that Karla had talked first. And while Jerry was serving his time in prison, he had no idea that she was burying him so deep that he might never get out. She now had an outlet for her hatred of him and his family.

In December 1987, she appeared before Sergeant Fantigassi of the Broward County Police Department and gave an interview for which she received a letter of full immunity for her participation in all crimes. Her testimony went into great detail.

She said that Jerry worked for Humberto Herrera and his right hand man, Jorge Gonzalez. Alberto Arrango was another cartel member who he also worked for, but Herrera was the main contact. Arrango was associated with the Colombian terrorist group, M-19, and visited Jerry often. She also said the Hank Maierhoffer was his front man for the Sylvania, Georgia airport. The Cartel paid Jerry about $2 million per trip delivering cocaine and that sometimes he would bring his own product to sell. There would be at least two trips a week.

When asked about Arrango and Herrera, she said they often visited at the Florida house because they liked to party as well as conduct business. Herrera especially liked the women. Since Arrango spoke little English, she would act as an interpreter so she got to know a lot about the business.

After the hijack incident at the Sylvania airport, Herrera insisted on bringing in Terry Cornell, a retired policeman from Chicago, to interrogate Jerry's employees. When Cornell arrived, he brought along his son, Terry Cornell, Jr. and Ron DeFranco. Jerry sent the older Cornell to Georgia to see if he can find any of cocaine that might not have been stolen. Terry Cornell, Jr. helps Bonnie tap phones to see if anyone is talking. He would also help drive the load cars to the airports where the cocaine was to be off-loaded. This eventually led to Jerry's arrest.

Jerry had Terry Cornell, Jr. take $400,000 to Montgomery to hire attorneys for his men. The attorney hired for Ron DeFranco was a Chicago attorney named Ken DeValle. DeValle later visited Jerry and said that unless Jerry paid him $1,000,000, his client would testify against him before the Grand Jury and Jerry would get indicted. Then Karla began getting phone calls from Terry Cornell, Jr. and heard a beeping sound that makes her think the conversations were being recorded. He also was acting strange around her. So Jerry had her call Herrera to see if he still vouched for the Cornell's; a courtesy, she said, to see if they would giveJerry permission to kill them if necessary. This became important when it was learned that Jr. was going to be indicted for helping Jerry. At that point, Jerry arranged for the Grand Jury room to be wiretapped.

She said he asked his long time friend and employee, Lee Curry, to see if it can be done, so Curry contacted an expert. Unfortunately, the man became worried and contacted the FBI. But there was no connection to Jerry because Curry refused to cooperate.

Meanwhile, Hererra and Gonzales continued to support Cornell, Jr. and said they'll have his father talk to him. But eventually, Gonzalez told Karla that the cartel released DeFranco and Cornell, Jr. to Jerry, to do with them as he saw fit. Jerry's first response was to cut off Cornell's tongue and torture him. Then, he decided to have him killed and buried where he would never be found, but not until he was tortured to see who he had talked to.

Karla asked Bonnie to find people for the job, and she brought down three men for the job. They brought several guns, including machine guns, AK 15s, and 9mm. Several of the guns were fixed with silencers. She said that one of Jerry's brothers provided the money. Eventually, she said, the decision was made not to use these men and instead hire Colombians. So, she contacted a man who worked for Arrango. His name was Alvaro Pelize. Pelize, she said, came from a terrorist group in Colombia. Jerry immediately liked the idea because he had faith in

Chapter 18

Colombians. Jerry then wanted the men Bonnie brought to take care of Larry Allen, who he doesn't trust and Ken Del Valle. They were to kill them both.

Pelize and two other men met with Karla and Bonnie to discuss the murder of Cornell, Jr. Karla hired a private detective to find out where Cornell was living and other personal information about him. The detective learned that Cornell had been kicked off the Miami police force for beating up a young black boy. She said that Jerry began having second thoughts about killing Cornell and instead wanted to do something that would make him suffer his entire life. There was talk about having Cornell's wife murdered, but Jerry thought that would be doing him a favor, so that was ruled out. A deal was finally agreed on where Pelize would pay the Colombian hitmen $20,000 within 24 hours of the hit.

She said the arrangement was that if Cornell, Jr. was killed and buried somewhere, then Jerry would go to trial because his disappearance would discourage anyone else from testifying against him. Otherwise, he was going to accept the plea agreement the government had offered.

One morning, around nine, Karla, some of Jerry's brothers, and some of their friends were sitting in a coffee shop at the Montgomery, Alabama courthouse when Jerry's lawyers, F. Lee Bailey and Ira Dement approach. Dement said, "Karla, I'm glad you think you did a good job." When she seemed puzzled, he explained that Cornell's mother had been murdered. It was the first she had heard about the hit, and she didn't think it was possible to get the money to them within 24 hours, so she feared for Jerry's family. She arranged for Jerry's daughter to be picked up at school and informed the others in his family that they might be in danger. Eventually, the Colombians received their money and no one else was killed. Karla said that Jerry was pleased by the murder, knowing that the son of a bitch would live everyday knowing he was responsible for his mother's death.

Then, when they went to trial, one of the prosecutors came up to Jerry and said that Cornell was still going to testify. Jerry looked at him and said he wasn't going to give Cornell the pleasure of testifying against him.

She said it was the way he was, but at that time she was so obsessed with him she didn't care. She said that she and others then took a bag filled with seventy grand as the remainder of the payment for the hit.

The mother's funeral was held in Chicago, and Karla said Jerry told her to get some men to attend the funeral and kill Cornell, Sr. and anyone else involved, just to put the icing on the cake. He wanted to make a point that there were consequences for testifying against him. She didn't try to make those arrangements, however.

In January 1988, she began the long process of telling the federal authorities her story, testifying against everyone involved, including her friends, associates, and the Colombians. For this, she was granted full immunity and placed under protection by the U.S. Marshalls. She had assisted the DEA in a "buy and bust" sting where she lured people, mostly Colombians, into bringing in cocaine to sell to her, only to be arrested. Week after week, defendant after defendant, the trial revealed her sordid life, both in Kentucky and in Florida with Jerry. She explained the code words cocaine dealers used when talking on the telephone, how the drug was transported, the major suppliers – she gave the impression she was an expert on cocaine trafficking. And this was from a 28-year-old woman who was a former prostitute for a small airline.

While this was going on, Jerry and Bonnie were corresponding via letters and telephone calls, taped by Bonnie who couldn't resist falling back on old habits. In February of 1988, the second month into Karla's testimony, the following conversation ensued between Bonnie and Jerry:

Jerry: What you doing?

Bonnie: Sitting here with my damn head a running.

Jerry: You're running out of one weather right into another, that change is what's doing it.

Bonnie: I know it. I got an article to read you. Hang on one second.

Jerry: Alright.

Bonnie: I went and got Trudy today (Trudy is her daughter, herself a drug dealer, who had been arrested on a variety of charges. She has two

Chapter 18

small children that Bonnie takes care of.). We got to go Thursday and see if we can't get her started in some damn program.

Jerry: Why didn't she try that thing down there, at least go down and talk to them?

Bonnie: Tomorrow I'm going to. The judge talked favorable to me. He said most people around here don't understand unless it's them that drugs and somebody on drugs don't realize they need help. You know, and all kinds of stuff. And I told him I was going to try to take her up there, and he said – well, he lowered the bond to a thousand.

Jerry: That's good.

Bonnie: Well, I went down there to put the thousand cash up and they had another. By God, I had to put property up after all.

Jerry: Man oh man.

Bonnie: Carrying a concealed weapon up here in Corbin. So, anyway I brought her home Okay, here it is. (She begins to read a newspaper article.). Cocaine dealer expected to testify. Confessed cocaine dealer Karla Espinal, whose recent testimony helped convict five people on federal cocaine charges, is expected to take the witness stand today at another drug trial. Ms. Espinal will be the government's key witness against two of her friends on trial for trafficking in cocaine. Jurors were told yesterday that Ms. Espinal would play a key role in the government's case against Roy Stout, 27, of Lexington, and Hector Ramirez.

Jerry: Ramirez?

Bonnie: Yeah, 45, of Miami. Stout, who operates Stout Flooring Company on Walnut Street and Ramirez are charged with conspiracy to distribute cocaine and possession of cocaine with intent to distribute. Their trial began yesterday in U.S. District Court in Lexington. Two other people who were to stand trial with Stout and Ramirez pleaded guilty yesterday. Darryl Wayne Thompson and his wife Terri Lee Thompson, both of Lexington, pleaded guilty to conspiracy to possess with intent to distribute one kilo or two pounds of cocaine. The Thompsons stood trial last week on other cocaine charges and were convicted. Ms. Espinal was the government's key witness against them.

Two weeks ago, Ms. Espinal helped the government convict three men who brought more than 28 pounds of cocaine from Miami to Lexington last November. Ms. Espinal was offered seven kilos or 15 pounds of cocaine last summer by friends in Miami. She didn't have to pay for it until it was sold. Ramirez came to Lexington to keep an eye on the cocaine and to collect the $125,000 Ms. Espinal was to pay for it. But Ms. Espinal, a drug addict, was unable to get rid of the cocaine and went to the horse park intending to commit suicide.

More conversation ensued about the amount of cocaine, then Jerry told her some bad news.

Jerry: Has Karla been down there, lately?
Bonnie: No, why?
Jerry: Do you know what the rumor is?
Bonnie: What?
Jerry: That that's where she's staying.
Bonnie. At my house?
Jerry: Yup.
Bonnie: Shit!
Jerry: That's what I told them. I said that is all fucking bullshit and get that straightened out right now.
Bonnie: Who in the hell thinks that?
Jerry: Well, I'll tell you that's what I heard last night. But I'll tell you when I see you who I heard it from, and it comes from some people and, you know, how I got ahold of it. But think about it. I told them, I said – I said, listen, I know that's all wrong and I want you to go back – don't just be satisfied now within your own mind. I want you to go back and tell them other people that's all wrong, because if you think about it –
Bonnie: Hell!
Jerry: – where they're going to run it at.
Bonnie: Right. I don't want the son of a bitches coming in here thinking the son of a bitch is here.
Jerry: That's right.

Chapter 18

There was more conversation regarding Karla, with the thought that she might have been the one who started the rumor she was staying with Bonnie

Jerry: Just to protect herself up until – now listen to this carefully. Just for this small period of time, just to protect herself up until court time, she's willing to let the motherfuckers come in here and kill you and the kids. Just to buy her what, three or four months?

Bonnie: Cause she's jealous of me having a fucking house. That's pitiful.

Some more conversation regarding Karla's willingness to say anything to get out of trouble ensued.

Jerry: If it helps her for eight hours, it don't make a fuck to this motherfucker how many people get killed.

Bonnie: Plus, that's what she's wanting here anyway. I'll say one thing. That son of a bitch is – she can –

Jerry: She sits around and thinks and breathes this shit 24 hours a day.

Bonnie: She must.

Jerry: It's not normal. She'll take a motherfucker's money, and she's scared that he'll do something, beat her fucking ass or anything like that now, she takes this and takes that, lies and steals every fucking thing in the world. Now her remedy for getting out from under the heat; well fuck, I done stole his money, I'll just tell this or I'll do that, and for this short price, I'll just have him killed.

Bonnie: And you know that shit don't bother her or nothing like that. She talks about that a lot. I'd say no, I ain't in on nothing like that Karla, there ain't no way.

Jerry: Well, everybody sees now though, I guess. Hopefully they do.

The conversation wound down with just idle chatter.

A month later, Bonnie was arrested for dealing drugs with Karla. Since Karla had already been granted immunity, she had no skin in the game and eagerly testified against her friend. Bonnie was found guilty and sentenced to 12 years in prison.

But as bad as it was for Bonnie, it was going to get much worse for others as Karla kept adding to her stories to the federal authorities. Already given full immunity for her previous testimony, she chose to continue to implicate anyone who had ever been involved with Jerry. She decided to tell about Jerry's escape plans from the jail as he was awaiting trial in Montgomery. It started, she said, when he was at the Miami Correctional Facility in south Miami. Jerry's plan involved his going to a dentist outside the facility. Through F. Lee Bailey, he was able to obtain permission to have the dental work performed at Jackson Memorial Hospital. Jerry had, according to her, made arrangements with Jorge Gonzales, a Colombian, to hire some men who would overcome the U.S. Marshalls, even if it required killing them, for which they would be paid $300,000. But at the last minute, Jerry signaled Gonzales to withdraw. Bonnie Anders was aware of the plan. After that, there was another escape plan that involved fake police cars. The plan was to intercept the Marshalls as they drove Jerry from the Correctional Facility to Montgomery to stand trial. But that too fell through. Then, after he was moved to the jail in Montgomery, she said there was another escape plan involving a jail guard who was bribed for the sum of $250,000. The police station was in the same building as the jail so in order to distract their attention while Jerry, with the help of the guard, walked out there were going to be several diversions. But Karla got drunk one night at her hotel and dropped a note with a description of the plan. It was found and turned over to the police.

Then, Karla dropped another bombshell. She said that in regard to the state charge involving Jerry and the shootout with the DEA at the airport in Madisonville, he had bribed the judge to make the sentence concurrent with the federal time, which meant he got away with the crime. She said that a friend of his, Babe Finley (He had owned the Wagon Wheel Tavern in Maryville where Jerry once worked) knew a man who was friends with the judge and was willing to pass along the bribe money of $216,000. For that, the judge would sentence Jerry to time that was meaningless considering the federal time he was already

Chapter 18

serving. She said that the judge's lawyer friend assured them of that. And it was agreed there would be no federal prosecution. She also said that the sheriff, who had been on Jerry's payroll back in the marijuana days, was to be paid a thousand dollars. The money was brought to the courthouse and after the agreed upon plea, was taken to the lawyer's office, counted and given.

With all this new testimony and her eagerness to testify against any and all of Jerry's associates, the federal authorities decided to reopen the case. The new charges would be racketeering and continuing criminal enterprise, where if found guilty, Jerry would probably never get out of prison.

The Immunity Letter for Karla:

Dear Ms. Espinal:

This letter will confirm in a formal way the agreement that has been reached as a result of certain conversations between your attorney, Honorable Stephen D. Milner, and a representative of the United State's Attorney's Office for the Middle District of Alabama, namely, the undersigned D. Broward Segrest, First Assistant United States Attorney. This letter is intended to state the agreed-upon terms and conditions under which you will furnish to the government information which you now possess regarding the LeQuire organization and its importation of cocaine into the Middle District of Alabama, and elsewhere, during 1982 and 1983.

Ms. Espinal, by signing the original of this letter, you agree to the following terms:

1. You will cooperate fully and truthfully with the government in its investigation of the LeQuire organization and in any other federal criminal investigation which may arise out of or result from this investigation. You will respond fully and truthfully to all inquiries addressed to you by representatives of the government, and you will testify fully and truthfully at any and all reasonable times and places before grand juries and against any and all defendants at the trial of

any and all cases arising from this investigation or any other such investigation.

2. It is the intention of the United States to grant you full use immunity and it is understood that your cooperation will be pursuant to testimonial use immunity. If you fully comply with the terms of this agreement, you will not be prosecuted by this office for other existing charges known to this office, or for potential charges based upon information supplied to this office by yourself.

3. It is understood and agreed that you must at all times give complete, truthful and accurate information and testimony. If, in the judgment of the attorneys for the Office of the United States Attorney for the Middle District of Alabama, you give false, incomplete or misleading testimony or information, or otherwise violate any provision of this agreement, this agreement shall by null and void and you shall thereafter by subject to prosecution for any federal criminal violation which this office has knowledge, including but not limited to perjury and obstruction of justice. Any such prosecutions may be premised upon any information, records, and/or testimony provided by you and such information, records, and/or testimony may be used against you.

4. This office is aware of the agreement entered by you with the State of Florid through your attorney, Stephen Milner, Esq., as confirmed by that certain letter from Kelly D. Hancock, Assistant State Attorney, Chief, Homicide Division, 17th Judicial Circuit of Florida, Broward County Courthouse, Ft. Lauderdale, Florida, 33301. It is understood and agreed that you will give complete, truthful and accurate information and testimony to grand juries sitting in this District, as well as the grand jury in the 17th Judicial Circuit of Florida, about your knowledge of a homicide which occurred on or about April 22, 1984, at 428 Lakeview Drive, Ft. Lauderdale, Broward County, Florida, which involved the death

CHAPTER 18

of Mildred Cornell. In the event that you provide said testimony in this District of the death of Mildred Cornell, and its implications in the District, you will not be prosecuted for your involvement in said homicide.

Chapter 19

Bailey was outraged that Federal authorities waited several years to bring charges after he was certain an agreement had been reached when Jerry pleaded guilty at the earlier trial. Now, the government was not only dredging up old charges in which to justify their RICO and CCE allegations, they were adding new charges such as an attempt to escape from jail while awaiting trial, and the murder of Mildred Cornell. He stated frequently that he, his co-counsel, Ira Dement, and Jerry were assured verbally that the Federal prosecutor had implied that no additional charges would be filed regarding the cocaine smuggling indictment. He appeared before the judge to plead his case and to vent his anger,

"May it please the Court, my good client is in somewhat of a different postures than any of the others, and although I applaud the scholarly argument which have been visited upon the Court, mine will be a little different.

"Now, in this two-week old case, which could best be described as some kind of unholy alliance between Miami Vice and the Beverly Hillbillies, it is perfectly apparent that the Government had one idea in mind, and that is to take a man who is already, thanks to the sentences he has already received, for the crimes he has admitted, is to use him as a vehicle to park his whole family, an acquaintance and a friend, in the federal hoosegow. And probably with the real purpose to get enough going so that the Government could go in and dig up the Tommy LeQuire farm only to prove their claims that the riches there to be false.

"My client has been badly mistreated by the law and the federal system, and I include myself in that, and Mr. Dement, the Federal prosecu-

Chapter 19

tors who were in charge of this office in 1984 and 1988, and Your Honor, for this reason. Jerry LeQuire has been denied substantive and procedural due process. It was contemplate by the people that put our Constitution together that we would remedy a great number of the ills in the system, which we rejected by forming the United States of America, and that was the Common Law of England. We outlawed confessions and illegal searches and some other things and mandated there be some promptness in the disposing of criminal accusations against people. The time itself was a defect, a corrosive that should be avoided whenever it could. We have speedy trials, and other provisions all pointed in that direction.

"When Jerry Allen LeQuire was contemplating indictment in 1984, he certainly had every reason to fear, knowing that the Government knew he had pleaded guilty to importing marijuana in Marathon, Florida, they had him cold up in Madisonville, Tennessee, with his fingerprints in a drug-laden airplane, and they had him cold in Montgomery, Alabama, that he might be indicted for a continuing criminal enterprise or a RICO. There have been a string of cases, and I know Your Honor is aware of them, because I have seen them cited by you, that requires the Government to exercise due diligence, and in the case of lack of due diligence, if it is sufficiently severe, to prevent the Government from prosecution.

"What we have here are two federal prosecutors, one the U. S. Attorney himself, John Bell, who didn't understand the law. He testified before Your Honor on November 18 that he didn't have three predicate acts and he couldn't indict Jerry LeQuire for continuing criminal enterprise, and that he made a conscious decision not to indict him for a RICO conspiracy. Thanks to the wisdom of sequestration, his assistant, Charles Truncale, then came in and contradicted him very flatly. Truncale said there was more than enough, and he was correct, to indict him for a continuing criminal enterprise, and he proposed that to the U.S Attorney, and he was rejected.

"Although I commend Mr. Bell's credibility to you on a higher plane than I do Mr. Truncale, I really don't care who you believe. The United

States had the power, and it had information, and it had the evidence to put Mr. LeQuire to trial for continuing criminal enterprise then and there on all the predicate acts of this indictment, and they consciously decided not to do so.

"In addition to that, where there is an extraordinary set of circumstances not contemplated by the practitioners of the law, and the victim is a citizen and the mistake is made by the lawyers, it's only fair that the balance fall against the lawyers and not the benefits. And Your Honor's ruling in this case, however correct it may appear to be on its face, which refused to estop the United States from bringing this prosecution because of a sterile record which did not contain that which it should have contained, I submit is unjust.

"I let Mr. LeQuire down, Mr. DeMent let him down, the Court let him down, and the prosecutors certainly let him down. Your Honor knows because the transcript makes it perfectly plain that I intended to put on an act before Your Honor for a single and legitimate purpose, and that act was to present Jerry LeQuire as a defiant person who was still a member of the clan who would not cooperate in my way and whom no one had to worry about. And that's for a reason I am sure was obvious and articulated by me, the mother of Terry Cornell was killed because people went there to kill Terry.

"Bell and Truncale both agreed Terry wasn't even a chief witness against LeQuire. What Terry was was the first person in any Federal Court who was going to stand up publicly and name Humberto Hererra and Jorge Gonzales and Alberto Arrango as suppliers of this dope. Indeed, until this indictment they were never mentioned, and you will notice they were not mentioned in the indictment brought by Mr. Bell and Mr. Truncale. Terry Cornell's mother was mistakenly killed because they wanted Terry to die before he could ever give that testimony. It wouldn't have hurt LeQuire much, but they didn't want it.

"We were all terrified that whoever had set that assassination in motion would have Mr. LeQuire next because it was perfectly apparent

Chapter 19

from what Your Honor heard about it that if anyone could have provided enough evidence to extradite Colombian kingpins into this country and make them stand trial, it would have been a Jerry LeQuire who had turned for the Government. And as I told Your Honor in chambers, and as I said in open court, and you acknowledged you knew something about that, it's not my practice to tell a sentencing judge that my client is in a defiant mode, but I wanted the public to believe that Jerry LeQuire would rather do 36 years than rat on his friends. That was what we set out to show.

"Now, I have never in my practice, and neither has Mr. DeMent, if I am to believe what he tells me, failed to cover the bases in a plea of guilty as to what the future may hold. It is perfectly plain to you, despite the claim of Karla LeQuire, that this was her bright thought, that the lawyers in Tennessee, confronted with this problem because they were not confronted in State Court, did cover the bases and the record at least addresses the matter of future prosecutions.

"Under these circumstances where it was known we were trying not to show any favors done by the Government for Jerry LeQuire, this is the only record where the record is absolutely silent so far as I know about the Government's right to prosecute him further for the acts that were already of record. Jerry has given an affidavit which is uncontradicted that had he known that he could in the future have been prosecuted, had he been told by anyone, including the Court it its allocution under the strained circumstances of this case, that he would have not pleaded guilty, and I think a fairly logical thing for anyone to have said and to have believed at this time.

"And the court says well, that's too bad, Mr. LeQuire, because Mr. Bell said the whole deal is what has been described, when that wasn't the case in his mind, in my mind, and in Ira Dement's mind, that Jerry LeQuire has to pay the price. We have circumstances where our attention was distracted, We had to describe something other than what we knew was the real purpose, of misleading the public. I shouldn't say misleading, of telling the pubic emphatically that he wasn't going to testify against anyone.

"And under those circumstances, if because we were distracted by that purpose, Jerry LeQuire didn't get the protection he was entitled to, he should get it now. The Court and the lawyers ought to take the blame for that, because your description of what happened to Jerry LeQuire is malpractice, perhaps, but it's not an excuse to make him pay the penalty for a mistake in the record."

Bailey brought up the marijuana charges and the DEA shootout at the Madisonville, Tennessee, airport, describing how the matter was finally settled with a plea bargain. But now the Federal government was reopening the case to substantiate the CCE and RICO charges.

Bailey said to the judge, "So I will ask your Honor to look at the record of that plea agreement and see if the remarks of Mr. Dedrick is enough to keep open the right of the United States to now put Jerry LeQuire on trial once again for bringing 1,052 pounds of marijuana into Madisonville in 1982, when he stood there in open court, was assured by his lawyers, the only thing he had to worry about was tax.

"This Federal prosecutor did not say Jerry LeQuire shouldn't later be prosecuted for one of these two offenses that require a predicate act, RICO or CCE, then; of course, our promise would not bind that event. He made no such statement, nor could we ever have anticipated. We were trying to wrap up this man's past criminal conduct so he could get some perception of where he stood in life.

"He pleaded guilty to all these offenses, he received a very substantial sentences. And what has happened since that time? Nothing. He has been in prison. We have no evidence in this case of Jerry LeQuire running a drug business from inside the prisons. We have had evidence that maybe one could believe that Ms. Anders had some contact with cocaine, although it's certainly not very specific or believable. We have ample evidence that Karla LeQuire, on her own, got into the cocaine business, she says she was an addict. None of that had been tied to this defendant, he has been sitting up in Minnesota at 15 below zero, visiting

Chapter 19

with his friends and on the telephone to his family and seeing them in prison.

"Now, was there a conspiracy between Karla and Jerry LeQuire? And we don't have any other involved according to the evidence I have seen, to bust him out of the Montgomery jail in 1984? Yes, there was. Could he have been indicted for that being a federal prisoner by the Federal government? Mr. Truncale says he considered it very carefully, and didn't indict him. Is it proper to now come back and put him on trial for that escape which we thought was packaged up in the deal before Your Honor and had every right to think? It is about as unfair as I have seen the United States get.

"All of these rights of Jerry LeQuire are really tied together, they smack of estoppel, they smack of prejudicial, unfair lack of due diligence by the government. They smack of laying back until now, we are disable by the passage of time and cannot cross-examine witnesses as effectively who claim lapses of memory, such as did Karla LeQuire for the only day in her life she ever heard that her husband was going to get socked in Federal Court by enough years to carve up any adulthood. Says she didn't remember. I queried whether that could have been done if everyone had acted properly and we are overwhelmed with Government evidence that the Government had what it needed."

Bailey continued this line of attack, questioning why the Government waited this long to bring up things like the murder of Mildred Cornell when Karla admitted to being the one who carried out the orders.

"To try to make an unholy link between the escape attempt," Bailey continued, "the prosecution of which was abandoned, the man was getting enough punishment at the judgment of the Federal authorities, and all these unrelated events, and to try to go back and pick up three crimes for which he could have been prosecuted, perhaps, diligently and promptly, in 1984, as a continuing criminal enterprise or a RICO is just patently unfair.

"I believe this case ought not to be submitted to the jury. I think that to the extent that there may be some federal in here which are triable, they have been so badly contaminated by number one, the character of the indictment, the opening of the prosecution, and the evidence which this jury has ever been subjected to, that to restore fairness in this trial to Jerry LeQuire is beyond the power of counsel, the Court and perhaps the all mighty Himself. Thank you, your honor."

Bailey's impassioned and reasoned arguments were met with denial. His statement that the prosecution had given verbal agreement that the plea ended all prosecution attempts was ignored, just as was his argument that the passage of time so badly contaminated the evidence as to make a fair trial impossible. In the end, the judge chose to allow the trial to continue.

With so many charges, the jury had its work cut out as the prosecution brought its case on everything from attempted escape attempts to murder. Karla spent days on the witness stand telling her long, elaborate story. She implicated all of Jerry's family, Bonnie, and his employees, including Hank Maierhoffer, who, to Jerry's surprise, would never stand trial. Bailey's defense tactic on the murder charge was to show the inconsistencies in Karla's testimony and to show that the real people who had something to lose by Terry Cornell's testimony were the Colombians. The following is a partial transcript of Bailey's cross-examination of Karla as he questions here relentlessly:

Q. Now, of the people that were involved in the smuggling of cocaine, Jerry was one who could have named the Colombians as co-conspirators, right?

A. That's correct.

Q. And you recall at the time, do you not, that there was considerable concern over the fact that the United States for the first time in years was successfully extraditing people from Colombia to try them in the U.S.

A. Correct.

Q. So that whereas the Colombians didn't seem to be doing much about the production of cocaine in their own country, we were going down and legally getting the kingpins and bringing them back citizens of Colombia; do you remember that?

Chapter 19

A. Yes.

Q. And there was great concern about that.

A. If they could be found.

Q. And people were shooting judges and attorneys generals of Colombia.

A. Yes.

Q. You had enough information, had you chosen to do so, to testify against Jorge and others in the United States and put them in as co-conspirators in a large cocaine operation, did you not?

A. Yes.

Q. And you are also aware that Terry Cornell had enough information so that he could have give such testimony; is that correct?

A. That's correct.

Bailey then asked her if Jerry's employees posed a significant risk to him should they agree to testify. He went through them one by one and she identified several, including Ron DeFranco, who was Terry Cornell's friend.

Q. Now, Terry Cornell was not involved in the Montgomery importation, was he?

A. He drove one of the cars up here.

Q. Terry Cornell did not have enough information to be a very effective witness placing Jerry LeQuire in Montgomery, did he?

A. Yes, I believe he had enough information.

Q. Well, I will inform you, both he and DeFranco testified he did not know enough to testify that Jerry was in the Montgomery importation; Terry Cornell has said that, has anyone brought that to your attention?

A. No.

Q. When, to your knowledge, was it first known to anyone connected with the representation of Jerry LeQuire, that DeFranco had become a government witness with the cooperation of Mr. DeValle? (DeValle was his Chicago lawyer.)

A. All I knew was that Ken DeValle had gone to try to the get the million dollars from Jerry, I was not aware that Ken DeValle represented

– there was a slew of lawyers – that Ken DeValle represented Ron De-Franco.

Q. You are aware, of course, that plea agreement was made with Ron DeFranco, and Ken DeValle, defense counsel, signing onto the agreement?

A. I would say maybe a week before the trial, the trial was going–

Q. How did you learn that DeFranco had flipped?

A. Jerry told me.

Q. Now, Mrs. Espinal, you were very concerned about what was going to happen in this Court at that trial, weren't you?

A. Yes.

Q. Your husband, whom you had never seen as a free man since you married him, was committed to doing eight years in a federal penitentiary, correct?

A. Correct.

Q. And if convicted in this Court, could have received a very heavy sentence as his colleagues already had, correct?

A. Correct.

Q. Do you remember a discussion with the lawyers and Jerry and you where it was suggested that if the Judge was giving people over ten years for simply being worker bees, that the queen bee would probably get double that time?

A. Yes, I do remember that.

Q. You did not want him to plead guilty or get convicted, did you?

A. I didn't expect him to be here for the trial.

Q. Now, Mrs. Espinal, you were never bashful about calling me up and asking me what was going on with the case; is that true? Drunk and sober, correct?

A. That is correct.

Q. Frequently you would get drunk and call up and harangue what was going on with Jerry's case, true?

A. That's correct.

Chapter 19

Q. All right, now what is the likelihood that if you expected Jerry Allen LeQuire to go to trial in a case where others had received severe sentences and he could anticipate, and you knew that his lawyers were off doing something else when they should have been preparing, that you would forget that fact, what is the likelihood, Mrs. Espinal? (This question goes to Bailey's claim that Jerry had already considered a plea days before Mrs. Cornell's murder, but Karla had previously stated she knew nothing about this.)

Q. What steps were being taken to impeach Mr. Ron DeFranco's testimony, if you remember?

A. I think at that time I had learned that Mr. Del Valle was Mr. DeFranco's attorney, and I think maybe records were trying to be gotten out of the jail.

Q. The fact that Ken Del Valle threatened Jerry and tried to fix the case wouldn't have anything to do with guilt of innocence, would it?

A. Well, at that time I believe we had learned, or I had learned that Ken Del Valle was representing Ron DeFranco.

Q. Mrs. Espinal, in truth you do not draw a total blank as to any recollection of any trial preparation being conducted on the 19th, 20th, 21st and 22nd of April, 1984.

A. No, because right on that Wednesday was when the escape note was found, and there were a lot of things going on.

Q. Exactly. You were very much occupied with concerns other than those of your husband, weren't you?

A. No, they concerned totally my husband.

Q. Did you carry from the prison a handwritten note which outlined a potential escape attempt which has been received in evidence which you have identified?

A. Correct.

Q. How long had you had the note?

A. About two weeks.

Q. Okay. And you had taken steps to effectuate this escape as outlined in the note?

A. Yes.

Q. Were the people in Montgomery on the 18th as we all sat in with Jerry?

A. I don't recall sitting in with Jerry, as you all sat in with Jerry, is that what you are talking about?

She was nonresponsive in her answer, and after many objections by the prosecutor, Bailey moved on to ask about the escape note she dropped.

Q. You were drunk. When did it come to your attention the note had been found?

A. The following morning. Mr. Dement told me that and had me fill out an affidavit.

Q. Okay, and do you recall being assured at some later time that the authorities would not prosecute you?

A. I believe the following day.

Q. Was the escape or the decision to escape predicated on the fact that you had come to understand with Jerry that the defense in this case was hopeless?

A. I believe Jerry told me it was hopeless.

Q. All right, so that assuming, if you will, that on the 18th, in the presence of three other people, Jerry was told that he would be pleading guilty the following Monday and that you were sitting there, would that have been any surprise to you based on what Jerry had already told you about the hopelessness of his case?

A. We were going to court.

Q. Isn't it a fact, Ms. Espinal, that when Mr. Dement and I told Jerry, along with my son sitting right next to you, that he took it like a man and you raised hell?

A. I don't recall being at that meeting.

Q. So if others testify that's exactly what happened, you couldn't possibly deny it, could you?

A. If other people said I was there, then I must have been there, but I can't recall being there.

Chapter 19

Q. Now, prior to this meeting, had you been involved with anyone in a plot to murder Terry Cornell?

A. Yes. Jerry asked me to talk to Jorge (Gonzales) and Humberto Herrera because Terry Cornell and his father were brought into our organization by (them). That was around the beginning of January.

Q. All right, you thought he might flip.

A. Well, and at that time there was a Grand Jury hearing coming up in Alabama.

Q. All right, and what did you and Jorge agree to?

A. He would talk to Terry Cornell, Senior and Junior, you know, make sure that, you know, they would stand straight. A couple of weeks later, Jorge said that they were having a lot of internal problems within the organization. Humberto had gone back to Colombia, and he would see what he could do about it.

Q. Tell us the next time you talked to him. When was the first time you talked with him about killing Terry Cornell?

A. The end of January. That Jerry felt it was Humberto's and Jorge's responsibility to take care of Terry Cornell, Jr. He said, yeah, we will see what we can do about it.

Q. In other words, as you sat there talking with Jorge, although no words were used to that effect, you understood you were requesting Terry Cornell to be assassinated?

A. Well, you, that's correct. I had done anything and everything that Jerry told me, and yes, I was perfectly willing.

Q. I take it you now feel some remorse about having participated in what you say is a planned murder?

A. Of course I feel remorse. I wish it had never happened.

Q. When was the next conversation with Jorge?

A. Roughly maybe a week later.

Q. Alright, and what was planned as of that? Had Jerry been indicted by that time of the conversation?

A. No.

Q. Was it known at this point that the architect of his indictment would be Ronald DeFranco?
A. No.
Q. Okay, was it thought that it might be Terry Cornell?
A. Jerry thought that.
Q. Jerry told you that his concern was Terry Cornell as a potential witness establishing his connection with the Montgomery importation?
A Yes.
Q. Was the purpose of killing Terry Cornell to prevent an indictment?
A. I believe to start with, yes.
Q. To start with. So you had no way of knowing, of course, when a Grand Jury might indict Jerry LeQuire, did you?
A. No.
Q. The first week of February, did you and Jorge agree that Terry Cornell would be killed?
A. Jorge said that he was, you know, working on it.
Q. We all expected an indictment to come out at any time in February of 1984, didn't we?
A. We didn't know.
Q. I am asking you whether or not there was any degree of urgency of getting rid of Terry Cornell before he could get an indictment against Jerry.
A. Yes, Jerry wanted Terry gone.
Q. Did Jorge agree to that?
A. Yes, he did. In the month of February, Jorge released Terry Cornell, Junior and Senior, from his organization, and gave them over to us, and therefore at that point other people were contacted.
Q. You testified earlier that you were well aware that Terry Cornell, if he had become a government witness, could easily cause the indictment of Humberto Herrera and Jorge Gonzalez, correct?
A. Correct.
Q. And you say that after agreeing to dispose of him so he couldn't be a witness, suddenly those people turn him over to you?

Chapter 19

A. Correct.

Q. Okay, so they really didn't care then if he causes their indictment, and they are not going to act on it?

A. They weren't worried about it; Humberto was in Colombia and Jorge, there were internal problems and they had moved all their, you know, offices and whatever, and I don't believe Terry Cornell had any way of knowing where they were.

Q. Are you telling this jury that Humberto Herrera and Jorge Gonzalez didn't care if Terry Cornell caused them to be indicted?

A. I don't know. The way I see it, when they released him, you know—

Q. You claim that Terry Cornell had enough information to cause Jerry to be indicted in Montgomery.

A. I believe he did.

Q. That's why you had him killed?

A. I didn't have Terry Cornell killed. Terry Cornell is not dead.

Q. We'll get into that. You tried to have him killed, didn't you?

A. Tried to have him killed under the direction of the person who told me to do that.

Q. Okay, now the situation is that despite the fact that Terry Cornell very clearly can implicate Herrera and Gonzalez, they have disclaimed any further interest in him, is that right?

A. That's correct.

Q. Even though it is known that he is talking with the government or at least suspected, they have said we don't care, you take care of him; is that right?

A. They said they were going to take care of him at first, they didn't do nothing about it, and then they gave us a release; Jorge had too many problems.

Q. Did you hold the understanding that the key to winning the case was to get rid of Terry Cornell right up until the morning when the trial was scheduled?

A. No, until maybe a couple of days before that.

Bailey's cross continued for a lengthy time, catching Karla in many inconsistencies by repeating his questions in slightly different forms, a tactic he used with all the prosecution witnesses. He repeatedly challenged her on her memory and truthfulness, often prefacing questions with the question of whether or not she was drunk or high when she made statement to officials. Then, he began questioning her about her confession of the murder to Sgt. Fantigrassi in Florida.

Q. When did you first learn that Mildred Cornell had been shot?

A. When you and Mr. Dement walked into the cafeteria here in the courtroom and told me.

Q. Tell us when that happened.

A. You and Mr. Dement came up to the table where we were drinking coffee.

Q. Where is this?

A. There's like a little cafeteria in the courthouse and Mr. Dement came up to me and said you killed Terry's mother.

Q. You, Karla, had killed Terry's mother?

A. That's exactly what Mr. Dement said and I said, what?

Q. Would you give us the rest of the conversation? He is accusing you of murder.

A. I said what? When did this happen? And he goes, last night. I said why didn't you call me and let me know last night so I could call the family and inform them for their security.

Q. You told Sgt. Fantigrassi something quite differently, didn't you?

A. No, I think I told him the same thing.

Q. Is this an act you were putting on with Dement? After all, you had ordered the murder.

A. Yeah, because we weren't–.

Q. You knew it was going to happen. You knew it was to be Mildred Cornell and not Terry.

A. That's right.

Q. And you knew it was to happen before Monday morning.

A. That's correct.

Chapter 19

Q. And here Ira Dement is saying you did it on Monday morning, is that right?

A. Mr. Dement said you all killed–

Q. And you pretended that you were surprised by all this, but of course you weren't, you were just putting on an act. Is that right?

A. That's exactly right.

Q. Why did you lie to Sgt. Fantigrassi?

A. I did not lie to Sgt. Fantigrassi about that.

Q. Have you listened to the tape recording?

A. No, I haven't.

Q. Did you tell Sgt. Fantigrassi the following: Question, "Was this prearranged, the plea, or was it something that came about at the last second?" Answer, "Well it depended on when the hit went down. If Terry Cornell, if he got snatched, we were going to court. If there was a hit, we were pleading." Question, "Okay. The hit – there was a hit but it was the mother." Answer, "Right, so we were pleading." Did you make those statements?

A. Yes, I did.

Q. Would you care to explain them in the light of your present testimony?

A. Well, that's exactly what happened. We did plea.

Q. You just told this jury on your oath that you never talked about pleading before Monday morning, didn't you? That was a lie, wasn't it?

A. That was not a lie.

Q. When did you and Jerry make arrangements that if Terry Cornell got kidnapped you would go to court, if he got hit or killed, you would plead, or if the mother got killed, he would plead, when did you make that arrangement?

A. I can't give you a date, I can't recall.

Q. Mrs. Espinal, please listen to the question. You have just described to Sgt. Fantigrassi a contingent arrangement where you either go to trial or plead, depending on what happens to whom. Now, was that true what you told the sergeant?'

A. Yes, that was true.

Q. Then it can not be true what you told the jury that there never was any talk of a possible plea of guilty until the Monday morning, can it?

A. Not between the lawyers.

Q. Between you and Jerry, there couldn't have been any such talk, can there?

A. Jerry may have mentioned it, but I don't recall him mentioning it.

Q. So you now say Jerry may have mentioned he might plead guilty if somebody got killed, but you don't recall if that's so, is that what you are now saying?

A. I know that if Terry disappeared we were going to trial, definitely.

Q. I asked you when that arrangement was made?

A. That was in January.

Q. The question is, do you see yourself in that transcript telling Sgt. Fantigrassi that you had made the arrangement to plead guilty if someone got killed?

A. That's what it states here. I made the statement on the tape. If this is the actual transcript of the tape of what I talked to him about. I talked to him for hours.

Q. You have no recollection of having told him an arrangement was made to plead if someone got killed, is that correct?

A. I know that he decided to plead guilty.

Q. Did you just tell the jury a few minutes ago that no talk or plea was ever had in your presence until Monday morning?

A. That's correct.

Q. Is this a lie under oath to Sgt. Fantigrassi or did you say that?

A. I said that, and I must have been mistaken. I did not intentionally lie, that is the way you are trying to portray me.

Q. Is this another instance where you have been caught and claim it's a mistake? Is it?"

A. Are you claiming that I am being caught at lying?

Q. Caught at lying. Is that what is happening here? You have been caught lying and you want to say it's a mistake.

Chapter 19

A. No, because I am not lying.

Bailey then pursued more inconsistencies between her testimony in Florida and what she has told this jury. He presses her on her testimony that the Madisonville, Tennessee judge was bribed – every charge she has made and catches her in discrepancies. By the end of his cross examination, which went on for hours, it is apparent that he has raised much doubt in the complete truthfulness of her testimony.

As Jerry listened to her testimony, he tried to remain optimistic. Bailey's defense, perfected by decades of experience, was impressive. But as witness after witness came against him, he saw Bailey struggle to counter their statements. Many of these were former employees who had spent enough time in jail to be persuaded to testify for their freedom, and Jerry understood. They were pawns in the game the prosecutors were playing. Some wouldn't look at him during their testimony; some implied they were only doing this because of family needs, but the government didn't care. With each witness, another nail was fastened to his coffin. Then, Terry Cornell came to the stand and seemed to be gloating as he stared in Jerry's direction.

The prosecution laid the foundation for why Jerry wanted him killed. The 30-year-old man told the jury that he had helped Jerry smuggle cocaine, had assisted in wire tapping, and in general had acted as Jerry's right hand man. He said that Jerry worked for Jorge Gonzalez, and that Gonzalez worked for Humberto Herrera. And that it was their cocaine Jerry smuggled from Colombia. He talked about the pilots by name, and he talked about his friend, Ron DeFranco. Then, he got into his mother's murder.

"When LeQuire was arrested in Fort Lauderdale, did you agree to testify before the grand jury?" the prosecutor asked.

"Yes. I received immunity to testify," Cornell said.

"Were you told to come here on April 23, 1984, to testify at Jerry LeQuire's trial?"

"Yes."

"And where were you living at that time?"

"428 Lakeview, Apartment 22, Fort Lauderdale."

"Did you live there alone?" the prosecutor said.

"My wife, mother and cousin were there with me," Cornell said.

"What happened after you left on the Sunday, April 22nd?"

"My mother was machine gunned," Cornell said.

"Were you planning on testifying against LeQuire the next morning?"

"I was."

"Now, tell the jury about the incident where Jerry LeQuire's son threatened you earlier."

"He chased me in his car," Cornell said.

The prosecutor paused a moment. "We'll come back to this later, but tell the court what Jerry LeQuire said about giving his brothers money."

"He said he gave each of them a present of a million dollars."

The prosecutor nodded to the jury. "How many houses did he have?"

"Six to ten from time to time," Cornell said. "He used them for his men to stay, to store guns and money. He kept a lot of money, more than I'd ever seen."

"Okay, do you know what happened to all that money?"

Cornell said, "He said he moved from place to place. That's what he told me."

Cornell's testimony would have amused Jerry under different circumstances. He was a little man trying to act the role of a big shot, all hat and no cattle.

"Did you feel threatened on another occasion, Mr. Cornell?"

"Yes, at the Atlanta airport. I had to get a police officer to escort me to the plane. It was the LeQuires." He cast a look at Jerry.

"Now, can you identify them?"

"No, but I heard the LeQuire name when they were checking in. One of them saw me and said, Hey, it's Terry." That's when they started chasing me."

"But after you got the policeman, nothing happened."

"I sat in the back of the plane; they sat in first class."

Chapter 19

"Now," the prosecutor said, "did you earlier in this room make a threatening gesture to the LeQuires, like pointing your finger them as though it was a trigger?"

Cornell shook his head. "No, but they pointed at me."

Having established that Cornell was privy to Jerry's secrets, the prosecutor finished with him. Bailey wasted little time in sin attempting to show that Cornell was a blowhard who didn't mind stretching the truth.

"Now Mr. Cornell, you have stated that you were a police officer for a period of time, but isn't it the truth that you were a probationary officer for over a year and terminated because you were not satisfactory."

"That's not true. I resigned."

"Yes, but only to avoid being fired, is that not right?"

"No," Cornell said.

"But didn't you put in for unemployment and the police department objected because you were fired?"

"I don't recall," Cornell said.

Bailey handed him a document. "This is a report from the police department discussing your termination. Have you seen this?"

"No."

"Well, is your commanding officer lying in the report when he says you were fired?"

Cornell hesitated before saying, "Yes, it's a lie."

"Now, tell me if you knew Jorge Gonzalez when you were with the police department."

"Yes. I did some investigative work for him earlier but I didn't see him while I was on the police force."

"Okay, now you're a private detective in Illinois, right?"

"Yes."

"Did you tell them that you had engaged in illegal activities and avoided prosecution by making a deal with the government?"

"The employment form only asked if you had ever been convicted," Cornell said.

"So, as long as you're not convicted, in your mind you have no obligation to report it, even though you're guilty. Now, Mr. Cornell, did you reflect to any degree since you had been in law enforcement on the consequences of committing the state and federal crimes while working for Jerry LeQuire?"

"No."

"So, you did it in a mindless fashion for the money, then."

"Yes."

"Okay. Now, you weren't a wealthy man when you left the police, so how many times have you held a thousand or two thousand dollars in your hand? Never, right?"

"Yes, that's right."

"But you don't remember how much you were paid."

"No, I don't remember," Cornell said, "there's been a lot of tragedy since then."

"Yes, but when you testified before the Grand Jury you remembered the exact amount, both for you and Mr. DeFranco, right"

"Yes, but.."

"Has something happened to your memory since you gave that testimony?"

"My mother was murdered."

"And that destroyed your memory?" Bailey said.

"It did a lot to it."

Bailey walked back and forth before saying, "Mr. Cornell, do you find it more difficult to remember things that you said happened than things that really happened?"

"I don't understand the question."

Bailey moved closer. "You don't understand the difference, do you?"

"That's an erroneous statement," Cornell said, fidgeting in the chair

"Now, you were hired by Jorge Gonzalez to come to Fort Lauderdale and investigate the Sylvania incident, right? And you brought Mr. DeFranco to assist. Now, would you tell this jury everything you then knew about Mr. Gonzalez?"

Chapter 19

"He's a Colombian in the import-export business."

"But at that time, you didn't know he smuggled cocaine?"

"I wasn't sure," Cornell said.

"You weren't sure. Now, how many times as a detective have you been employed by a Colombian drug kingpin?"

"Maybe twenty or thirty."

"So you knew that Mr. Gonzalez worked for an even larger drug kingpin named Humberto Herrera, did you not?"

"Yes.

"But when I just asked you to tell us what you knew about Mr. Gonzalez, had you forgotten that fact?" Bailey said

"I really didn't know what Jorge did. I understood that he was alleged to be a drug dealer."

"Is that how you described it under oath to the Grand Jury, that he was alleged to be drug dealer?"

"I don't recall."

"How about his associates, did you know they were drug dealers, Mr. Cornell?"

"We had gotten several referrals for business from him."

"Okay, did you know about the extradition treaty where we could go into Colombia and bring back drug dealers?"

"Yeah."

"And you knew that judges and others were being murdered in Colombia to discourage any extradition cooperation, did you not?"

"Yes."

Bailey said, "Okay, did you know Alberto Menendez?"

"I'm not sure. I know several people named Mendedez."

"Were they clients, Mr. Cornell?"

"Two of them were. I did electronic sweeps for them."

"And did you know any other people who were connected to Gonzalez and Herrera?"

"I did."

"And these were people you knew before you knew Jerry LeQuire. Does the name Rotera International mean anything to you, Mr. Cornell?"

"It's an import-export company that sends things into Colombia," Cornell said. "It's a legitimate company."

"But didn't you say under oath that it was a front for Jorge Gonzalez's drug operations?"

"I can't remember," Cornell said.

"All right. Now, do you know Alfonso Calle German?"

"He works for Jorge."

"Do you know Salomon Ackerstain?"

"He also worked for Jorge," Cornell said.

Bailey smiled and continued to name drug dealers who were associated with Cornell through his business. He also got Cornell to admit that he often listened in on conversations on phone lines he was tapping.

"Now, do you think that this information you heard could cause trouble for these men if the authorities knew about it?"

"Yes."

"In fact, you have said that you could have testified, right?"

"Yes."

"Would you agree that Jorge Gonzalez is a dangerous killer?"

Cornell shrugged. "It's possible."

"Didn't you tell the Montgomery Grand Jury that he was a killer?"

"Yes, I guess so if that's what the transcript says."

"Let's discuss your immunity, Mr. Cornell. You went to the government in December of 1983 asking for immunity if you would testify, is that correct? You would sell your testimony in exchange for no prosecution."

"That's right."

"Now, you had several guns in your apartment, didn't you. One was what is called a machine gun, and the reason for these guns is you had concern that somebody might want to do you in?"

"No, I'm a gun enthusiast," Cornell said.

Chapter 19

Bailey walked away, then turned and said, "Everybody knew that your friend, DeFranco, had turned, just as they knew you had turned, true?"

"Yes."

"And you both talked to the Grand Jury, but – have you ever seen an indictment in the United States of America where Jorge Gonzalez is named?"

"No."

"Okay, you didn't give any testimony in Montgomery regarding Jorge."

"I was going to do it at the trial," Cornell said.

"And it was to be at this trial that you would implicate Gonzalez, knowing that his Colombian friends were quick to kill those who put them in jeopardy."

"Yes."

Bailey turned to the jury and looked at them for a moment. "Now, Mr. Cornell, did you hear DeFranco's lawyer, Ken Del Valle, threaten Jerry if he didn't receive money?"

"He didn't threaten LeQuire," Cornell said.

"Look at page 54 of your Grand Jury testimony and see if you told the Grand Jury that Del Valle was threatening LeQuire."

"Well, there was a money dispute between the–"

Bailey snapped at him. "Do you wish to change the testimony where a moment ago you swore that you never heard Del Valle threaten Lequire?"

"It must have slipped my mind," Cornell said.

"Do you understand the meaning of extortion, sir?"

"Yes."

"Did Del Valle extort LeQuire on that day?"

"Yes."

"Then, tell us about the extortion," Bailey said.

"I don't recall all of the conversation."

"Is it because you're making it up, Mr. Cornell?"

"Why would I lie to the Grand Jury?"

Bailey shrugged. "Why would you lie to this jury? Obviously, you are lying to one of them, wouldn't you agree?"

With that, Bailey wound down his cross, leaving Cornell a bruised witness.

Cornell's problems followed him after the trial. He became involved in Chicago politics and used leverage to obtain a number of positions. In 2003, he was named a parole supervisor for the Illinois Department of Corrections by Governor Rod Blagojevich, now serving time in prison. But Cornell was forced to quit the job once it was learned that he had not been entirely truthful in the application process. Though he told the press that he quit because the job was boring, HQ spokesman for the Corrections Department said she was not aware of a resignation letter

Cornell was also indicted on four perjury counts stemming from criminal cases where he testified he was a Miami police officer for five years, while it was determined that he had been released six months into the job. He was eventually placed on probation. Before that, he worked for the Intercounty National Insurance Company that was charged with a $100 million fraud. He had been hired as a bodyguard and later was made vice president of legal affairs.

He readily boasts that he was the one responsible for taking down Jerry.

Jerry was acquitted of murder but found guilty on the RICO and CCE charge. He was sentenced to 60 years. Bonnie was also found guilty and sentenced to 14 years but her case was overturned on appeal and a new trial was granted. Jerry's son and two of his brothers were also convicted.

And Karla went into witness protection.

Chapter 20

When Jerry was arrested, Hank Maierhoffer's son asked his daddy if Jerry was going to kill him. It was a logical question given Maierhoffer's betrayal. Fortunately for him, his part in Jerry's demise was unknown for several years, and might have remained unknown if not for an anonymous letter sent to Jerry stating that Maierhoffer worked for the CIA. A copy of a document substantiating the claim was attached. It was a book segment about a retired brigadier general saying that he worked with Maierhoffer at the CIA both in the Middle East and later in America.

Maierhoffer had been involved in drug busts as early as 1974. He, along with several others, was captured when the pilot informed authorities of a marijuana smuggling activity. Maierhoffer testified for the government, who later said they had erred by not recording his oral confession, so they had no recourse but to release him from all charges.

"Cochran, joined by Hornsby, complains that the trial court erred in refusing their requests for certain material to which they felt they were entitled under the Jencks Act, 18 U.S.C. § 3500(e) (2), and the rule of Brady v. Maryland, 373 U.S. 83, 83 S. Ct. 1194, 10 L. Ed. 2d 215 (1963). First sought was any record made by Agent Richel of his conversation with government witness Maierhoffer following the latter's arrest. Both Richel and Maierhoffer testified, and the trial court's inspection of Richel's file confirmed, that no substantially verbatim record was made of Maierhoffer's oral confession; therefore, the Jencks Act was not applicable. See Palermo v. United States, 360 U.S. 343, 79 S. Ct. 1217, 3 L. Ed. 2d 1287 (1959); United States v. Roberts, 455 F.2d 930 (5th Cir. 1972). Defendants also claimed that Richel's file contained Brady material in the form of prior inconsistent statements by Maierhoffer

and information that he was involved in other criminal activities. However, the testimony was that no statement, inconsistent or otherwise, was recorded. And Maierhoffer's insistence that he had made no deal in exchange for his testimony made irrelevant any activities for which he had not been prosecuted. Also sought by the defendants was a report prepared by government agent Walker covering a conference he had with the pilot Sims when he first reported the smuggling scheme. An in camera examination by the trial judge confirmed the government's statement that Walker's report contained no exculpatory Brady material. We will not go beyond the trial court's finding to encourage shipping prosecutor's files to the appellate court whenever the defense cries Brady. Since Sims did not testify at trial, the Jencks Act is inapplicable."

In the mid 1970s, Maierhoffer was involved in another marijuana bust. He owned a DC-3 airplane and allowed a man name Joseph Abel to use it from time to time. According to testimony, he was approached by the DEA and told that they suspected the plane was being used to smuggle marijuana. They *asked* Maierhoffer for permission to place a beeper on the plane to track its movements. Subsequent to his agreement, the men were arrested and convicted.

But the biggest drug bust involved his old friend and co-worker, General Russell Bowen. Brigadier General Russell Bowen was a pilot in World War II flying P-38's. He received the Distinguished Flying Cross and the Distinguished Service Medal and was said to be the youngest P-38 fighter pilot at that time. He was eventually asked to join the young intelligence agency which was called the Office of Strategic Services, or OSS for short. Later, when the OSS was disbanded by President Truman, a remnant remained to maintain the organization and Bowen was one of these seventy-five people. They later formed what is now the Central Intelligence Agency.

Bowen held many jobs during his OSS/CIA tenure, including starting up airlines in South America that served as covers for the CIA. In the 1960s, he reported to William Casey, who later became Director of the CIA. Bowen dealt with both the Medellin and Cali drug cartels. These cartels provided cocaine to the CIA, which would then be sold to finance

Chapter 20

their operations. He eventually became soured on the CIA's involvement with the selling of drugs and openly voiced his discontent, believing that his reputation would carry some weight. But in 1982, he was ordered by his CIA handler to fly to Medellin. He was to take one CIA agent and return with another. But before leaving Medellin, 800 pounds of cocaine were loaded onto the plane and when he landed, he was arrested. The airport where he landed was Plantation Air in Slyvania, Georgia, the same airport that Hank Maierhoffer had purchased for Jerry, and the same airport where Jerry's cocaine was hi-jacked. Adding to this, Bowen's CIA handler was none other than Hank Maierhoffer.

Bowen was not allowed to present evidence that he worked for the CIA or his involvement with Maierhoffer, and spent several years in a federal prison. The sequence of events that led to Bowen's removal as a CIA threat was eerily similar to what happened to Jerry. He became a problem and was removed.

Maierhoffer later removed his operation from Fort Lauderdale to the Plantation Air airport, the same airport in Sylvania where Jerry's cocaine had been hi-jacked and where Russell Bowen was arrested. Jerry was certain that the planes the authorities confiscated were moved there as well. There is a credible possibility that the CIA had operated from this facility for nearly a decade before Maierhoffer *purchased* it for Jerry.

A natural question to ask is why would the CIA be interested in Jerry? To many readers, the idea of the CIA being involved in drug trafficking is far-fetched, a preposterous concoction of right-wing extremists. Yet, there have been countless accusations stating just that fact. In 2014, the Huffington Post wrote an article discussing the CIA-cocaine connection. They referenced Pulitzer-Prize winning journalist Gary Webb's stunning expose about the connection between the CIA, the Contras, and crack cocaine, and how now, almost 20 years later, people are coming forward to substantiate his claims. One of the more interesting recent revelations concerned the role of the CIA with the Contra rebels. According to Webb, the Contras would be handed bags filled with money obtained by the CIA sale of cocaine. But it began long before Webb's book. In 1985, then Senator John Kerry launched a Congressional investigation and found that the CIA was complicit in the drug trade, so to discount Jerry's claim as fabrication that he was contacted by the CIA to carry weapons to the Contras in exchange for his freedom to smuggle cocaine, pales in the light of other information.

And then there is the case of Harold Rosenthal. Rosenthal, according to those few he had confided in, stated that he just walked out of the federal prison in Memphis. Which begs the question: how? I have visited many prisons and it just isn't possible without a lot of help, and high-powered help at that. But my inquiries were stonewalled and eventually I grew tired of butting my head against a wall. And was it a coincidence that he contacted a friend, who was also a friend of Jerry's, to ask for help the get to Colombia? Perhaps, but you have to wonder. In any case, after Jerry left Medellin, Rosenthal continued to operate, but he, as Jerry predicted, made a mistake by attempting to become involved in Colombian politics. While living in the Atlanta area, he had worked within the Civil Rights movement, and was respected by the leaders, but getting in Colombia policies proved to be his undoing.

In the middle of the afternoon, he was yanked from his car and flown to the United States to stand trial for drug smuggling and escaping prison where he was serving a 31-year sentence.

A newspaper story stated, "Federal grand jury indictments were unsealed Monday charging 53 people with smuggling $3.8 billion worth of cocaine into the United States, the authorities said. Harold Rosenthal, of Atlanta, named as ringleader of the gang, was accused of trying to arrange the murder of drug agents to avenge his arrest and protect other members of the ring. An extensive undercover investigation by Federal, state and local authorities led to the indictments, which charge that some 5 tons of cocaine were brought from Colombia into Georgia, Florida, Tennessee and Pennsylvania from June 1982 to September 1983 in 14 shipments. The indictments were unsealed in Atlanta, Miami, Los Angeles and Little Rock, Ark.

Chapter 20

"Associate Attorney General D. Lowell Jensen said the investigation, in which 2,700 pounds of cocaine was confiscated, uncovered the largest cocaine ring ever in the United States. He estimated the amount of cocaine brought into the country annually at 30 tons to 60 tons.

"Mr. Jensen praised the Colombian Government for its help in the investigation. 'The Minister of Justice and the Attorney General of Colombia both deserve great credit for this enormous assistance,' he said. 'We believe it marks the beginning of a new era of cooperation between Colombia and the United States in drug enforcement.'

"The indictment asserted that members of the smuggling ring were supported by Bahamian immigration and customs officials who permitted planes carrying cocaine to land at West End Airport in the Bahamas. Mr. Rosenthal was serving a 31-year sentence for drug smuggling when he escaped from a Federal facility in Memphis three years ago. He was arrested by Federal agents last fall while he was stuck in traffic in Bogota, Colombia.

"A Federal grand jury in Miami indicted Mr. Rosenthal and three other persons on charges of trying to arrange Mr. Rosenthal's escape from the Metropolitan Correctional Center in Miami, where he was being held after his capture in Colombia. Officials said Mr. Rosenthal was being held in the Atlanta Federal Penitentiary."

He was tried and convicted, and his claim to be working for the CIA was not allowed into evidence.

A federal appeals court Friday upheld the racketeering and drug smuggling convictions of Harold Rosenthal and seven co-defendants in what the government described as the largest cocaine ring in U.S. history.

Rosenthal, a former Atlanta bail bondsman, was sentenced to life in prison without parole and fined $425,000 after his 1984 conviction on charges of racketeering, running a continuing criminal enterprise, importing cocaine, possessing cocaine with intent to distribute and conspiracy to import cocaine.

The Federal indictment charged that the smuggling ring imported $3.8 billion worth of cocaine into the United States in 14 months, using the equivalent of a small air force to fly the drugs from South America and the Caribbean.

The convictions followed an 18-month undercover investigation by federal agents. During the nine-week trial in U.S. District Court in Atlanta, Rosenthal contended he was working for the Central Intelligence Agency and ran the drug operation as part of his CIA duties.

In another story: "Harold Rosenthal, a former bail bondsman, was found guilty today of directing a drug trafficking ring that Federal agents said brought more than five tons of cocaine into the country from September 1981 to January 1984. A Federal jury found Mr. Rosenthal and eight others guilty of drug charges after three days of deliberations that climaxed a 10-week trial. Defense attorneys said Mr. Rosenthal was conducting the smuggling with a special dispensation from the Government because he was spying on Marxist groups in Colombia for the Central Intelligence Agency. The prosecutor, Craig Gillen, said in his closing argument that Mr. Rosenthal and his co-conspirators were motivated by greed.

"Mr. Rosenthal was arrested in Bogota, Colombia, a year ago. He had escaped in 1981 from a Federal prison in Memphis where he was serving 31 years for drug smuggling."

But there was more to this than just the trial, as this letter published by the New York Times, as part of a continuing dialogue with a Times editor, details.

From the Procurator's Office of the Soviet Union:

Sir:

I thought the written part of our dialogue on prisons was over ("Inside the Soviet Prison Called VS-389/36-1," letter, Dec. 26, 1987; "Soviet Penal Institutions: See for Yourselves," letter, May 16, 1988; columns by A. M. Rosenthal, April 23, 1987, Jan. 19, 1988, May 17, 1988 [and today]). I was wrong.

Chapter 20

A bulky package of information about inmates in the Federal prison at Marion, Ill., America's strictest security prison, was delivered recently to me at the Procurator's Office of the Soviet Union. There are 350 inmates in this "super-max" (super high-security) prison, whose name terrifies prisoners throughout the United States. One of them is Harold Joseph Rosenthal, a political prisoner serving a life sentence. It is he who wrote me.

Harold Rosenthal, a white, has been active in the black civil rights movement since 1957. In 1963, he was thanked for his activity by the Rev. Dr. Martin Luther King Jr. Mr. Rosenthal was on the Federal Bureau of Investigation's list as a "subversive element" for many years and was arrested several times. In the 1970s, he went to Latin America to support revolutionary movements, including the Sandinistas. One of his colleagues says he did this selflessly, through the force of his convictions, and he called him a socialist. In 1983, Mr. Rosenthal was kidnapped by United States intelligence in Colombia, taken to the United States and sentenced to life on charges of "politically motivated crimes of arms and drug conspiracy." As I see it, some people doubt the legitimacy of applying United States laws to a person kidnapped in another country, as well as a number of other aspects of the charges.

"If my politics were capitalist instead of socialist, I wouldn't be in prison right now," Harold Rosenthal, prisoner 08075-020, wrote me. "Lieut. Col. Oliver North, William Casey, Gen. Richard Secord and many others did the exact same thing I did. The only difference is I traded in arms for the liberation movements and in aid of the people, whereas Colonel North and the Central Intelligence Agency trade in arms and drugs for the contras trying to overthrow the people's government of Nicaragua. Because I follow my politics and conscience, mine is a 'crime,' while theirs is not. I will exchange prison cells with any Soviet prisoner. When the United States Government wants you to release prisoners, have me brought to Russia in exchange."

One remark: It isn't acceptable to us when someone in some other country categorically states that some person in the Soviet Union has been sentenced without guilt, and he or she should be released. We won't emulate this unwise practice. As a lawyer, I'm well aware that the letter from Harold Rosenthal and his lawyer represents the opinion of only one side, and there can be other opinions.

I feel obliged to mention an apprehension voiced by Harold Rosenthal: "Whenever a prisoner says anything about the prison system or goes against it in any way he suffers the reprisals....an example is Leonard Peltier...He is put in the hole for months on false charges. Prison officials tried to get another prisoner to kill him."

I would hope that this letter will not in any way worsen Harold Rosenthal's situation.

I would like you to know that nine Soviet citizens described by A. M. Rosenthal(no relation to Harold) as "prisoners of conscience" have been released. Those pardoned are V. Shmelyov, P. Ruban, V. Ostroglyad, V. Kalinichenko, A. Svarinskas, B. Romashov and G. Prikhodko. Two others - G. Astra and M. Niklus – had their sentences reduced and have both been released (Mr. Niklus even visited me at the Procurator's Office).

As of July 15, six people belonging to the group A. M. Rosenthal has referred to are still in prison, sentenced for anti-Soviet agitation and propaganda. As far as I know some of them are now being considered for early release. IVAN RAKHMANIN Moscow, July 27, 1988. The writer is a procurator in the Soviet Procurator's Office.

In appealing his verdict, Rosenthal and another defendant, Philip Bonadonna of Coral Gables, Fla., argued that the trial judge was wrong to limit the evidence they were allowed to present about the alleged CIA link. But the appeals court rejected that argument and said the CIA connection, even if it existed, was not a viable defense.

Jerry returned to prison knowing he had received what would probably be a life sentence. Bitter and disillusioned, his thoughts were filled with anger at life. He had always known the risk but never had he imagined such a harsh sentence would be applied. Sixty years! Maybe he should have accepted the government's offer to testify against the Colombians.

Chapter 20

Dead outside prison or dead inside, what was the difference? But it was too late now. Karla had seen to that.

How he hated her! She had ruined the lives of everyone associated with her. He hoped the Colombians found her and made her suffer for what she did.

He tried to correspond with his family, especially his son, but it was difficult. Bonnie kept in touch, for which he was glad. She had refused to testify against him, even though he knew she was offered a deal.

He sensed her frustration in her letters and knew she was also wondering why she hadn't cut a deal. While she was careful not to say anything direct to him about her feelings, she was not so hesitant to her friends.

Dear Sandy:

Lee Fugate (her lawyer in the RICO trial) was very pleased with the hearing. I think we will win all of this mess, including Atlanta. I've got to worry about 14 years I have in Ky. Fugate is not going to the Supreme Court with me on Ky., because he didn't get paid for it or Ala. He's a little upset with me. There's nothing I can do about it. Bailey needs to talk to Fugate unless Jerry has told him not to. I'm to the point of don't know what's going on.

I'm not going to write Jerry anymore. He hasn't answered my last letter from 6 or 7 weeks ago. I always thought he would be there for me or at least my family, as long as I was there for him, but he sure hasn't been. I'm really disappointed, and a fool I guess, but I'm honorable. I've lost my family, home, cars, jewelry, everything I've loved or had, trying to help Jerry by not being another Karla, and he has never tried to even buy Trudy a pack of cigs or buy my babies a hamburger. I've really been a FOOL, but I have my HONOR. My family and friends told me constantly how stupid I am. They don't know I'm afraid of them. I could have gone home and saved everything, everybody, the first day I was arrested, but I wouldn't agree to put Jerry in an electric chair, I wouldn't corroborate Karla's testimony. My granddaughters are even separated, but I have my HONOR.

Bonnie, according to statements credited to her, was now seeing the stark reality of her future. And if another chance for freedom ever came, she was going to take it.

It came sooner than anyone could have expected.

Chapter 21

Not content with sending Jerry away for 60 years, Karla came up with another bombshell. She talked about a terrorist plot to extort Jerry's release from prison. The plan was to blow up power transmission lines, a naval vessel, airport facilities, a dam and a nuclear plant; then to advertise to the media that the bombings were part of a terrorist group's protest of the United States' policy in South America. Jerry, through his lawyer, would then contact authorities and say he could provide information to stop the bombings. In return, the government would give him an early release. According to Karla, they had arranged for a fall guy to take the blame for the bombings. Charged in her testimony were Jerry, his son and brothers, a few friends, and Bonnie Anders.

The trial was held in September, 1991, in Atlanta.

She said the plan began to evolve in May or June of 1985, when Jerry was in the Minnesota State Prison. According to Karla, Jerry said it would work because of Muammar Gaddafi's terrorist activity and the fear it brought.

The trial was part circus and part "Let's Make a Deal." One of the defense witnesses was one of Karla's lovers while she was married to Jerry, who said she boasted that if she was ever caught with cocaine, she'd get her freedom by trading information about Jerry. And Bonnie chose to trade as well by backing up Karla's story.

The "terrorist activity" for which Jerry was accused consisted of damaging a couple of electrical transmission towers, not exactly front page news. But the prosecutor was quick to point out that a plan doesn't need to be successful to be the subject of a conspiracy.

Both Karla and Bonnie implicated Jerry's brothers and son in the conspiracy, claiming they did all the work. Bonnie said that one of his brothers tested the dynamite to see if it was good and that Jerry would sometimes call four times a day to check on the progress. Little by little the stories added up until the prosecution and defense began repeating their questions.

One of the defense lawyers explained to the jury that Bonnie got her undergraduate degree by listening to Karla's Montgomery testimony, then got her graduate degree by reading the available information prior to this trial. More than once, the judge seemed to have difficulty in accepting the testimony.

However, it was Bonnie's corroboration of Karla's story that seemed to carry weight with the jury. She echoed everything Karla said, almost to the word. It was a neat package.

The prosecutor summed up the case to the jury by quoting Robert Burns: "The best laid plans of mice and men often go awry."

The defense attorney said that the government's story was a "very poorly written script." In his closing remarks, added, "Now, I must confess that in listening to Mr. Weinstein's (federal prosecutor) opening remarks, I wasn't sure if we had been in the same courtroom during the entire three weeks because there were statements made, characterizations made of the evidence that are just not so. He appealed to emotion using inflammatory language. Rather that to appeal to your logic, he appealed to your emotion. All of us have grown to be suspect of dealing with important issues rather than rational thought process. Now, I don't want you to misunderstand that my failure to respond to each and every point raised by Mr. Weinstein is a concession or admission as to the point he tried to make. It is physically impossible to do that because I have 25 minutes.

"I'm going to ask you both now and when you listen to my argument, as well as when you are deliberating, to utilize your analytical skills, to divorce yourself from sympathy and prejudice and from emotion, and to make inquiry, perhaps similar to what you have done when you listened

Chapter 21

or observed a movie, perhaps a thriller or who done it. And perhaps you were entertained and amused by the movie, but you were sadly disappointed because it just didn't make any sense; there were real gaps in the logic, and the story just didn't hold together. I would suggest to you that is what you witnessed here the past three weeks. It is an appealing story and it has some legitimacy at first blush, but when you start looking at it and analyzing it and asking yourself some difficult questions, it doesn't make any sense. And it that kind of analytical thinking that I'm going to ask you to approach in this particular case.

"Now, the story that has unfolded the past three weeks suggests a very poorly written script in which some of the actors have forgotten or flubbed their lines. In considering this case and more specifically the indictment which you will have an opportunity to go through, I ask you to ask yourselves if this story is true, what things should have happened that didn't happen, and what things happened that shouldn't have happened. You have a right to make that type of inquiry. You are not there as sponges just to absorb whatever is thrown at you. And you have to assess for yourself credibility and believability of this story.

"And there is a very important portion of an instruction there that tells you that if you believe that certain witnesses – i.e. Karla, Bonnie, Zamora, Presswood – if they gave you intentional falsehoods, that they lied about material evidence, you don't have to analyze and scrutinize to determine which is a lie and which is truth. The Court has told you the law says you can throw it all out because when a person lies about material things, there is a suggestion that perhaps they lied about other things, and the law does not impose upon you the sometimes impossible task of deciding which lie to believe.

"I'm going to ask you or invite you to consider when analyzing testimony of those people, ask yourself does their respective segment of portion of the story fit or mesh together? Can you reconcile their differences by just an innocent loss of memory or is it something just a little more insidious? Is it an inept attempt to fabricate a story that just doesn't make sense similar to my analogy of the move? Does it flow? Does it make sense? Does it come out the way it should have if this conspiracy, if this grand scheme in fact existed other than in the minds of people after the fact to garner special consideration from this Government so that these people can escape punishment for some very serious crimes they committed.

"Now, don't get bogged down on character. To that extent, I agree with Mr. Weinstein. Let's not have this case determined upon the relative badness of the respective players. There is plenty of that going around. This is not, as I told you in my opening comments, a contest between sinners and saints. The issue is what is the truth.

"Now, character is fair game for assessing truth, bur what I'm suggesting to you is it should not drive or dictate your decision. It is a consideration. And that works both for and against both parties. Let's decide this case not on some mud slinging and name calling; let's decide this case based on what the facts are, what the truth is.

"The defense in this case is and always has been that there are certain historical events that did happen. We have, contrary to the representation of Mr. Weinstein, have never suggested that certain events did not exist. The Orlando house did exist. There is no doubt there were two explosions. There is not doubt there were prison visits. That is not the issue. The issue is is there any rational connection between any of those consistent with this scheme or theory that the Government has tried to sell you?

"I would argue that consistent with my opening remarks, that there *has* been a conspiracy, and that was a drug conspiracy. That was the purpose of Bonnie Anders, Karla, Presswood, and yes, even Ms. Zamora. Remember Ms. Zamora? She is the one that Karla said knew everything, but when we got her on the stand she didn't remember anything. And remember some of the questions concerning a courier and some of the evidence concerning what goes on with the drug conspiracy? Ask yourself, isn't that what you observed during the last three weeks? And aren't they attempting to kind of retrofit or engage in revisionist history to now portray it as something other than that?

Chapter 21

"Now, please try and keep in mind the historical chronology of this because I think it is important in assessing the credibility of Karla. Karla doesn't tell the story until almost two years after it happens, and then there is another year and a half or so that passes and then she testifies. What is important, ladies and gentlemen, who is sitting there during this whole presentation? Bonne Anders. She was going to school. She learned what the story is, and then she realized that her memory wasn't all that great, and when she didn't learn enough at school, she tries to get additional information through the investigate reports so she can get it down just right. Well, whether she did or not, we know that she didn't get it down just right. There are not just little things about dates. Forget dates. What about the sequence of events? If A happens, then B should happen, and C and D. And is that the way it was explained to you? No, it wasn't. We are not saying that because someone can't remember the exact month five years from now that is a lie, of course not. But what is important is that if someone was a part to some kind of plan that is as farfetched and nonsensical as this, wouldn't you remember the basics? And did they remember the basics? About the only thing consistent was they were pointing the finger at Jerry LeQuire. They got that down right. But what about the rest of it?

"Now Karla had every opportunity in the world to talk to Mr. Presswood and Ms. Zamora prior to them ever being interviewed. So in response to the logical question, well, Mr. Trost, how did these people get on board? Well, that is how. It is no big mystery. Karla was quite capable, both physically as well as the mind set to have talked to those people and gotten them on board. Again, what is the incentive for them to join the club? They have got exposure.

"I would suggest to you that what you heard her the last three weeks indicates a failed attempt to create a conspiracy that never existed. To, as I mentioned earlier, retrofit a drug conspiracy and to make it into something grandiose. Each and every one of them have an abundance of motive and an abundance of reasons to do exactly that.

"Now, I would like to talk briefly about the explosive devices. Let me begin be addressing the concerns made by Mr. Weinstein. Again, I'm not sure I heard the same testimony he was referring to because I believe the evidence showed that the expert that was called by the defense refuted each and every point made by the government's expert. Yes, Mr. Weinstein asked him a hypothetical that was totally irrelevant to this case and got what he thinks to be a significant confession. But it didn't. The expert clearly indicated that the devices weren't related, there wasn't a signature, and there was no relevant value in this Government theory that these devices in '85 and '86 somehow tie in these devices in '78, or the Jefferson City bombings for which Jerry was found guilty. I can't change the fact that Jerry LeQuire was found guilty. That is a fact. We are not here to insult your intelligence by suggesting anything else, but what is important is to explain how he was convicted of what. He was convicted by two fingerprints, and we explained to you how they got there. Did you hear any evidence to indicate that he had the ability or the knowledge to manufacture anything? No. But the Government asked you to make that leap of faith because he was convicted; therefore he had it, and you didn't hear that.

"Remember the whole theory ladies and gentlemen is that Jerry LeQuire is the mastermind. He is the one that has the specialized knowledge. And remember the Government says that this knowledge was not transferred through some kind of unknown, undefined method; it was done through Karla and primarily through Ms. Anders. And remember the cross-examination of those people. Did their responses to some of the questions strike you as people that had technical knowledge of devices? To the contrary. By Bonnie Anders own admission, she would have blown them up had the devices that were found at the scene been prepared the way she was supposedly instructed to do so. What does that tell you? We are not suggesting that there weren't two explosions, but what it suggests is that Bonne Anders and Karla had nothing to do with these explosions. And if it didn't, isn't it reasonable to conclude that neither did any of these defendants? And make the

Chapter 21

Government explain that to you. Because if they can't, the whole plan falls apart. Do we just wink at that and say, 'Well Government you did a pretty good job but, you know, these are kind of bad people, and I think maybe we will give you the benefit of the doubt'?

"That isn't how it works, ladies and gentlemen. It is their burden. Don't let them get away with it. Don't let them insult your intelligence. Make them prove their case. Mr. Weinstein commented on missing evidence and inferred that 'Jeez, the defense has subpoenas available to them so why didn't they bring it in?' Well, you know why. Because we can sit here for the entire three weeks and not say a word, not lift a hand, and that is perfectly okay because it is their burden. It is *their* burden. And it is not a response to a sloppy case or case that doesn't make any sense of case that doesn't prove what it is supposed to prove, to say well, it is not my fault, to say the defense didn't do anything to show these people were innocent. That is not our burden.

"Let's look at some of this missing evidence. And the reason why that is important, why you should be put in the position of having to decide which of the lies of Karla and Bonnie and some of these other people are true when there could be hard evidence to support and substantiate the Government's theory. Why didn't they bring these people in, why didn't they bring this evidence in? You heard there are phone records available, flight records that are available, theft reports of dynamite and incident reports of dynamite, and you would expect that if a guard got beat up and a dog shot that somewhere there are witnesses to substantiate this. What about phone calls made to the Miami Herald since one of the critical aspects of this so-called scheme was to convince the Government that we have a bunch of loony terrorists going around indiscriminately bombing things. Now why, I ask you, would people – *these* people –go through all the trouble, expense and risk and then forget the most critical aspect of the whole thing? Someone just forgot to call the Miami Herald?

"And where is the dynamite? They couldn't find anything, but they did produce these people who say you can take their word for it since they have no interest other than to just tell the truth. And what about

Karla? She is indeed a piece of work. And you heard what a loving, loyal wife she is because she told you. Forget the scheming, forget the duplicity, forget the theft, forget the fact that she solicited murder from two different people of her husband. Forget all that; that is a minor indiscretion. Girls just want to have fun, I guess. And remember the testimony of Mr. Carver who said that in 1985 Karla told him exactly what she going to do. She is going to make a deal. When she gets caught dealing dope, as she did, she is going to come here and fabricate a story and she doesn't care where the chips fall. And she is not going to be restrained by the truth because she had creative genius and she doesn't have a conscience to preclude her from coming in here and insulting your intelligence by giving the testimony she did.

"Sure, Jerry is not the nicest guy in the world, and he is spending a lot of time in prison, but he has the same rights as you and I. And don't you take the shortcut, the easy step of just rubber stamping what these people said because it is convenient, and you don't want to be bothered by thinking through it. That is your duty, and I know you good citizens will do your duty.

The jury, perhaps weary from it all, took less than two days to reach a verdict. Jerry was convicted of conspiracy and transportation of dynamite.

After sentencing, Jerry was sent to Marion, and he was angry that Trost hadn't talked to the judge about where he should be sent. He expected, given certain statements the judge had made in chambers, implying that the case was suspect, that he would be sent to a better facility. So, he complained through official channels and received this response from the lawyer:

Dear Jerry:

Unfortunately, as has been too often the case, your attitude and sarcasm interferes with your judgment. For the record, I filed a proposed order with the judge the very next day after your sentencing, copy of which is enclosed. I told his clerk the importance of having it signed

Chapter 21

and delivered to me as soon as possible. I intended to deliver a certified copy to the BOP and Marshall's office as soon as the judge signed it. I checked with the clerk telephonically on a daily basis thereafter to find out the status of the order. The judge did not sign it; instead he signed the standard Judgment of Conviction, incorporating the "designation language" in it. I did not receive it until after they already moved you. Jerry, I don't know what the hell else you expect me to do.

Frankly, you are naïve if you believe that the BOP's action would have been affected even if they had the judge's order before they shipped you. How could you listen to that garbage?

As to your cryptic comments about tapes, I don't have the slightest idea what you're talking about. I am not interested nor am I going to defend or be responsible for what other lawyers did or what you think they did. I communicated my position to the judge and to Weinstein (prosecutor) personally. Get off my case! The slime bag knows what I think of him, and I await the opportunity to take further punitive action against him.

By the way, before you totally write me off as some useless appendage, did you give any thought as to how and why you got concurrent time? Do you think it was because the judge just liked you or can you entertain the possibility that I did my job at sentencing and communicated to the court the misinformation and improprieties offered and expressed by the prosecution during the trial of your case?

As to your appeal, suit yourself. I have enough to keep me busy, and I don't need the practice. Frankly, I don't see any practical advantage we can gain other than to rub Weinstein's face in it a little more. Just give me some direction so I don't waste my time and run the risk of being accused of furthering some grand conspiracy.

Give me a call if and when you can. I am sincerely sorry for your suffering. I stand ready to continue efforts to help wherever possible.

For her cooperation, Bonnie's sentence was reduced, and soon she was a free woman. There was also an agreement for her incarcerated daughter. And Jerry went from prison to prison, all but forgotten by society.

He never heard from Karla again, and the only news he heard about Bonnie was when a woman, identifying herself as her daughter, said Bonnie had died. It was a lie.

Jerry was contacted by several Colombians who had been incarcerated, and they relayed messages of gratitude from Cartel leaders. Herrera said he would do anything Jerry requested, and Jerry believed him. Jerry was known throughout the prison system as a "stand up" guy for refusing to testify. When a convict's lies got Jerry sent back to Marion, a few months later he was approached by an unknown convict in the prison yard and said for payback he had nearly beat the liar to death in another prison.

Such was the prison code: You didn't snitch; you didn't lie to authorities about an inmate; and you minded your own business. The prison grapevine was better than any mail system; if something occurred in another prison, or something was planned to occur, the inmates usually knew in advance. Jerry, because of his Colombian connections, was treated better than other inmates. Once, he was housed with John Gotti and the head of the Cali Cartel, the most powerful Cartel leader in Colombia with the exception of Pablo Escobar. But his connections were also a double-edged sword because the wardens, perhaps getting orders from higher up, often went out of their way to make his life miserable. More than once he was warned that with one screw up he would return to Marion.

Because he was a "lifer" and a stand-up guy, Jerry was often used by the inmate called the "shot caller," so named because he gave permission for things to happen within his domain. If the shot caller deemed someone needed punishment, and that could mean anything, it happened. You couldn't hide from the shot caller. On a few occasions, Jerry was there for life or death decisions.

Mostly, he minded his own business, read books, and researched cases similar to his, in hopes of seeing light at the end of the tunnel. He was moved from prison to prison, which made it difficult for him to have visitors.

Chapter 21

Nearing his thirtieth year of imprisonment, he died on May 14, 2014. Although he was cremated with no service, thousands of people made inquiries about his arrangements.

Afterword

My last conversation with the CIA/FBI concerning Jerry was when I pressed them about Hank Maierhoffer. Their comment was that while they would "neither admit or deny that he worked for them, it was safe to say he no longer did." And that was easy to say because he had died several years earlier. Many others involved with Jerry, however, are still living, and most of them have struggled to put their lives together. One such person was one of his pilots, Maurice "The Hat" Roundy. After serving his time on the smuggling charges, he became entangled in a bankruptcy fraud case and spent several years in prison. He is out now and lives in South Florida. Those of Jerry's brothers who remain alive have become productive citizens but his son is serving life in prison without the possibility of parole, after committing armed robbery shortly after being paroled for an earlier charge. Karla died from alcoholism and according to her daughter was tormented by her past. Her daughter described her as a loving person who was unable to control her desires. She had not discussed Jerry and the daughter only discovered the connection when she found her mother's diary.

According to anonymous information I received, Humberto Herrera is living in the Miami area, but the person was too fearful to divulge additional information. The real Richard Martin, whose identity Jerry pilfered, said that he had experienced much difficulty because of the stolen identity.

As I look back on this book, there are many questions that remain unanswered. I still find it difficult to accept the Government's position

Afterword

that the end justifies the means. I wonder how they could use the testimony of a woman who admitted she was complicit in the murder of Mildred Cornell to go after Jerry, who was already serving significant time. Was it simply to put another notch in their belt? Only they can answer. I think the case of Jerry LeQuire shows the dark side of our justice system, and I will no longer look at any legal problem as black and white. I know this much, his story is more complicated than what is commonly thought.

I interviewed Jerry for nearly four years, in four different prisons, and in that time we became friends. It seems strange in retrospect that two people from very different backgrounds could find a common thread that bound them together, but life does not always pick and choose logically. That, I believe, is what makes us so unique. Our eyes, even perhaps our souls, are capable of seeing more that what is apparent.

Over time, we came to trust each other, and I believe that within the constraint of his circumstance, he attempted to be honest with me. It wasn't always easy for him because at times the questions were hard, even though I strived to show sensitivity to his duty as a prisoner. In his world, there are duties that if denied can result in harsh penalties. In his 30 years of imprisonment, he had seen all kinds of people come through, some to visit, some to stay, and he understood better than most of us the role of agendas in friendship. But he soon realized that my agenda was just to write the book, not to pass judgment, and certainly not to discover some desired secret knowledge, but just the book. Yes, I openly second guessed many of his decisions, and we often discussed these, but always civilly.

Since I wasn't allowed any recording device or writing instruments, I was forced to remember our conversations, which meant I asked the same questions repeatedly on visits. Soon, I began concentrating on the consistencies of his answers and found them remarkably okay. He was a student of geography and loved to discuss different countries, but his favorite country to discuss was Colombia. He enjoyed his time there, not for what he was doing but for its beauty. And he would often say that when he got out we were going to visit Colombia. That was fine with me.

He loved his family, his daughter and son, their children, and talked about them with some regret that he might never see them again as a free man. During such a long time of visiting, we discussed many topics but the one that always put him on the edge of his seat was religion. Amusingly, he had converted to Judaism because it allowed him to have healthier meals in prison. He even corresponded with a Rabbi. He had read the Bible through and through, heard all the talk about his need for salvation, and rejected most of it. He would often tell me that he didn't deserve any form of salvation, and I would counter by saying that in the eyes of a perfect God, why did he think his sins were any worse than mine? And then the discussion would increase in intensity.

I often sent him books – he loved John Grisham – and signed him up for USA Today. I also sent him spiritual books and encouraged him to learn certain meditation techniques. He tried. He had an inquiring mind and was open to suggestions concerning both his present and future life. There were those, of course, with good intentions who pounded him with the words of the Bible, using them as one would use a sledgehammer, but it rolled easily off him. He had seen and heard too much to easily accept that he could be a new man with a simple confession. Yet, that is what I told him; not just that forgiveness was his for the taking but that his walk with God had only stopped because he chose to stop; it had nothing to do with God. I told him what I believed – and he listened. No one knows what was in his heart when he finally left this world, after being treated for pancreatic cancer.

I understood that he was a person with bad intentions because I sensed that just below the surface was a volcano ready to erupt. We discussed his penchant to strike out and reason later, how if he ever became a free man that would get him into trouble. I didn't know him earlier so perhaps he had always been that way, but I suspect that prison hardened him, honed his emotions for survival. He did not argue with my observations, or not for long. Once, he wrote a letter out of anger to someone close to him. During my research I came across the letter and couldn't believe its intensity and viciousness. Upon further research I determined that his accusations were based on things that weren't true, and when I confronted him with the truth, tears welled up in his eyes. He wondered how he could right this terrible wrong, and for the first time I sensed his understanding of what we had been discussing. This time his quick reaction had resulted in an estrangement he badly wanted to repair. He asked me what he should do and I suggested that he write a letter asking for forgiveness. He protested that he didn't know how to do this, and I knew it was true because it wasn't in his nature, but it was something he alone needed to do. I told him not to worry so much about form but to simply speak from the heart. His letter was beautiful and resulted in a dialogue that would have, I'm certain, eventually led to a healing. Unfortunately, he died before it could happen.

He reached out to other inmates who were in need. I observed this firsthand on a few occasions. Once, he said that one inmate never had any visitors and no one sent him money to purchase things at the prison store. He needed shoes and other necessities, but most of all he needed someone who cared. I promised to help, so I sent the man a small amount of money. His gratitude was immense for such a small thing. But sometimes my help backfired. After Jerry died, I received a letter from an inmate saying that Jerry owned him money, and I should pay. I ignored the letter.

Jerry and I, because of my frequent visits, became well-known in the system. At all the prisons, the guards knew who I was. Some resented me, but most were glad I was there. At one prison, the guards were hostile and forced us to sit in a cluster with other visitors. I warned them that our discussion might be offensive, but they seemed more interested in Jerry's story than visiting with each other. This was the same prison where I had to complain to higher authorities to have his books and newspapers eventually delivered to him, and the same prison where we had to go through a lawyer to learn that he was in the hospital.

After a local newspaper ran a front-page story about my writing of the book, the word spread throughout the prison system like a wildfire. Within days, authorities at the prison where he was incarcerated reacted. He was told this would ruin any chance of parole. Prison officials fear scrutiny. For a long time I felt guilty at my naivety, but Jerry did his best to assure me it was his fault as much as mine. We vowed to fight for his parole, and I promised I would do all I could to get him a great lawyer. I was confident that he deserved to be released after serving 30 years, when such a sentence would never occur under modern guidelines.

One of my many observations after spending so much time dealing with the prison system was that it doesn't work. And it will never work. Most of the inmates I saw were young, black or Hispanic, and were there for drug offenses. Many of them, according to their families, came out of prison with worse drug problems than when they entered. Most of them were there for non-violent crimes. Most of them were uneducated. Many of them dealt with drugs because they saw no other way to survive. Mandatory sentences, while making it easier on authorities, is questionable.

Jerry was fiscally conservative and socially liberal. We shared that together. He disliked the Republican Party and hoped that one day Hilary Clinton would be president. He liked Obama, even though I sensed some old South feeling about blacks. He appreciated the role of the CIA, even given the possibility that they might be the cause of his imprisonment. He believed that they controlled the world, and that very little of consequence happened without either their knowledge or approval. For that reason, he suspected that the next president would either come from the Bush or Clinton family because they had the closest ties to the CIA. One of his friends was Aldrich Ames, the CIA agent convicted of selling information to the Russians. They played chess together, and he said most of the inmates liked Ames. Another of his friends was the head of the Ayran Brotherhood.

In prison, whoever harbored thoughts about aging making him weak, had only to cross him once. He didn't care how old or how large, if you wronged him he sought retribution. This earned him additional respect from both guards and inmates. Once when he was late arriving for our visit, a guard informed me that he was being kept in his cell while another prisoner was being moved. No further explanation was offered, and I didn't question Jerry about it. I imagine it was someone who Jerry didn't like.

He prided himself on staying in excellent physical condition and often boasted of the pull-ups he could perform. He had little use for those who used religion as their ticket out and had more respect for a mass murderer than a child molester. While he liked many of the guards, he fiercely disliked the wardens, calling them pinhead bureaucrats.

He talked with regret about one of his former girlfriends, Bonnie Miller, who was killed in a car wreck. He wondered what his life would have been like had he married her instead of hooking up with Karla. He introduced me to one of his bootlegger friends, now dead, and told me stories about robberies and murders his friends had committed. And he talked about money the authorities said he had hidden.

"They dug up my brother's farm," he said, almost laughing. "If there was money, they really must have thought me to be stupid." I never asked him it existed but he would often bring it up, as though to see if I became interested. I told him I sure didn't want to receive a FedEx package stuffed with hundred dollar bills. Once he asked me if I thought the feds had any right to the money if he ever got out. But that's about as far as our conversations went. But the interest has not waned much over the years for those who were around when he was arrested. Nearly 300 million is a lot of reasons to wonder.

He would ask me what I thought he could do to make money if he became free, and I actually began exploring support groups. He was woefully out of date with technology but seemed to have an interest in learning. He was an excellent typist and offered to help me write a book about his prison experiences. He wondered how much a good, used Mercedes cost, and what it would take to rent a nice apartment? And though, as I have admitted, I knew deep in my heart he was still capable of violence, I was going to speak on his behalf at the parole hearing. Thirty years is long enough!

When the story appeared that there was the possibility of him getting paroled, it sent fear through some people. One lady who had betrayed him had someone contact him to say she had died, but he knew it wasn't so. And he didn't care. He urged me to contact her for a meeting, just to observe the fear in her voice. I didn't. But I am certain it wasn't retribution violence that would cause him trouble, but the violence brought on by his quick temper.

No matter how much we discussed this problem, he couldn't be deterred. It seemed ingrained in his DNA. He was the perfect candidate for anger management classes. His excuse was that it was the way God made him, so I suggested he ask God if that was true. God doesn't talk to me, was his reply. I said he needed to allow God to find him, then. But I could tell that he had grown weary of knocking on the gates of heaven and seeing them not opening. I gave him books to read as assignments, then we discussed them on future visits. He enjoyed philosophical discussions and assured me he was trying. He said it was difficult to shut out your thoughts in prison to think only about God. I could only imagine. All the soil of past gardens sprouted fruit at night, when inmates were left to the solitude of their past indiscretions. And he sat in his cell and observed this drama unfold. Screams, tears, pleas – he would describe them to me. Each sound had its own meaning.

Jerry, as a function of survival, was skeptical about inmates, especially those assigned to his cell and cellblock. Once, he mentioned a new cellmate who said he was from Maryville and who asked a lot of personal questions. He asked if I would check on him. Aware that my information might dictate the man's fate, I only reported that I was unable to find out much about the man, but in truth I was certain he was lying. The man was moved to another cellblock shortly. Why was he there? Jerry said the authorities liked to spy on him. Another man he wanted my help with was a lawyer who was in prison for running a Ponzi scheme. He claimed to be innocent and was certain he would win the appeal and soon be on the streets. After checking the facts, I told Jerry the man had swindled hundreds of millions, angered the judge, and would probably never get out of prison, unless there was a miracle.

And a miracle was what Jerry needed because I soon realized that the authorities were going to do all in their power to deny him parole. Someone who knew something about how they thought said that his refusal to testify against the Colombians was, even after 30 years, a sore spot with the establishment. They wanted vengeance, not justice. And in my short experience, I could see this as a distinct possibility.

The authorities treated inmates as a bad slave owner would treat their slaves. They aren't human, just cattle to be herded from place to place. On one occasion, Jerry was diagnosed with a medical condition, according to what he was told. What medical condition? They refused to say. Can you imagine? They wouldn't tell him and certainly wouldn't tell me. But it required him to be moved to another facility with better treatment facilities. What prison? You'll know when you get there. I felt my anger build until I wanted to scream. Where are you taking him? None of my business.

A week later, I learned he had been moved 600 miles away. But they still wouldn't explain his medical condition. At that point, I began writing letters to Washington. Oh, I'm sure there are reasons. After all, you're not family. No, I said, but the family didn't know either. Ahh, well we'll see. When I talked with Jerry, he said they wouldn't even let him look out the windows of the airplane. After all, there are no windows in a cattle truck. I look up at the sky and cry, where is humanity?

So, when I spoke of God's love, this is what Jerry bounced the words against. I wanted to scream, "Look at me – I can show you!" But I would be gone and he would be left alone with this. Look inward, Jerry, I begged. Don't let them define you.

During our visits, I looked around and asked questions about inmates. He usually knew the answers. Each prisoner had a story. Some inmates, he said, were worthless human beings and needed to be put away. Some were a victim of circumstances. What was he, I asked.

"I deserved to be in prison but nonetheless the authorities lied and deceived me," he said. "I don't deserve what I got."

"Did you kill Mildred Cornell?"

"I was acquitted," he said.

"Did you bribe the judge in Madisonville?"

"Yes," he said, smiling.

"Did you plan escape attempts?"

"Yes, but not like Karla described."

I never asked, "Have you hidden $300 million?"

A friend of Jerry's asked me, "Do you think he has the money?" I laughed and said, "He told me he gave it to you to hold." There was no further mention of it.

When he talked of Karla, it wasn't with bitterness. He claimed to have no knowledge of what happened to her, nor did he seem to want to know. He was, however, happy that I had made contact with one of his former pilots, and urged me to visit him. I was always a little reluctant to discuss some of his former associates because I didn't know his feelings toward them. Had he been keeping score?

We discussed music, what he liked and didn't like. He would email me song titles and ask if I enjoyed them. He liked songs with messages; I didn't. I tried to get him to listen to jazz; he wouldn't.

He used the email system regularly and wrote letters sparingly. Stamps cost money. He had a distinct writing style and in most of his writings would end with "Your friend, Jerry." Our friendship meant something to him, as it did to me.

He worried that his death would come in prison, not from an illness but from poison. He believed that John Gotti had been poisoned. "It's the easy way for them," he said. The last time I saw him was right before he was to begin treatment for his cancer. He seemed in perfect health. We visited for three days, four hours each time. We told stories, shared a few memories, and acted as though nothing had changed. I said I would visit him the next weekend, but when I arrived he had sent an email

Afterword

saying he was too sick to see anyone. It was our last correspondence. He died shortly after that.

I hope he had found peace.

About the Author

RICHARD BIGGS, a former engineer, is a writer living in Knoxville, Tennessee. His earlier book ,There Is No Hope Here, is the story of poverty in the Appalachian region of eastern Kentucky. You can visit his website at http://www.richardbiggsbooks.com

www.ingramcontent.com/pod-product-compliance
Lightning Source LLC
Chambersburg PA
CBHW071904290426
44110CB00013B/1271